# BECOME THE
# EXCEPTION

# BECOME THE EXCEPTION

BY

## MIKE MARCHEV

MBA, CTC

GREYHOUND PRESS
COLONIA, NJ

# BECOME THE EXCEPTION

Copyright © 2000

Michael A. Marchev, MBA, CTC

Cover design by: Ad Graphics, Tulsa, Oklahoma

Printed in the United States of America.

For information write
Greyhound Press
40 Autumn Ct., Colonia, NJ 07067


Marchev, Michael A.
Become The Exception
1. Sales   2. Success   3. Motivation
ISBN 0-9702547-0-9 (pbk)
FIRST PAPERBACK EDITION
10  9  8  7  6  5  4  3  2  1

*Dedicated with love and affection to my wife, Barbara, whose values, sense of humor, warmth, understanding and friendship have made me the happiest married author on the planet,*
*and*
*to all the people I have befriended over the past thirty years who have contributed in countless ways to my professional and personal growth. You know who you are . . . and I thank you.*

*"Hey Angelo! Why don't you try selling something so you can tell me what it feels like."*

*– President of a large electronic component manufacturing company sensitizing his sales manager to a corporate objective.*

# TABLE OF CONTENTS

## SECTION 4
### CORRECTING AND AVOIDING COMMON MARKETING AND SALES MISTAKES

## SECTION 5
### MORE STRATEGIES FOR MULTIPLYING YOUR BUSINESS OPPORTUNITIES

## SECTION 6
### WINNING OVER YOUR PROSPECTS AND CLIENTS

# Author's Foreword

*You have to sing like you don't need the money.*
*Love like you'll never get hurt.*
*You have to dance like nobody's watching.*
*It has to come from the heart, if you want it to work.*

          – Kathy Matea, Country Western Singer

It is all in front of us. Future successes along with future failures. Shining moments coupled with a few unfortunate regrets. As a popular saying goes, yesterday is a canceled check; tomorrow is nothing but a promise. Today/now is all we really have to work with.

The good news is that today/now is all we really need. There is much to be done and much we can do. There are people to help, objectives to achieve and fun to be had. With a little bit of time and some reading effort on your part, together we can accomplish a great deal.

This book is a milestone in my sales career. It is my contribution to you, your family and your future. It was not written to impress you — anybody can write a book. My reason for writing this book is to get you thinking in a healthy, pro-active way that will serve you throughout the rest of your sales career.

This book was written specifically for people who have something to do with "selling." This target market actually includes over six billion people — the population of our planet. Believe it or not, virtually every person on our planet, at one time or another, in some shape and form, will find themselves selling something to somebody — an idea; a car; a house; an interview; a raise; a pardon; you name it.

This book is about health . . . about peace of mind . . . and about making money. It is about doing things right . . . and doing the right things. It is about being successful . . . and having fun doing what you do. This book is about insuring that your daily eating habits improve.

Like most of the business-related books you have purchased over the past few years, no one is going to force you to read this book from cover to cover. But I would be doing you a disservice if I didn't recommend that you "Become The Exception" in this regard and budget some quiet reading time to do just that.

Why do I think this book is worth your investment of time? Four reasons:

1. For over thirty years I have been practicing and studying the art of salesmanship. I have learned the hard way that much of the hoopla found in popular sales books doesn't do much to build careers because very few people have the discipline to follow these academic suggestions. This is not to say that many book strategies are not sound. They just are not practical.

2. My ideas and stories will work for you because they are simple, logical and realistic. I can say this emphatically because I am a simple, logical and realistic person. And as the saying goes, "If I can do it, anybody can do it."

3.  The information on the following pages, in addition to being valid, is easy to read, easy to digest and easy to implement. There are only a handful of 25-cent words in this book, and those, I hasten to add, were inserted by my editor who thought he would get paid more by driving me, along with my 6 billion readers, to Webster's Fifth Edition now and then. *He was wrong.*

4.  I suppose there is one more reason for reading this book. Whether you paid for it or not, it is now in your possession. If you are reading this now, you might as well give the rest of the thing a shot. Who knows, you might surprise yourself and find some amazingly useful ideas perfectly suited to your personal style.

If life is about success . . . and failure . . . and winning . . . and losing . . . and friends . . . and loved ones . . . and experiences . . . and wishes . . . and regrets . . . and competing . . . and laughing . . . and crying . . . and thinking . . . and reflecting . . . and sleeping, then I am living a textbook life.

If this book, in the slightest fashion, can assist you with any one of the facts of life listed above, then I will consider the last thirty years of my life validated. The fact that this book took five of those years to write is of little significance. Those years along with this morning are yesterday's news. As my college football coach, Vic Fusia, was fond of reminding us, "The hay is in the barn." I'll confess that I along with sixty-five other jocks between the ages of 18 and 24 didn't have a clue what he was talking about at the time. Thirty years later, I finally understand his message. The hard part is over, the work is done, it is now time to enjoy the fruits of our labor.

Your future and your sales career are still in front of you. What you do today will largely determine what you harvest in the years ahead. I sincerely want it to be a bumper crop. If you allow me into your world for a brief time, I can help more than you could ever imagine.

Let's begin to take the steps that will help you "Become The Exception."

– Mike Marchev

# Introduction

# Become The Exception

**M**any Americans seem to have been stricken with the disease "quit-itis." They quit everything too soon. It is almost an epidemic. From marriages to diets. From jobs to exercise programs. The malady is even more acute in the sales profession.

This book will help you "Become The Exception" to this sad statistic. You can become among the elite of the sales world who know how to keep a prospect and convert that prospect to a loyal client. Learning how is not going to be painful. In fact, it will be a wonderful adventure.

After a prospect first rejects a proposal, fifty percent of sales people stop calling. Another twenty-five percent stop calling a prospect after a second rejection. But, the vast majority of all sales happen after the fifth contact.

Is this bad news? Well, for the quitters it is. But for salespeople schooled in the art of selling, this statistic is exciting news. Why? Because seventy-five percent of your competition is quitting long before it is time to quit. All you need to do is figure out how to stay in the game through those five initial blows to your ego.

We are about to create a systematic, consistent, persistent, do-able program . . . a program that is realistic and that you can stick to. We are going to groove into your swing a sequence of events that will ensure you establish a relationship with prospective clients and grow your business.

## Overcoming The Two Big Obstacles

Two initial obstacles that all salespeople must come to grips with are fear and time.

The first of these Big Obstacles is fear. Fear of rejection. Fear of people not liking you. Fear of people saying "no." Fear that people will think you're a pushy, arrogant salesperson.

Ladies and gentlemen, fear is okay. Fear comes with the territory. Every professional, from athletes, actors, speakers, to (yes) even politicians, feel a little fear surface when they go into the game. So, when it comes to exhibiting a little fear, you are in good company. I still feel it after thirty years. Once you know that fear is a given and is okay, you will be well on your way to clearing this obstacle.

A second way to control fear is by feeling comfortable with yourself and your product. In other words, know what to say. And that's one of the major objectives of this book. We are going to spend time designing a roadmap to where you want to end up . . . not by scripting each and every word, but rather by giving you the tools to confidentially choose your own words.

The third way to deal with fear is by committing yourself to the selling system I give you in this book. Fear is often a by-product of hit-and-miss tactics. Think of selling as a "system" of behavior that inevitably leads, if followed, to success. Half of your competitors quit after the first contact because they do not *know* the system. The next twenty-five percent of your competitors quit after the second contact because they do not *believe* in the system. It takes a consistent and a persistent system of activity to arrive at the point where a sale results. You must believe in "The System."

You must also understand that by definition some people are going to say no to you; some people aren't going to want to talk to you; some people aren't going to want to read your proposals; and some people aren't going to want to grant you an interview. That's a reality which The System defeats. The difference between a professional salesperson and the wanna-be is that the pro knows the difference between what is acceptable rejection and what is not.

Big Obstacle number two is time. You have twenty-four hours a day to achieve your objectives if you designate all twenty-four for business. I'm betting you have a few other areas of your life that warrant some attention — families, little league games, church groups, playoffs, computer problems. You must realize, however, that nothing happens unless you devote time effectively. Sure, you probably feel like you spend a lot of time "on the job." You identify prospects, make lists, read periodicals, newsletters and magazines. But most salespeople spend time avoiding the moment of truth when they must face the prospect who holds the awesome and humbling power of rejection in his voice. This book will teach you to use time effectively and will actually create more free time for you to enjoy life (with the requisite bucks in your jeans).

## Do You Believe?

You cannot sell anything effectively, or represent anything or anyone effectively, unless you firmly believe in what you are doing and saying. If you don't believe in your company . . . if you don't believe in your product. . . if you don't believe in your agents . . . if you don't believe in yourself, then all the sales training in the world won't make you a success.

Perhaps you think of sales negatively. You may not enjoy telling friends that you are in sales because somewhere along the line you were totally turned off by some amateur salesperson. Don't think of yourself as another one of "those guys." Think of yourself as someone in the business of helping people solve problems. The days of the fast-talking, fast-walking, wheeling-dealing, high-expense-account salesperson are yesterday's news. We are polite people trying to find real solutions to real problems. Regardless of the service or product you represent, you have some hardware, some people, and some intelligence. You have something of value to "bring to the party", so you have nothing to be ashamed of. Yes, the people are right, you are in sales. And lucky for them that you are!

## The "Know It All Before You Call" Myth

Most would-be salespeople get hung up in the early going because they think they need to know everything about their product or service before approaching a prospect. They get the ASK Pie Chart backwards.

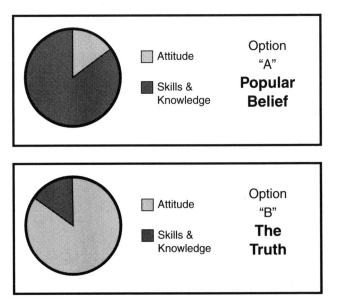

It is very admirable and important that you know what you are talking about. But to be successful selling, the pie chart you select should be letter "B." People migrate to positive attitudes. Enthusiasm is infectious. The most well-informed salesperson in the world, when diagnosed by a prospect to be short-changed in the personality department, is going to wash out of this game early and without fanfare.

Eighty-five percent of your success depends on communication and attitude. The remaining fifteen percent involves industry and product knowledge. That may sound backwards to you, but your knowledge will increase as you initiate sales contacts and learn from your mistakes. The knowledge will come once your attitude and people and communication skills are being applied in sales situations.

So, when you net this all out, your job is to talk to people, ask questions, internalize the information, offer proposals, fix problems and move on to the next opportunity. Do this, and your knowledge will take care of itself.

## The Golden Millimeter

The difference between winning and losing is usually just a fraction of effort. This is as true in selling as it is in any profession. The people making the sales and the money do not stand head and shoulders above those who are not "doing the job."

I remember seeing an article in Sports Illustrated depicting a downhill ski racer with his goggles in place and snow flying furiously. The caption read:

*"How does it feel when you measure success in hundredths of a second?"*

In the Olympics, the gold medalist and the fourth place runner-up are always just a couple of blinks of an eye apart.

19

Think about it. A blink of an eye separates the winners from the losers — 100ths of seconds, a difference barely measurable. I call this The Golden Millimeter and it applies to the sales profession, too.

---

## The Golden Millimeter

**Think of your career as the Olympics of business — highly competitive, but you only need to do a little more than your competitor to win.**

---

All you need to do is send a few more letters or make a few more phone calls, make a little more effort preparing prior to your next presentation. You don't have to beat the other guy by twenty-five miles. You just have to be a little bit better, a little bit faster, a little bit more creative, a little bit more responsive to your prospects' needs or problems to move the gold to your side of the table.

This book will help you design a system to travel that Golden Millimeter to success. Here is what we will accomplish:

- You will gain a clear perspective of what the sales job entails and how a well designed system will result in increased sales volume.

- You will find sales concepts that make sense for you and that you can immediately put into place in your own organization.

- You will learn how to select from among the many proven ideas and concepts in this book, those that you can personally "connect" with and implement to achieve success.

Let's face it, you are not going to implement twenty-five, thirty, or forty new ideas as a result of reading this book — even if you find that many you like. That's what is affectionately known as blue-sky thinking. Instead, I want you to look for that one nugget . . . that one concept or idea that you feel could improve significantly your present way of doing business.

Peter Drucker, the management consultant, believes that as you attend a seminar or listen to a cassette program, you should try to identify one personal weakness and look to replace it with one new idea. If you can do this, then the seminar was worth your investment of time and money.

But just don't look for what you need to change as you read this book. Look for the positives, too. Confirm where your current methods are correct and effective. I've given many seminars where people have said to me, "Mike, it's refreshing to know that I'm doing a lot of things right." Accept with pride those things you are already doing well. That's a big part of the fuel you need to propel you to the next level.

## Unshuffle Your Deck

In my live seminars, I invite two salespeople to compete. I hand out a deck of cards to each person. One deck is shuffled. The second deck is in order by suit, low cards to high cards. Then I look at my watch (like a tense, pressured prospect or client waiting for a response) and I say to the competitors, "I need a seven of clubs for our meeting next week." Who do you think is the first person to deliver the correct card?

I then ask for a second card. "I need a five of hearts for our conference tomorrow." Which salesperson is first to deliver the goods? Finally I say, "I need the King of Spades for a meeting this morning!" You already know who is going to win.

The person whose deck was ordered properly will cut through this assignment like a piece of cake . . . a no brainer. The person with the shuffled deck would have to start at zero each time and sort through the pile of cards one by one to deliver on my otherwise simple request.

The point I make at the conclusion of the contest is that salespeople will come up short of the competition if they fail to design a *system* of prospecting, closing, and ongoing client servicing. When you don't take the time and effort to get your deck in order (remember the Golden Millimeter), chances are you won't be the first to deliver the goods. Playing with a shuffled deck is a head-on-collision waiting to happen. This book will help you put your deck in order.

As soon as you take the time to put your deck in order, you will begin traveling that Golden Millimeter toward becoming a very successful sales professional. Let's start right now.

# SECTION

# SHATTERING FOUR THRESHOLD MYTHS

## Chapter 1

# Myth #1:
# Selling Is A Numbers Game

Undoubtedly, you've heard this one before: "Selling is a numbers game." Make the calls, make the presentations, work your way through enough people, and eventually you will make a sale. I'm not saying this is totally false, but raw volume does not necessarily produce success. And even if it does, it's the hard way.

Rather than thinking of sales as a game of large numbers, begin to think of sales as a game of darts. By aiming your effort (the dart) at a clearly defined target (your pre-qualified prospect dart board) your chances for hitting the mark (a sale) are greatly enhanced. Contrast that mindset with a pure numbers game, where you buy a lottery ticket or throw a handful of marbles up in the air hoping one or two land in a paper cup.

If you want to save yourself a lot of time, money and frustration, know who you would like to do business with. Your chance for success is much higher if you direct your efforts conscientiously toward a list of defined prospects. This concept is called "Bracketing."

## Bracketing

Bracketing is the *systematic process* of zeroing in on a designated target. Let's use the game of golf as an example of bracketing in action.

During a Merrill Lynch corporate golf outing I attended in Tucson, Arizona, Al Geiberger was the guest PGA golf professional. He was positioned on a par 3 hole all afternoon as each foursome of company representatives played on through. Al's job as guest pro was to hit a fifth shot on behalf of the team to see if he could score a hole in one.

Before the first group arrived, Al hit a single shot to check the distance, wind and range. This first shot fell a little short and to the left of the flag stick. Mr. Geiberger mentally recorded the results. After making a few mental and mechanical adjustments he hit a second ball and watched its flight. This time the ball landed a little long and to the right of the flag stick. Again, he adjusted his mechanics. His third shot was pin high and left. After making the final adjustment, his fourth shot was right on the money. After mentally recording and "locking in" the swing mechanics for shot #4, he could then duplicate the shot, impressing the bajeebers out of each passing foursome. Al was within six feet of the pin for the rest of the afternoon.

This is how bracketing works — a trial and error, adjustment setting exercise designed to zero in on a given target. Bracketing in sales works the same way. First, you have to lob some effort in the direction of a specific goal (your specified prospects). Then, watch what happens, make an adjustment, and try it again. Keep on tweaking until you have a method that results in the prospect becoming a client.

Here is a specific sales bracketing effort you can try on for size. Make a list of five qualified prospects you have decided you would like to do business with. Next, write down three ways you can improve awareness of your products or services among these prospects. (For ideas on awareness programs, see the chapter in Section 5 titled "How To Increase Your Visibility.")

Initiate the awareness program and record your results from the first round attempt. Now, make some adjustments to the program and try again (either on the same five prospects or on a new set of five). Record and adjust again. Continue until you are, as the pro's say, "in the zone." Finally, apply your refined method to a new group of targeted prospects.

One caution: Bracketing will not necessarily work with prospects you have not qualified. Try this and you are really back to the old lottery numbers game. Trying to bracket here is like Al Geiberger trying to drop his shot near the hole when the winds gust on and off up to 40 miles per hour and come from all different directions at any time. Likewise, unscreened prospects are coming from all different directions in terms of what they want and need. You'll miss the green and get discouraged.

Let others waste their time chasing raw numbers. Identify your target using the system I describe in Section 2 and then use bracketing to become successful by design. There will be very little luck to your sales campaign.

# CHAPTER 2

# MYTH #2:
# YOU MUST LIKE PEOPLE

Many people preach that a primary prerequisite to be successful in sales is that you must "like people." The implication is that you should have the innate capacity and desire to cozy up to just about everybody . . . or at least everybody with a bankroll in their wallet. I am not a fan of this postulate.

You see, I have traversed the United States many times, worked in eighteen countries on five continents, and observed countless people on airplanes, in post office lines, at restaurants, toll booths, and department stores. I have watched people drive cars, run races, attend classes, and root for their kids at high school athletic programs. For over fifty years I have watched people do just about everything people can conceivably do on this planet. (Well . . . almost everything.)

Here is what I have concluded: The world has its quota of nasty, insincere, and negative people who I consciously choose to have nothing to do with. More accurately stated, I don't like them or what they stand for. And I don't have any intention of entering their world and trying to change them.

(How's that for an "I am a salesman, therefore I like all kinds of people" endorsement?)

On the other hand, during these same travels, I have met many fine, upstanding, fun and creative human beings running around our planet trying to creatively figure out how things work while maintaining a healthy sense of humor and appreciation for reality. These people are the ones who I want to be around . . . learn from . . . and even try to emulate. I like these people.

So, let's give this "you've got to like people" thing a different twist. If you want to minimize your stress, have more fun and earn more money, begin spending more time looking for and doing business with people toward whom you have a natural attraction . . . people who are honest, hard working, fun, intelligent, enthusiastic and easy to be around. It is also a good idea to take a little more time than we often do to understand people better. After all, many nice people just don't know how to make a good first impression. It would be a shame for you to prematurely cross them off simply because they have a lot of bad hair days.

Where does it say you must do business with (or, what's worse, seek business from) everyone who wants your service or product? That's a myth. You may feel a little out of joint right now and be saying to yourself, "Is this guy saying that it is okay to be prejudiced?" No! Not at all. Take a deep breath and read the above again. I am saying that it is okay if you don't do business with rude, unhappy, belly-aching whiners. That is all I am saying, and I will say it in a court of law if you insist on hearing it under oath.

If you are going to bust your chops servicing people to the maximum of your abilities, you might as well do it for people who will appreciate your efforts. You will bring more energy and positive attitude to your job every day. And that translates into more success.

## CHAPTER 3

# MYTH #3:
# REJECTION COMES
# WITH THE TERRITORY

Picture yourself in a large city like New York on a Saturday morning. The sun is shining and it is a perfect 72 degrees. Life is grand, you are feeling good, and you have a full day to just "enjoy" before meeting a friend for a mid-afternoon cocktail at the Plaza Hotel.

You decide to take a stroll down one of New York's famous avenues when you spot a woman on the corner with four suitcases and three small children tugging at her skirt. She's trying to get her entourage into position to cross the street. Parcels are balanced, kids in tow, just waiting for the signal to turn green. Being of sound mind and strong bone, and in no particular hurry, you approach the woman and politely ask if you can be of assistance.

What is her reaction? Despite the fact that this is New York (where a multitude of reactions are possible) the alternatives really only boil down to two.

- **Reaction #1:** You appear to be a godsend. "What a gentleman!" she thinks. She appreciates this unsolicited sign of kindness and doesn't know what to say. Everything she ever thought about New York City must have been wrong. You feel good about yourself having helped this family safely across the street. You bid them all a sincere goodbye and continue down the avenue whistling a happy tune en route to your appointment with Mr. Chivas in the Plaza's Oak Room.

Now let's rewind the tape and look at the exact same situation with a different outcome. Woman and children are at the light, in position and ready to make their move. You ask if you can help. Same woman . . . same predicament . . . same street . . . same city. You use the same words with the same sincere tone.

- **Reaction #2:** She gives you a questioning look, pulls her children close, and fires back a terse and unappreciative refusal. In so many words, she says: "Buzz off, creep, or I'll call the cops."

How would you feel and react to this kiss-off? I'll tell you what you would do if you were a confident professional with the appropriate dosage of self-esteem flowing through your veins. You would start whistling a happy tune and head out in search for that bracer with your name on it down at the Plaza's Oak Room. After all, it's no skin off your nose if this woman doesn't allow you to make her life easier. That's her problem, not yours. You offered relief. She had the opportunity to accept it or reject it. Your response in both situations should be the same: Ease on down the road with a bounce in your step.

But that is not how most people respond. You might: (1) try to convince the woman that you are a nice person and that she has nothing to fear; (2) take the rejection personally and get somewhat miffed, thereby making your afternoon less enjoyable; or (3) shrug it off, but not before uttering a few expletives to yourself. All these responses betray your emotional interpretation of events: You think *you* have been rejected. Wrong!

Many sales courses will tell you to keep a stiff upper lip when you are rejected and don't let it get you down. But once you accept the proposition that *you* have been rejected, you have given up the psychological high ground and put your self-esteem into retreat. Simply put, you need to reject the notion of rejection. (Got that?)

Once you understand that all you are trying to do as a salesperson is help people, every outcome should be the same. If prospects don't want your help or choose not to deal with you for whatever reason they conjure up in their minds, it is not your problem. You simply have to locate another package-burdened, kid-totting mother of five.

Whether prospects accept your services or not should be no more important to your self-esteem than whether a lady lets you escort her across the street. The average salesperson can't seem to come to terms with this. They let prospects alter their emotions, personality, and feelings toward life. This makes no sense.

- Can I help you cross the street? Yes or no?

- Can I hold the door for you? Yes or no?

- Can I help you with your next buying decision? Yes or no?

- Would you like me to get you a warm cup of coffee? Yes or no?

- Can I help you decide on which computer system is best for your growing business? Yes or no?

Regardless of the response, you are the same person, with the same amount of product knowledge, experience and competence and with the same objective, i.e. to feed your family on a regular basis by finding people you can help. Don't tell me it is more complicated than this . . . because I am not buying it. After thirty years of flailing away at this business, it finally dawned on me that the people who decided to do business with me simply said "Yes," while the others simply said "No," (or in many cases, "Not yet").

If you stop linking, no matter how subtly, your sense of self-worth and accomplishment to a prospect's response, then selling ceases to be hard work and instead becomes a game. (Digging holes on a Scottsdale, Arizona highway in the mid-afternoon sun with a pick ax on a 105-degree day — that's hard work.)

## No Chaser

If the lady crossing the street refused your help, would you feel it necessary to dig for an explanation? Of course not. So why do so many sales managers demand that their sales people dig out the answer to "why not" whenever a sales opportunity goes south? Chasing for an explanation to "no" usually focuses the salesperson on rejection. (It also often drives a wedge between the manager and salesperson.)

In general, the most healthy mindset for you to have is:

*"You, Mr. Prospect, have made a decision to attempt to move forward without my services. I'll be here when you come to your senses and change your mind. It's not my responsibility to straighten you or your company out."*

Think of how you would look to the prospect. He has just rejected your proposal, but you don't seem to be overly bothered by the "rejection." The prospect thinks: "Why isn't he upset about not winning my business?" The implication: You are too much in demand by other clients to be overly concerned. The prospect may very well wonder if he just made a mistake.

If the prospect is willing to share the reason with you, I say go for it. You may learn something useful, but be careful. Even if a prospect tells you why he selected a competitor, chances are the reason given is not the real reason. It is often a polite reply designed to accelerate your immediate departure.

If you still insist on finding out "why" a prospect has rejected your service (not you), try this approach. "Mr. Smith, may I ask you two questions regarding our recent proposal?" This small courtesy can pave the way for some meaningful dialogue by accomplishing two things. First, it eliminates your concern that you might be treading on thin ice or unfriendly territory. Second, it clearly indicates to your prospect that "the interrogation" will be brief.

Question #1: *"Is there a specific reason why we failed to earn your business?"*

Question #2: *"In addition to that, is there another reason?"*


The second answer will usually be the *real* reason.

# CHAPTER 4

# MYTH #4:
# STRESS IS INEVITABLE

A nother myth in our profession is that stress, like rejection, is inevitable. In truth, the two often do travel together, weighing down the carrier. But is this condition necessary? Most definitely not!

During my live presentations I ask people in the audience if stress plays a role in their everyday work environments. Without exception everyone nods in agreement and the room is salted with giggles and laughter. (Ask the same audience if they have some disease, and you get a very somber response. Yet stress can become very debilitating. So, why do so many people take stress so lightly?)

It's obvious that a lot of sales professionals feel stress. But stress does not have to rule your life. You were not born with stress. It is something that you allow to happen. Stress is self inflicted in many if not most cases and is a by-product of pretending that the world operates differently than it really does.

When our imperfect world, on whose game board we all must play, follows its natural course, we object to its imperfection and thereby create stress. In engineering, stress results from the application of a constant force to an immovable object. In life, the force is your expectation and the object is reality. You pretend . . . you guess wrong . . . you have stress. But, once you learn to go with the natural flow and rhythm of the world (by all means stopping long enough to change what needs to and can be changed), you will become more effective, efficient and pleasant to be around.

Here are a few examples of ways we can pretend ourselves into an uncomfortable and unhealthy stress level.

Expectation: *"The airlines will never mishandle my luggage."*

Reality:    If you travel often enough, your turn will come when your bag doesn't reach the connecting flight or falls off the airline's truck.

Result:    When your bags don't turn up on the carousel, you get stressed and allow it to ruin your day, your vacation, etc.


Expectation: *"It's Tuesday afternoon at 5:00 p.m., there should not be much traffic."*

Reality:    The world (and all of our metropolitan areas) is filling up with people. I personally have seen the population of our planet double since 1949. Some-one smarter than I am said it will double again. There are fewer and fewer hours in the day when you can beat the crowd at the supermarket, the mall or the highways.

Result:    When you leave for a very important appointment and don't allow enough "fudge time" for the little fender bender, street cleaning, or guys painting the white lines during rush hour, your stress level will build as you realize you'll be late for your appointment.

Expectation: *"Your teenage child understands why you dictate the rules you do and will never miss curfew."*

Reality: By and large, any human being under the age of 20 is pretty much lacking the adhesives in his cranium necessary to have rules stick in memory.

Result: When he meets his first love and decides that he would rather spend a few more minutes with her than scamper home to make daddy proud, parents get bummed out and wonder where we went wrong. The resulting stress level would pin a 5 on the Richter scale faster than you can get out the words "Good grief, do you know what time it is?"

Expectation: *"The world is "creep-free" and everyone who calls us on the telephone is squared away and knows exactly why they have called."* (While we are in this dreamland, we also pretend that they will speak in a clear, audible fashion and respect our time.)

Reality: Along with a population explosion (and increased sales calls) comes an increasing number of less-than-squared-away individuals.

Result: When the caller turns out to be less than polite, we take this confrontation personally and allow our blood to boil for hours.

Doesn't it make more sense to accept the world and all its nuances as they are . . . maybe even with a modicum of humor? Hold onto this reality:

## Bad things happen to good people.

Be ready to field some uncomfortable goings-on in your life. And when they happen (and they will happen) flash back to this chapter, take a deep cleansing breath and repeat to yourself slowly the New Jersey stress-relief mantra:

## FUH GEDA BOU DIT!

And then get on with your life.

## Looking For Easter Eggs

If you want to be more successful, you must learn to lighten up. Selling isn't as much work as you are probably making it out to be. I want you to reach back to your youth to get a new mindset.

Think about the game we all played during Easter as kids — hiding and finding painted hard-boiled eggs. Our parents, or the Easter Bunny, salted a few eggs around the house for us to find and jubilantly declare as our own. The youthful battle cry was:

*"Get out of my way, I'm looking for eggs. I will look everywhere and I'll find those little jewels if it is the last thing I do. I'm on a mission, so get out of my way."*

There was excitement, laughter, and anticipation. There was a competitive spirit. But, whether you found a bundle of eggs or not, this was fun!

The exuberance of the Easter Egg hunt always intrigued me. If finding a few lousy tasting, hard-boiled eggs was so exciting as kids, why don't adults share the same fascination when searching for new business that could net some crisp, folding paper adorned with pictures of dead presidents?

Not unlike the eggs, potential customers are salted (hidden) throughout your territory and waiting to be found. They may be unrecognizable at first glance or hidden within some organizations. But they are out there. When approached with the same competitive spirit, playing "finding the customer" can be pure exhilaration — and lucrative! (I'll show you how in Section 2.)

Remember, you didn't find an egg everywhere you looked. But sometimes with the help of a little clue ("you're getting warmer") you managed to zero in on the magic oval.

The same holds in the hunt for customers. As you prospect and engage in conversations and meetings you uncover clues — clues that can often lead to a close.

There is one more point that we often forget. Whether it's a member of the opposite sex, an Easter egg, a prospect, or virtually anything else that is not immediately within our grasp, the fun and enjoyment often comes with the hunt. Don't overlook this when the prize comes in the shape of a new customer.

# A BASIC
# SALES SYSTEM
# THAT WORKS

# CHAPTER 5

# PROSPECTING — THE PRELIMINARIES

So you have decided to go into business. Congratulations. For the sake of an example, let's say you have decided to start a travel agency. (Throughout the remainder of the book, I'll use the travel agency example because I find that the "Thank you Mike" perks from travel agents are a lot more fun to use than, say, those from tractor manufacturers.)

You heard that business travel could supply a consistent flow of clients so you want to go out and sign up a few good accounts. Most people in your position, I'm sorry to say, would hire an outside salesperson and say, "There are millions of companies out there who travel for business purposes and who need our services. Don't come back without a bunch of new clients."

This is a mistake. The deck is shuffled. Most people get so excited about their new venture they just jump in the water head first and wonder what happened within a year or two. Let's do a little walking before we break into a run.

If you worked for me, the first two weeks you would be at your desk or in the library creating a game plan so you would know exactly what we wanted to achieve every step along the way.

## Divide And Conquer

The first step would be to outline a logical sales territory. Let's go to school by learning from a couple of the more successful companies. Take a look at IBM and Xerox. They have zone managers, territory managers, divisional managers and national managers. They break down the country into saleable sections. They cut the whole pie into pieces.

Small business owners fail to see the logic of this simple yet winning strategy of "Divide and Conquer." They insist on trying to be all things to all people . . . everywhere. When I ask travel agents in my sales seminars, "Where's your territory?" they answer "New Jersey" or "Illinois" or "My territory? It's anywhere I can find a client."

If you're going to be successful and your territory is "everywhere" then you better be able to tell me everything about "everywhere." Say you think your territory is New Jersey, and I ask, "How many corporate accounts are there in New Jersey?" You answer "Thousands." That doesn't tell me anything. That doesn't give me any confidence that you are on top of things.

Let me explain what I'm driving at from a different angle. If you're playing basketball, you are playing the game "on the court." Football players play football "on the field." Clearly visible white lines mark out of bounds from the actual playing surface. You need to be on the field or on the court to be in the game. The same is true in ice hockey. You need to be on the ice to be playing hockey. If you are not on the ice, you are *watching* hockey.

Salespeople, to be effective, also need a well defined arena, a court, a field of play. In the game of sales, this is called a territory. And until you know exactly where your defined territory is, you cannot begin to create an effective prospecting and sales system.

Get this as straight as you can as early as you can. You can't go out and sell everywhere effectively. Your brain can't comprehend "everywhere," so you will fail to systematically prospect what really should be your territory. Instead you will eventually short-circuit with sales overload and become another statistic on the "former salesperson" chart (the fastest growing chart in American history).

The solution is easy. Define your selling territory. Start defining it as it relates to your specific place of business. In our travel agency example, your territory may be a set distance around your office from where your "product" is distributed.

Think small in the beginning. A mile from your business might be a good starting point. I know what you're thinking. "I already have accounts five miles away. Why should I be confined to such a small area? There is action out there, and I want my piece of it." That's fine. Keep 'em. But I still want you to define and start developing a territory one mile from your primary location. Trust me. This is the only way to do it.

Once you define your territory, make it your business to know what's in that area. Let me ask you a question. Do you now know where every business office is within your one-mile territory? Have you called every one? Are there any new startups which could be insulated or hidden? Is there a new suite of offices in your territory with twenty-five guys who could use your product by the ton?

My point is this. There are many of these "little gold mines" near your office that you are not presently aware of. (Often they don't look like prospects . . . until they become clients.)

Why be concerned locally? Because all things being equal, if your business is equal to the competition in every other way, the single factor that separates you from the rat pack is your proximity to the prospect's front door.

Once you have defined the territory, two challenges common to start-up business efforts must be faced head-on immediately. The first one I call your "Awareness Factor." Simply put, not enough people beyond the confines of your immediate family and friends know that you are alive. You are just another Yellow Page line paying rent down on Main Street.

Your second problem negatively affecting your future eating habits is that once prospects know you are alive, they don't (yet) have a single reason to choose you as a provider of goods and services.

Your objectives just became clear. You have to make sure more people know you are alive, and then you have to give them plenty of reasons to want to do business with you. Once you realize the importance of this last sentence, the game becomes fun, and you will be in for the ride of your life.

## Reality Check

You must be realistic when creating a prospecting game plan. If you create an overly ambitious plan that will cost an arm and a leg, it's not going to work (unless you were smart enough to cash in your Internet stocks at the top). So your plan has to fit your budgetary constraints.

Time is another issue. You have little league games, on-call chauffeuring duties for the kids, church functions and other personal commitments. You want to get ahead, but you don't want to put yourself in the bondage of sixty to seventy hour workweeks. The system I am going to outline can fit into any time constraint and still work for you.

Let's put a ribbon on this territory thing by citing one last example. Say we just opened a flower shop on the upper east side of New York City on 76th Street and Third Avenue. We are as excited as two people can be. I'm the flower arranger, and you are my only salesperson. After we open up and toast our success, I send you almost eighty blocks away down to Wall Street to sell flowers. Does that make sense? Of course not. In New York City every two blocks has a shop where you can buy a bouquet of flowers. Every two block square has a drug store, a grocery store, a liquor store. Every two block square has everything you could ever need. The shop owners in New York City are smart enough to realize that their territory is two blocks . . . and that is a big enough territory because it is filled with people. Therefore it is a foolish waste of time and energy to run down to Wall Street to find a customer. We have plenty of would-be buyers in the immediate vicinity.

Many small businesses, including travel agencies, establish a business presence on Main Street and then start running all over the countryside trying to sell their product. A little discipline is needed here. Define your territory and then start digging.

## Hit The Books Before The Bricks

The next step involves a little research. You want to find out how many people within that territory might have a reason to talk to you or have a use for your service. Here's another example.

Suppose your sixteen-year-old daughter wants to make a few bucks to go see *NSYNC. Babysitting is a natural, but she doesn't drive. And for purposes of our example, Mom and Dad's Limo Service is closed. (Clearly this is a fantasy example.) So, her territory has to be limited to walking distance from the house.

Is every house within a mile a good prospect? (Again, fantasy strikes . . . assuming any teenager would walk a mile.) Of course not. Many homes don't have children. Many homes have children, but they are old enough to have already copped

*NSYNC tickets from a scalper. Obviously, just because a house was built within her territory, doesn't mean it automatically qualifies as a prospect for baby sitting services.

But once your daughter has identified those specific houses with kids between six months and ten years old, her job of selling baby sitting services becomes very straightforward.

The same is true for small businesses. Once you have defined your territory, you have to identify all the potential customers (prospects) in it. One easy way to get started is to visit your town library and ask your reference librarian for help. Every state publishes these resource tools. These books cost about eighty dollars apiece, but you don't need to buy them. (If you are "e-powered," go to the appropriate state's ".gov" web site and start surfing.) For example, if you are selling to industrial or manufacturing companies, ask to see your state's Industrial Directory.

These resources are typically organized by town and/or county. Decide what towns or counties fall within your defined territory. You will find the following information listed for each manufacturing company: The name of the company, address, phone number, products they make, sales, square footage of the plant, when it was established, number of employees, and corporate officers (e.g. chairman, president, treasurer, purchasing agent, controller, etc.) You will find out who the directors are, who they bank with, and who their accounting and law firms are. All this information is going to be listed on a single page, and there will be thirty companies per page. Now this is called jumping out of the blocks on a mission.

Here is where salespeople who take shortcuts make a costly error. The companies listed on these pages are not prospects. By definition they are nothing more then "suspects" at this juncture. Here's the difference. When you *think* someone has a need for your service, they are a suspect. When you *know* they have a need for your service, they become prospects.

How can you tell the difference? Phone the company and say,

**MM:** *"Good morning, my name is Mike Marchev from Small Company USA. I am updating my mailing list and at the same time asking two questions to complete a survey. Do you have time to help me out today?"*

They will say "yes". . . or they will say "no." If they say no, do not take it personally. But in 99 out of a hundred calls, they will say yes. You then say,

**MM:** *"Does your company travel for business purposes?"*

They will say yes or no. If the person says "yes", the company might be a prospect. Follow with this question,

**MM:** *"Does your company use a travel agency?"*

The person will answer either yes or no. If yes, that is a pretty good clue that they might be a prospect. If they say that they don't, ask another question,

**MM:** *"Does that mean you book tickets directly with the airlines?"*

Once again they will respond with a yes or no. That's all you are looking for right now. You don't want to try to sell anything or give the impression that you are eager to gain entry into their work environment. They didn't ask you to call, so in effect you are an intruder.

Remember, at this stage of the game all you want to find out is who uses your type of service or product so you can determine if they qualify for your prospect list or not. When companies eliminate themselves from your prospect list, don't interpret this as a bad day at Black Rock . It isn't. Quite the contrary, it is good news. Your success rate will improve the more tightly you define your prospect list's qualifications. You can't afford any deadbeat candidates on your list. You must become highly disciplined at building your prospect list. That means controlling your natural salesperson's optimism. No, that octogenarian couple that runs the "No Chew Luncheonette" is not likely to franchise the concept and begin flying all over the country. Scratch them off the list.

So, that's how you get started, but this job is never over. You must continually look for new names for your prospect list. Growing your list will soon become a very enjoyable and rewarding part of your business.

Now, I can hear many of you saying, "but I don't sell to manufacturing companies."

The State Industrial Directory was an example. I still want you to make contact with your reference librarian. Naturally, I suggest that you use the appropriate directory that makes the most sense to you.

## CHAPTER 6

# THE TEN STEP SYSTEM

The preliminary steps of defining your territory and identifying the prospects that inhabit it are really part of a larger ten-step prospecting system. And following The System inevitably leads to success. So, let's hit the basic elements of The System. The steps in order of implementation are:

1. Specify
2. Quantify
3. Identify
4. Qualify
5. Present
6. Satisfy
7. Collect
8. Measure
9. Expand
10. Repeat

## Step #1: Specify

This step involves defining your territory. Remember ice hockey has a playing surface. When you are on the ice you are playing the game. Once you remove yourself from the ice, you no longer can score.

As mentioned in the previous chapter, we can't be in all places and be all things. The smaller you make your territory, the faster you will understand what it is you need to do. The secret is to have enough people in your territory to allow the system to work effectively. This leads us directly to . . .

## Step #2: Quantify

Start by finding all potential "suspects" within one mile of your main facility. Then, branch out slowly and methodically from this starting point, block by block, half-mile by half-mile, and you will become very knowledgeable about your territory.

As you quantify you should maintain a file to keep organized. You can build files several ways. Some are more antiquated than others but the key is to do what works for you whether that's three-by-five cards or your computer. (I use a software package from Symantec called ACT.) Your file, once completed, is the most important information in your possession. It will help you focus on the task at hand, help you differentiate dead end contacts from suspects from prospects, and save you countless hours when it is time to "touch bases" with your prospects. This is the way that you will position yourself miles ahead of your competition.

You also need to update your file systematically. Like just about everything else in life, this is easier said than done. If you can update your prospect file once a year, you are doing okay. Twice a year is time well spent. Treat it as a scheduled inventory day. The information can and does change. (The fastest way to let your prospects know that you're not up to speed or sincere about doing business with them is by addressing your letters to somebody who left the company two years ago.)

## Step #3: Identify

Identify which companies/people in your territory are actual "suspects." You do this by developing a profile of your target customer. It is a real stress-buster once you figure out who you want to do business with. You don't have the luxury of trying to do business with everybody. You have to devote your energies on targets who have a high probability of providing you with a return on your investment. You start this process by developing a profile.

To develop a target profile, focus on who you currently enjoy doing business with and who is producing revenue for your company. Make a list and jot down all those companies that you enjoy doing business with on the left side and companies you do not like working with on the right. You will probably find a pattern. The companies you like to do business with may be close to your company, travel internationally, pay on a credit card program, have a similar size, come from referrals, etc. If you look hard enough, you will see some trend.

Once you identify the type of organizations you like to do business with, and compare them with the companies that turn you off, you can begin to concentrate your efforts on suspects who are "good-guys." I'll bet you dollars to doughnuts that you are spending a great deal of time trying to land a new client that, prior to developing a target profile, will fall on the wrong side of the page. Doesn't it make more sense to spend your time developing more of the good guys? I think you can take this to the bank:

**The companies you enjoy doing business with will prove to be the most profitable relationships.**

# Step # 4: Qualify

Determine which of the identified suspects in your territory have an interest in what you are doing . . . these are your prospects. This involves a little telephone work and a little market research (as we mentioned in the previous chapter). But don't get intimidated. You only need to ask a few questions to a handful of people.

It is now time to rate your prospects. Although it may not sound like a righteous thing to do, you can't treat all prospects the same. Some need more time. Some are more profitable. You must rate your prospects to allocate the proper resources to each one.

Here is a fast and easy way to do it. Think in 3's. A, B or C. One, two or three. Red, yellow or green. Let's use A, B and C. Under the A category list companies that you consider to be "home runs." You would do anything short of breaking the law to service these accounts. They're big spenders. They're local. They are financially strong and pay promptly. Whatever your reasoning is, you want these accounts. There shouldn't be more than a few prospects on the A list. (I'll tell you why in a minute.) These are the real beauties.

The C list is comprised of companies that would be nice to have but do not warrant any effort on your part now. In other words, if a C prospect walked by your front door, you wouldn't necessarily stop what you are doing to bring him in. (With an A prospect, you'd be shooting out of your chair to offer him a cup of coffee). There will only be a handful of C prospects on your list.

Most of your list will include B prospects — those are the ones that you're going to work on from eight-thirty to five, Monday through Friday.

Why categorize prospects? Time. Consider this true experience which happened to me. I called on a company on my A-list several years ago and said,

**MM:** *"Mr. Jones? Mike Marchev. Can I come by and introduce our program to you?"*

**Mr. Jones:** *"Mike, I hate to waste your time. We're very happy with the company we are currently dealing with. Let me save us both a lot of time and effort."*

**MM:** *"Okay."*

About four months later I made a routine follow-up call on Mr. Jones.

**MM:** *"Mr. Jones, Mike Marchev here. I'm following up on our last phone conversation. I want to make sure everything's under control."*

**Mr. Jones:** *"Thanks, Mike, but nothing has changed. We are still happy, and I see no reason for a change. I appreciate your interest."*

I called Mr. Jones a third time a few months later and he responded the exact same way.

**Mr. Jones:** *"Mike, everything is under control. Thanks for calling."*

After the third call I began to feel like a nuisance. I thought that I'd better lay low for a while. Jones seemed like a nice man, and I didn't want to bug the guy.

About a year later as I was sorting through some old files, I remembered that I hadn't spoken to Mr. Jones for a while. I called him. He was very nice and asked how things were going. He then said,

**Mr. Jones:** *"Mike, I wanted to call you but I lost your card. I thought of you when we wanted to change vendors last week but I didn't know how to get in touch with you."*

Was Jones responsible for contacting me, or was it my job to stay visible throughout the year? I blew it. I wasn't around when the ball was fumbled. I decided right then and there that I would never lose another account for lack of visibility. So, I created the A- List.

This Wednesday I want you to ask yourself this question, "Is there anything I can do for my A prospect this week?" Many if not most times the answer will be "No." You've done everything you can do to this point in the relationship, and you are up-to-date with this prospect. Ask this same question for every single prospect on your A-List. When next Wednesday comes you ask the very same question. "Is there anything I can do for any of my A prospects this week?"

Why Wednesday? Wednesday is the perfect day because you have plenty of time left in the week to respond appropriately to your question. If you waited until Friday to ask, you would put off any needed action until Monday, and all your good intentions would probably get washed away over the weekend. Remember,

**Professional salespeople
have to keep their hands on the buyer's pulse.
You do this most effectively utilizing
an A, B and C prospect category list.**

## Step #5:  Present

Next, you need to convince your prospect that *you* have the solution to his or her problems. This will take some time. (Stay tuned for the concept of Seven Customer Contacts . . . what I call the Seven See's Strategy.) You need to develop a relationship to convince the prospect that you are worthy and qualified to perform the task at hand.

As a salesperson, you are your presentation. You're selling your presentation. Your number one job is to develop and master your presentation. Fine tune it to a three (phone), or five to eight minute (live) presentation. Tighten it up and make it flow seamlessly.

Have you ever talked into a cassette recorder and developed your presentation by listening to yourself? The first time you do this is going to make you cry. You're going to realize that you don't have your act together. Have you ever video taped your presentation? You may wish for a quick death (or, in my case, plastic surgery). The point is: Take your presentation seriously. Have someone listen to and critique your presentation. Use today's tech tools to see yourself as others see you.

If you were in my motel room prior to my giving a speech: (a) I'd have some explaining to do to my wife, and (b) you'd think I was a lunatic. I bounce around the room "warming up" — what all professionals do before they perform. I look in the mirror and practice.

If you want to put more distance between you and your competitors, add enthusiasm to your presentation. If you do not believe in your company, or the owner, or the employees, or the industry, this will come across to your prospects. When you believe, this too will become apparent and will draw prospects and opportunities to you like a moth to a flame. What's more, when you believe you can easily work through rejection.

Enthusiasm. Develop it. Believe in what you're doing — or change jobs.

## Step #6: Satisfy

Once you have been given the opportunity to service the account, you have to perform the service with the same professionalism as when you sold the service. You've talked the talk, now you have to walk the walk. (I'll give you some specific suggestions in a later chapter.)

## Step #7:  Collect

Once you've rendered the service and the customer is pleased with your efforts, quickly collect the monies that are owed you. If this sounds obvious to you, join the club. But, you'd be surprised how many people provide a service and never get paid for one of a zillion reasons. The most frequent reason is that they don't have a *system* in place to automatically collect invoices. (There it is again, the need for a system.)

## Step # 8:  Measure

At regular intervals after you have converted a prospect to an active account, you need to measure the value of your account quantitatively and qualitatively. This is very important. Ask yourself how you feel about the relationship. Do you feel good about the account, the possibilities and the future? Or do you resent having to deal with those "low lifes"?

I can make more money for you, improve your bottom line, and put a smile on your face without selling one thing. How? With this advice: Identify your deadbeat accounts — the handful of people whose attitudes are dragging you down . . . people who want the moon for the price of a Big Mac.

Once you identify these "repeat offenders," I wouldn't be rude, cruel or impolite. Simply suggest that your relationship needs some fixing and provide them with one or two options. They can change their attitude (or fix whatever the repeat offense is) or you would be happy to help them select another source who will respond better to their style of doing business (like, say, Attila the Hun).

Measure your relationships with current clients because they may not be doing you any good, and in fact, some may be doing you harm. Trust your gut feelings. Do this every six months.

## Step #9:  Expand

Expand the services you provide to your client base. Brainstorm how else you can help your clients. Can you help with vacations? Ground transportation, like limousines? Can you help them organize business meetings? Provide accounting assistance with incentive programs? Help them buy theater tickets? Challenge and press the envelope on your (or your firm's) concept of the services you provide.

For example, if you are a corporate travel agent, take the position that you provide executive services. Your clients don't need you just for tickets. They don't need you to simply book a hotel or a rental car. Their secretaries are intelligent people and can call the car rental agency directly or any airline on a toll-free number. You are a provider of executive services. And your services are not found so easily by dialing 1-800.

## Step # 10:  Repeat

Now that you have The System running smoothly and you know the steps by heart, you simply do it again. Repeat the entire process. That's how The System works. You are, in all probability, in a business where the realistic expectation is that you can aspire to hit singles and not homeruns, just like the rest of us. That's not a negative statement. You can score a lot of runs with a long succession of singles. Once you get The System set up, you just repeat it and repeat it and repeat it. Or, as they say in my home state of New Jersey — bada bing, bada bam, bada boom!

Let's look at more ways to feed new prospects into the "Repeat the Process" step.

# CHAPTER 7

# FEEDING YOUR SYSTEM WITH NEW PROSPECTS

You've set up your System and now you want to follow Step #10 of the previous chapter which said, "Repeat the Process." One problem. You need to feed the system new prospects. (That's like saying to George Foreman, "Don't worry, George, whenever you are hungry, I'll find you a burger.") You've defined your territory and now you're identifying people who have an apparent interest in your service. In a previous chapter I suggested business directories as a fast and effective way to begin the process. If you are going to keep The System operating, you need lots of tools to find prospects. Here are other proven sources of prospects.

## Client Referrals

Approach a handful of satisfied customers. The best time to do this is as soon as a customer congratulates you or thanks you for a job well done. You can then say without hesitation,

**Salesperson:** *"Thank you for saying that. Incidentally, do you know any other people/companies/ associations who might enjoy learning about our service/program?"*

Be a little cautious when asking customers for referrals. Your client might not want to take the time, take other people's time, or personally endorse things. If the client says no or dodges your request, be smart and let it drop.

One other suggestion. Build into your System a "referral letter." Keep a form on your word processor, and whenever you complete a job for a client, send it out soliciting two things: (1) a brief note of recommendation; and (2) the names of any people the client thinks may benefit from your services.

## Ask Prospects

Another good method for building your prospect base is by asking prospects. Many salespeople assume that if a prospect doesn't buy from them there is no potential left in the relationship. Not so. A prospect can and should be asked for referrals. You need to create a recognition in the prospect of your professionalism before asking for a referral. But if you are perceived as credible, trustworthy and ethical, your prospect will have no qualms about referring you to others.

When you approach a prospect who is totally happy with his service provider, he would be nuts to switch just because you appear somewhat squared away. His failure to entertain your offer has nothing to do with you or your company. Simply say,

**Salesperson:** *"It is refreshing to hear that you are a satisfied customer but perhaps you know somebody who is not so happy."*

You then ask for a referral. If you don't get one, you are not a clown. You haven't set yourself up for rejection. This is nothing more and nothing less than a professional way of doing business.

## Company Leads And Orphan Clients

This source is often overlooked. Your own company probably has highly qualified leads buried in file cabinets — former customers who have done business with you years ago but for one reason or another have stopped. When you unearth a former client, you call them and say,

**Salesperson:** *"Mr. Jones, I understand that you once did business with us and you stopped for reasons that are unclear to me. I'd like to learn what problems might have upset you so I can fix them and ask you to give us another opportunity to work with you."*

(I am not suggesting you parrot my words. If you like them and you can say them naturally, by all means, be my guest. Chances are you will feel better using your own words. Either way, you get the drift.)

By farming your own file cabinets you will find without question some qualified prospects who have a use for what you provide.

## Your Company's Employees

Some time back, I had been working with a company for two years, when one of our employees came up to me and said, "Mike, I don't know if you're interested in this or not, but my next door neighbor works for IBM, and I think he's connected somehow to the purchasing department." My immediate response was, "Where have you been for two years?"

My permanent response was that a good way to build a prospecting list is to ask your own employees if they know anyone who might have an interest in what you do.

People who are not marketing oriented do not think about sales. They think about operations. So, if you approach some of your employees and ask them who they know — neighbors, friends, relatives — who might be interested in what you do, you're going to uncover some potential prospects with a personal connection to someone in your own company.

## Friends And Social Contacts

Friends and social contacts are another area that many salespeople fail to capitalize on. I'm sure you have some friends that don't know what you do for a living. Take the time to write them and explain exactly what you do. Then ask for referrals.

How about memberships in civic and professional organizations? You can't join them all, but you can join the Rotary Club, Chamber of Commerce, P.T.A. or any clubs that are of particular interest to you. (Of course, you should not join just to sell something.) You will join to learn, to network or to congregate. Along the way, you will have ample opportunity to explain what you do for a living.

## Centers Of Influence

A center of influence is someone with above average visibility, reputation, or Rolodex in a position to point you toward prospects or steer prospects to you. He or she is someone important to you for one reason or another. There are centers of influence in every facet of life.

To ask a favor of someone who is going to influence the opinion of others, you've got to have established a certain level of rapport. Be sure that this person understands the benefits you have provided other clients as well as the type of prospects you are interested in.

## Canvassing

Canvassing is a term used for cold calling. It used to be known as "chasing smoke stacks." There's a right way to do it and there's a wrong way. Here's the way I do it.

First, you can't afford to just cold call. Ringing doorbells and walking into companies unannounced to make a sale runs the risk of labeling you a nuisance. Consider these two methods: First, politely and unassumingly walk into a place of business and ask for information. If your territory is like mine in New Jersey, every building has a sign hanging on the door saying "No Soliciting." News Flash! You are not a "solicitor." A solicitor by definition is someone who is attempting to sell something. You're not selling anything. Think of yourself as entering this office seeking information.

Walk up to the receptionist feeling very squared away with your card in hand and say,

**MM:** *"My name is Mike Marchev, Corporate Travel Systems. Since I was in the neighborhood, I would like to find the name of the person in your company responsible for making travel decisions. I'd like to write the person a letter and introduce our services."*

You are not selling anything. You are looking for a name. The receptionist will provide you with a name every single time. Then say,

**MM:** *"Excuse me, but do you have an envelope?"*

They will give you an envelope every single time. On the envelope is the address of the company neatly printed. Write the contact name on the envelope along with the name of the person who just gave you this valuable information. (This is a good idea because chances are you will call that company in a day or two and it's nice to say, "Mary, remember me? I was the fellow who came in and asked for that envelope the other day.")

Do you see how easy this is? Turning to leave you have your envelope and you have the name of the contact. But a thought strikes you. You turn and ask the receptionist,

**MM:** *"Excuse me, but does Mr. Smith ever see anybody unannounced?"*

Most of the time they will say "no" and suggest you call for an appointment. But from time to time you will get lucky. You have absolutely nothing to lose. As long as you are polite, you can try this little gambit without apology. If the person does grant you some on-the-spot face time, your solitary mission is to introduce yourself.

**MM:** *"Mr. Smith I appreciate your coming to see me. My name is Mike Marchev. Is there a time next week when I can meet with you to introduce our service? It will take about fifteen minutes. I think you'll find what I have to say to be very interesting."*

Most people caught by surprise will only be seeing you out of natural courtesy and they will appreciate your professionalism in not trying to sell something on the spot.

Here is the second method I use to canvass: Walk into an office unannounced and say,

**MM:** *"Excuse me, I was driving by and couldn't help but notice your sign on the front lawn. What is it that you do here?"*

Again, you're not selling anything. You don't go in with your bag of tricks or your brochures. Often, the receptionist will feel unqualified to answer in detail. The receptionist will call Mr. Smith and say, "Mr. Smith, someone's at the front desk asking what we do." If you're lucky, Mr. Smith will come out to check out the action.

> **MM:** *"Mr. Smith, Mike Marchev is my name. I was driving by heading for the Bigelow Company and I saw your sign. I was curious to learn what your company does."*

True story: I have had plant tours as a result of walking into companies unannounced and showing an interest in what they do.

## Conventions And Trade Shows

These are always good places to pick up leads and capture names. Again, you are not there to sell; you are there to identify prospects. You approach a booth and introduce yourself.

> **MM:** *"My name is Mike Marchev. I know you're busy and trying to sell. Here's my card. When you get back home in a couple of weeks I'd like to call you. I think I have something that you'll want to hear about."*

They will take your card 100% of the time, if only to get rid of you. After all, they paid a huge rent to stand on a 10 x 10 square foot piece of convention center to do what you just did for free. Yep! They'll take your card every time. Take their card as you leave. Now, you have a person's name to follow-up with, and you have a common denominator, the show.

## Directories

As mentioned in Chapter 5, be sure you check your local library for information, and introduce yourself to the reference desk librarian. (Consider her the Captain Kirk of the book stacks — helping you to boldly go where no salesperson has gone before . . . to seek out new leads and new prospect locations.)

## Networking

The purpose of networking is to make contacts with people who have a common interest and to utilize their contacts and experiences. Don't for a minute think that networking is only about you. An equal, if not more important, piece of the networking puzzle involves you helping others achieve their goals and objectives. In fact, I strongly urge you to give before you get.

Professionals meeting and helping professionals — that's what networking is all about. Several years ago I joined the New York City Sales and Marketing Club. At the time, they held luncheons once a month and often featured a guest speaker. At every meeting I would meet ten to twelve new people, swap business cards, and find out what they all did for a living. It was fun and I looked forward to each meeting.

Networking may occasionally appear to be a waste of time. But when it works, it pays big dividends. It's effective because nobody gets upset that you're hustling — the arena is set up for working and interacting. You don't go there if you don't want to meet people and find out who's doing what and how they can help each other.

## The Sunday Newspaper

Every Sunday morning I pour myself a cup of coffee and open the newspaper. I turn to the Help Wanted Ads and clip advertisements of companies in my area. I figure the companies that are hiring are growing and probably need to buy supportive materials and services. The ads are usually sorted by industry. So, if you know your target industry, the prospecting becomes very focused. In many of the ads you can find a contact's name or an address. Some even have phone numbers.

Every Sunday, you will find about fifteen or twenty new opportunities. Simply clip the want ads from the newspaper and on Monday morning, as soon as you get to work, make some phone calls.

## Direct Mail

This is one of my favorite ways to add names to my prospect list. Direct mail positions you as a professional organization and will prove instrumental in getting you in to speak with decision makers. If administered properly, your prospects will call and ask to see *you*.

## Newsletters Produced By Your Prospects

Try to get on corporate mailing lists if you can. Getting on a prospect's mailing list can be very rewarding because the latest information comes right to your door periodically with contact names, phone numbers, calendars, events and much more. How cool is that?

## Ride The "Terror Train"

An actual survey some years back uncovered the one thing that most professionals feared literally worse than death — public speaking. But if you can get by the terror of the first few times, you'll find speaking is a fabulous prospecting tool. Why? Because it positions you as an "expert." You are The Authority. (Relax . . . you do not need to know all the answers to be an "authority." The proof: All those Wall Street analysts interviewed on TV who sound impressive at the moment, but turn out to be wrong about as often as they are right.)

You can make opportunities happen. Regardless of your industry, I am sure you have some information that many clubs and organizations in your town would find interesting. You simply write an introductory letter and say, "I'm available to speak on ABC. If you would like to learn about ABC, give me a call. I'll be happy to fill in on short notice or help whenever I can."

Professional organizations will call in response. They are always seeking people to speak at weekly or monthly luncheon programs. Just write a brief letter and say you're available. Period. All Aboard!

You can see from the above suggestions that there are many ways to find prospects who can use your service. Consider yourself a gorilla warfare commando. If you are like most entrepreneurial companies you probably don't have the dollars and the people to do big promotional projects. That's okay. Use your energy and cunning to try a few of the things I just mentioned. Launch a luncheon speaking grenade here, a direct mail missile there. Commandeer some newsletters.

What you're trying to do, and this is very important, is to identify people to put in the top of your funnel to sort out as suspects or as bona fide prospects. Do this and you will have more and more customers.

## CHAPTER 8

# MAKING THE TELEPHONE
# YOUR WEAPON OF CHOICE

One of the most important weapons you have to implement The System is your telephone. But as with any weapon, you need to be trained in its proper use. Most people do not enjoy "putting themselves on the firing line" so they avoid (without realizing it) using the telephone. They fuss with prospect lists, enter endless information on their computer database, analyze and study their product or service — all the while subtly avoiding the thing they have to do to succeed — make the call!

This next statement you can take to the bank. The more you pick up the telephone, the more money you are going to make. It's a direct relationship. Let me repeat that in a strict mathematical formulation:

### Picking up the telephone + dialing = $

What outcomes can occur as a result of your picking up the phone? Let's list the negative outcomes. The person on the other end of the phone may not want to speak with you; may not be interested in what you're talking about; may hang up on you; or may be nasty or rude.

Chances are that you have exhibited all of these behaviors at one time or another when some unsolicited caller dialed your number. This does not make you a bad person, just a disinterested one. In all of my selling days on the telephone only two people have ever been nasty to me. Many people have not been interested. That's okay.

The good things that can happen on the telephone far outweigh the bad. Here's a list: You may have a very pleasant conversation; find somebody who is interested in what you do; schedule an appointment that leads to new business; learn something that will lead you to an entirely different strategy; get a tip on a hot internet stock that sends you into immediate retirement on a beach in Hawaii. (I put that last one in to be sure you are paying attention. Obviously, I haven't experienced that positive outcome yet. But, believe me, the good things far outweigh the bad things.)

## Re-Orient Your Reason For The Call

Let me give you an attitude that will make it easier for you to use the telephone as a marketing tool. Most people don't enjoy calling strangers because of the anxiety associated with "selling" on the telephone. We all naturally fear (or at least dislike) rejection. And when you try to "sell" on a first phone call you are bound to get a lot of what feels like rejection. So don't try to sell on the telephone. You can't sell on the telephone. Re-orient yourself to a new objective — a new goal of calling:

### You are not calling to sell.
### You are calling to schedule an appointment.

If I told you to sell me a toaster on the telephone, or sell me a car, or a trip to Tahiti, picking up the telephone would become a very painful experience and hard on your stomach. You might even stumble on your words. But if I said call me and simply ask if I can meet you for lunch, that would be very easy.

Here is how it might sound,

**MM:** *"Hi. My name's Mike Marchev, from Corporate Travel Systems. I'd like to take you to lunch to outline a very attractive service that we offer corporate clients."*

This is a no brainer. You don't have to rehearse a formal sales script or worry about handling some bizarre objection. You are simply calling to schedule an appointment. You are not a crook. There are only two types of people in the world — those you can help and those you can't help. Your single purpose is to find out which category this particular prospect falls into. And the cleanest way to accomplish this in short order is via a personal meeting. That's it. Start using the telephone for the purpose it was designed — to make appointments.

Here are a few telephone techniques which will help you land that appointment.

## Maintain Control

When you call a prospect, *you* are initiating the call — it's your dime and your idea. Therefore, you should be in control of the call. Many people initiate the call and then pass control to the other person. Don't let this happen to you. When you call, I want you to immediately identify yourself, your organization, and who you want to speak with.

In the majority of cases, the gatekeeper will say, "What's this in regard to?" (I know that's what they are going to say because that is what Alexander Graham Bell was told on his first call.)

I want you to answer the gatekeeper's interrogation in a clear, polite fashion. (Remember, you do not have a hidden agenda or any intentions of manipulating anybody, so don't feel defensive.)

Instead, you want to come across with an air of confidence — an *expectation* that, of course, Mr. Big would want you put right through to him. People will respond to you on the phone the way they decode your confidence level. If you appear unsure of who you want to speak with or what you are calling about, the gatekeeper will cross you off as another cold call, put your name on that little pink piece of message paper, and use it to dispose of her gum. Be confident and you will maintain control and take the script away from the gatekeepers. They will interpret your call as a professional call and will pass you along to the person you would like to speak with. (I realize that it doesn't always work this way. More on tough calls in a minute.)

## The Best Time To Call

My message in this chapter should be clear. Get on the phone and call people. You may think of a million reasons why you can't or shouldn't, but all of them are bogus. Examples:

- *"It's only eight-thirty in the morning. Let me give Mr. Caffeine an opportunity to have his first cup of coffee."*

- *"It's almost lunch time. I'll call right after lunch. I don't want to bother Mr. Pritikin at lunchtime."*

- *"It's December 12th and I don't want to call Mr. Claus this close to Christmas."*

- *"It's Monday — it's too early in the week."*

- *" It's Friday — too late in the week. "*

There are a million reasons to avoid the telephone. But there is a best time to call somebody. NOW! Whenever you think of it.

When the idea hits you. When that person enters your mind. When what you are reading triggers a prospecting idea.

I call most prospects before eight o'clock in the morning and after five because I know that decision-makers usually come to work early and stay late while gatekeepers often leave pretty close to schedule. I also call people during lunch. Many executives eat lunch at their desk while the gatekeepers are away from the phone. When the phone rings you'll often find yourself talking directly with Mr. or Mrs. Big.

## Create What-If Scenarios

Once you make the call, you know that only a few replies are likely after you ask for an appointment. You know what all the options are. So prepare by spending a few moments playing "what if."

Here is a useful analogy. What do professional firefighters do when they're not putting out fires? Do you think they play pool, wash the engines, or play cards? How about throw a frisbee in front of the firehouse or watch a brawl on the Jerry Springer show?

You would be wrong. What firemen do between fires is have "what-if-scenario" meetings. They ask themselves what would they do if the grocery store downtown caught fire during rush hour, or the only high-rise in town broke out in flames on the eighth floor? They assign specific tasks well in advance so when the fire alarm sounds, each and every person on the force knows exactly how to respond.

You and I are not in the business of fighting fires but we can learn a great deal from these people. Professionals, regardless of the industry, go through the same type of preparation. What if. . .? When you prepare in advance for at least the most probable outcomes, you will be more successful.

Let's try a sales example using the travel agency analogy. You make a call:

**MM:** *"This is Mike Marchev from Mike's Do It Right Travel Service. I'm calling Mr. Smith to schedule an appointment."*

**Gatekeeper:** *"Mike, are you a travel agency?"*

**MM:** *"Why yes I am."*

**Gatekeeper:** *"Mike, let me save you some time. We are totally pleased with who we are using to make our company's travel arrangements."*

Is this a stretch, or do prospects actually say that? (The foregoing is called a "rhetorical question.") The gatekeeper/prospect can also say:

- *"Mike, the president's wife is a travel agent."*

- *"We don't use travel agencies."*

- *"We just changed travel agencies recently."*

- *"Mr. Smith is not in at the moment."*

- *"Mr. Smith is in a meeting which is probably going to last until the Supremes reunite."* (If you hear this one or something like it, you may want to re-charge your self-confidence unit for a while.)

- *"Mr. Smith's on vacation."*

- *"Mike, we don't travel that much."*

- *"What could you do that our present agency is not already doing?"*

As you make more and more calls, you will adapt this list to ten or fifteen responses that typically come at you over the phone when you ask for an appointment.

We will look at some of these responses and suggest how you can get past each one in a moment. But first . . .

## Avoiding The Death Pause

What you want to prevent at all costs is what I call the "Death Pause." The "Death Pause" goes something like this:

**Ron Rookie:** *"I'm Ron Rookie from the A.B.C. Travel Agency. I'd like to speak to Mr. Smith to schedule an introductory meeting with him one day next week."*

**Gatekeeper:** *"Ron, why should Mr. Smith do business with you?"*

**Ron Rookie:** (Silence — not prepared for this question.)

Silence is all that can be heard over the telephone line — a sickly, loud lack of sound . . . the Death Pause. If you are a live, breathing human being, your stomach will be the first thing to go. Your nervous system will kick in full blast, and you will start to sweat. Next your hands start shaking and you wish you had never called in the first place. You become totally humiliated as you don't have a clue what to say. The silence is getting louder and you can feel your heart beating through your shirt. You know you have to say something fast. But what? You hear yourself making a noise. You are speaking. You say,

**Ron Rookie:** *"Well, in case you change your mind, I'll be happy to help you."*

You then offer to send some literature, which the savvy gatekeeper agrees to, knowing that this is the sign that you will soon be hanging up. You hang up the phone and don't know whether to start crying or reach for the want ads to find a new job in accounting.

This entire negative scene can be avoided with a little work up front. Do your homework and recognize the fifteen logical responses that might surface during your call. Consider it "insurance" against the Death Pause.

## Handling The Most Common Responses

Remember you are not a crook, and all you want to do is ask for an opportunity to meet with somebody. If the prospect doesn't want to meet with you, you don't particularly want to meet with the prospect. You are looking for people who want to speak with you about the product or service you are offering.

Because my personality and your personality are probably different, I can't put the words I might say in your mouth. You have to write your own script for your own "what-if" scenarios. Ask yourself, "If my prospect says this, what would I say back?" Then literally create the script. Try it, and over time keep refining it.

For example, how would you handle the "We don't travel that much" scenario? A lot of salespeople might respond with, "Well, how much do you travel?" Or "How many people travel?" Or "How big is your travel budget?" In other words, they start firing questions in response to avoid the Death Pause.

Here's the way I would handle it.

**Gatekeeper/Prospect:** *"Mike, thanks for calling. We don't travel that much."*

**MM:** *"This may sound funny to you but that's exactly why I called you. My company specializes in firms like yours which don't travel that much. It's been our experience that most of our competitors are chasing the IBM's and the G.E.'s and the companies with large travel budgets. We have found that there are a lot of companies like yours*

77

*whose travelers really need the services we provide. We purposely target local businesses that don't travel as much as the big corporations. It'll take me about fifteen minutes to outline our program to you. You really don't have very much to lose."*

Do you want companies who don't travel that much at the top of your list? Probably not. But you have to read through the smoke. The gatekeeper/prospect wasn't awaiting your call and probably didn't initially focus on what it was you were saying. The immediate knee-jerk response was to get rid of you and get back to whatever he or she was doing. The reason you were told "We don't travel that much" was to get you to hang up first.

Having done your homework, you know that this was a possible scenario and you are ready. When you answer your prospects with an intelligent, polite, "Yes, however", you will find yourself getting more appointments.

I mentioned that a lot of salespeople start firing questions over the telephone to avoid the Death Pause. Here are my thoughts concerning this practice. The person you just called doesn't owe you a thing — including answers to your questions. If you are going to ask a question, I recommend you ask permission before going to Q&A. It really irks me when I make a call and the person answering the phone simply states, "That line is busy, please hold." Boom! All of a sudden I'm listening to "If I Say You Have A Beautiful Body Will You Hold It Against Me?" on country music station KCOW. If they simply took three seconds and asked, "May I put you on hold?" I'd be happy to listen to Willie Nelson sing "You Shouldn't Mess with the IRS."

The same principle holds true when you want to ask a prospect some questions.

Compare these dialogues.

**Rookie:** *"Mr. Enchilada, where do you plan to travel next month? Where have you been? How much do you spend on travel each month? Do you go first class or coach?"*

**Prospect (thinking to self):** *"Who is this bozo? I don't owe him any answers and I don't know why he wants to know."*

Now try it my way.

**MM:** *"Mr. Banana, may I ask you three questions concerning your travel habits?"*

**Prospect:** *"O.K."*

Then you can fire away because the prospect gave you permission to ask. Remember: Before asking the questions, ask permission to ask questions.

Back to asking for an appointment. Once you realize that you are not going to get the appointment, you should shift gears and try to learn something that will help you the next time you decide to try again with this prospect. You might say,

**MM:** *"I understand. Personally, I wouldn't change either if I was totally happy with who I was doing business with. Before hanging up, may I ask you three questions? Is your annual travel budget closer to ten thousand or one-hundred thousand dollars? Do you ever travel internationally? Do you have a central travel coordinator or does each individual secretary book your travel?"*

Ask two or three questions that will help you position the prospect as an A, B, or C candidate.

## Penetrating The "Ditchboard"

A constant hurdle in telephone marketing is circumventing the infamous switchboard — or as I sometimes call it, the

79

Ditchboard, because the job description requires the operator to "ditch" all salespeople. Let me give you some ideas on this.

First, if you find yourself being screened at the switchboard, don't get annoyed with the operators. For every call they handle from a squared away individual like yourself, they get two hundred from a bunch of clowns dressed like professional salespeople. Understand that the people trying to "ditch you" is doing nothing more than their job. Be nice because you'll only get into the castle if they open the gate.

When a switchboard operator screens you, thank her (or him) politely, get off the phone, wait a day or two, and then call again. But, before hanging up the first time get the gatekeeper's name so the next time you call you can address her personally.

**MM:** *"Hi Mary, this is Mike Marchev. I spoke with you last week. You told me that you thought your boss was totally satisfied with the agency you are doing business with. May I ask you a question? This is very important, because I think we have a service that Mr. Smith is going to find very interesting. How would you suggest I go about getting an appointment with him?"*

In other words,

## To get the Gatekeeper to play on your team, ask for help.

Do this and you will position yourself as someone who means business because very few salespeople return a second time as quickly as you did. You weren't arrogant. You had no tricks up your sleeve. Your job is to schedule an appointment with Mr. Smith, and you are politely persistent and tenacious. What's more, you respectfully asked the Gatekeeper to share her expertise as to how to navigate the obstacle course. This won't always work, but the odds are pretty good.

Another way I have gotten past switchboards is by saying,

**MM:** *"Could you please connect me with the sales department."*

Most switchboards consider this a good thing. Sales is something that helps everybody at the company eat regularly. If you ask to speak to somebody in sales, very few operators will ask you "why." Once you are connected to the sales department you then say,

**MM:** *"I'm not sure if I'm in the right place. I'm trying to find the person responsible for making your travel decisions."*

Correct directions are usually forthcoming.

The important mindset to keep is that you're not trying to sell while using the telephone (in most cases). All you're trying to do is schedule an appointment to introduce yourself and your program.

When you do succeed in scheduling an appointment, don't quit on this "upper." Many salespeople decide that it's Miller Time and stop calling. Don't. When you get an appointment, your energies are up. Your voice is up. Your program worked. You become charged and excited. Make another call right away. You will find yourself on a roll. You will be more confident. As professional golfers say, "You are in the Zone." Don't take yourself out of the game now! Continue to place at least ten more calls after you managed to schedule an appointment. Everything will be working for you.

When you decide to start your telemarketing program, block out a specific time each day to make your calls. Know that there will be a sense of rejection in this exercise by definition (unless you follow the mindset I gave you in Chapter 3), but don't stop calling. You may have to make a hundred phone calls to talk to fifteen people to get six presentations scheduled to get one piece of business. Those numbers are not high or low. Your numbers will be what they will be.

Remember,

## The more people you call, the more money you're going to make.

That is how it works. Make those calls.

# CHAPTER 9

# PROSPECT MEETINGS THAT GET RESULTS

Our profession has an old saying, "Selling is a contact sport." This means that to sell something, you must meet with the prospect. You have to put your face in front of people before you can establish rapport and make them feel comfortable enough with you to do business with you.

You've been working hard to identify and pre-qualify prospects. You've been contacting individuals asking for a few minutes of their time so you can outline your program and its benefits. So what if everything you have done actually works? What do you do if your prospect agrees to a personal meeting?

Many salespeople who are successful getting appointments fail when it comes to being prepared to meet with a prospect and take the relationship to the next level. All too often these salespeople resort to what comes naturally — reciting their company's brochure. They almost become a talking brochure. If you simply recite your firm's brochure ("we have eighteen people; we've been in business fifteen years and we're the best") your prospect's eyes will glaze over slowly but surely, like he's watching a potato grow.

Most prospects are intelligent and polite. So, if you are granted an interview, you will find that prospects do not throw you out of their office even when you show up as a talking brochure. They will probably look at you, nod their heads, and pretend they are interested in what you are saying. In reality, there is a very good chance they are thinking,

> **Prospect (thinking):** *"This is all pretty trite. When are you going to tell me something I don't already know? I canceled my root canal for this!?"*

Trouble is, you won't know your prospect is writing you off since he'll be smiling and nodding politely.

Go in prepared. Meetings like this don't grow on trees. You've got to know exactly what information you are going in with, and, I hasten to add, exactly what information you want to take away from the meeting.

Here are some general guidelines to help make your meetings more productive.

## Cram For The Exam

Think of your preparation for the meeting like the proverbial "cram" for an exam. The topic: Your prospect's business and industry. These days, you can almost begin and end your research on the Internet.

Research the company's web site and an additional industry site. Another good source of information for large public companies is www.sec.gov — where the Securities and Exchange Commission archives all public company documents. Here your best source of information is a form called a 10-K.

This form is like a super annual report, with all kinds of information about the company's business, operations, officers, and financial results. Depending on what you are selling, this information can be incredibly valuable. At the very least, you will immediately win the prospect's respect when you demonstrate that you took the time to know about his company's business and operations.

## Lights, Camera, Action

Treat every presentation like it's an event. You are on stage before a captive audience. Warm up and treat the meeting as a unique opportunity. Believe that every prospect will listen if what you have to say is worth listening to. Remember that enthusiasm is contagious. Look alive and show your enthusiasm for your product or service.

People usually end up doing business with people they like. So, one of your primary objectives in going to a meeting, other than to fact find, is to make this new person feel like a friend. Focus on getting the prospect to feel comfortable with you. If you go with that objective in mind, you probably will find something about the prospect that you like. That creates a very valuable chemistry.

## Mirror, Mirror On The Wall

The prospect may want to know something about you, too. But, keep your description of your qualifications brief. People who "sell" their qualifications come off as insecure or pompous. Keep your self-description to two or three minutes (practice with a watch). Then focus on showing a sincere interest in your prospect's business. Almost every sentence that comes out of your mouth from there on should have a question mark planted at the end.

## Take Along An Enforcer

You want to impose a discipline on the meeting that will give you the best shot at success. So take along an "enforcer." Go in with a written agenda to hand to the prospect. Tell the prospect that you took the liberty of outlining, say, eight main points you would like to touch on in the next fifteen minutes. (These should be designed to fact find and uncover "hot buttons" as well as show your qualifications.) Then *ask* if you can proceed.

By using a written agenda, you give the prospect (a) confidence that you are a professional who respects the prospect's time, and (b) an opportunity right out of the blocks to amend your presentation as he sees fit. When the prospect buys into your agenda, there is no need to hurry or guess later on.

Another reason to lead with an agenda: When the prospect shows an interest in the agenda, you will sense this and become more comfortable. Plus, if the interview drifts away from the planned presentation, having a written agenda will pull the discussion back to the points you wanted to make and the questions you need to ask.

## Run The Prospect Through Your "MRI"

Your fundamental mission in the first meeting is to uncover the prospect's hot buttons — his problems, concerns, reasons for choosing one service provider over another, goals, etc. This is in-depth diagnosis, like a hospital CAT scan. You are going to run the prospect through your own custom-designed "MRI" (Marketing Research Inquisition) while keeping him much more calm and contented than the typical patient is when they are run through the donut.

Here are some basic questions you should use in your MRI.

- *When are you looking to buy an "XYZ"?*
- *What feature do you find most attractive/important?*

- *Can you explain why you feel this way?*

- *Of all of the reasons people buy XYZ's, why did you pick that particular feature or benefit as the most important?*

These questions can be tailored to fit any service or product you are selling. With these questions, you are throwing the ball into the prospect's court and asking him to define his hot button.

Let's use shopping for a car as an example. Ask people what feature they feel is most important in a car and the answers might include: image, gas mileage, price, durability, reliability, safety, color, radio, speed. What is important to one buyer is not important to another. So, by fact finding you locate the hot button needed to close the deal. I once explored for the hot button of a would-be car buyer and closed the sale solely on the sound quality of the speakers built into the rear seats. (True story.) Have you noticed that Ford finally found this hot button? They recently featured their Delco radio products in car commercials!

Let's try travel. Ask your prospect what service is most attractive/important when selecting a travel agency? Among the many possible answers are: proximity, years of experience of agents, international capabilities, other major clients currently served, Internet booking capabilities, payment plans, meeting and conference capabilities, etc.

Once you find a potential hot button, probe it with more questions. For example,

**Salesperson:** *"What do you mean by international capabilities?"*

**Prospect:** *"We look for somebody who is familiar with the airports in France and Germany, and who can help us with international customs regulations, exchange rates, and visa and passport paperwork."*

**Salesperson:** *"Of all the important factors you could have named, what made you choose this one?"*

(Some very specific reasoning is about to surface. )

**Prospect:** *"Because ninety-nine percent of our travel is overseas."*

By asking these questions, you learn the customer's concerns and focus, which allow you to start forming a strategy to address these specific needs.

Here are a few more fact-finding questions you can ask:

- *How do you handle your travel presently?*

- *What is it you like most about your present agency?*

- *What was the service or attribute that determined your selection of your present agency?*

- *Is there anything you don't like about the way your travel is being handled?*

## Clarify & Confirm

This may sound like a cliché, but not too many people do it — you have to listen to and understand what the prospect says. More importantly, you should always clarify any ambiguity or trace of a hot button by saying,

**Salesperson:** *"Mr. Jones, let me see if I'm hearing you correctly. Your most pressing concern is . . ."*

Repeat your current understanding of the prospect's needs and get confirmation. Then you can address the need accurately. While doing so, salt in your qualifications and experience as they relate to his need.

# Life After Death

Remember, there are only two kinds of people — those who are (or can become) interested in what you represent and those who are (or will) not. The latter group might have given you a slot on their calendar because they didn't know how to say no. Most experienced salespeople know within ten minutes if they are on the same wavelength as a prospective client. As you get more familiar with The System and your confidence level builds, you will get better at distinguishing the two before you go to the meeting phase. Meanwhile, view these dead-end meetings as a great place to practice your presentation and meeting skills.

# Obscene Gestures

Reading body language is another skill you will want to develop over time. As you grow more confident in what you are saying, you will gain the flexibility to focus at the same time on the other person's non-verbal communications. Often this is quite enlightening (and amusing).

If a prospect picks up a pencil and starts tapping it, you can bet your burger that this guy has tuned out. If he picks up the mail and begins opening envelopes, you have burned your welcome to a crisp. Other telltale signs of your imminent demise: glancing at a watch, or quickly answering an incoming phone call.

Early in your career, you may witness all these "obsceni-ties" of body language. These episodes of embarrassment and frustration come with the territory. When these occur, your agenda (or your presentation of it) is not working. The best advice: either move through the remainder of the meeting quickly, or be disarmingly honest by telling the prospect you

89

feel like you are not addressing his concerns. Ask again what they are. Remember, what doesn't kill you makes you stronger.

## No Thanks, Dr. Kervorkian

A slow form of suicide is the act of trying to sell somebody something when they clearly and steadfastly are refusing to be sold. Yes, tenacity is a virtue in the sales business. But as Kenny Rodgers said: "You've got to know when to hold 'em and know when to fold 'em." Don't keep spending time with somebody who is not interested in you and/or your product. Life is too short. Part company amicably and move on.

## The Follow Up

You've made it your business to talk with more people, gone in with an agenda, and run your MRI. Now that you have all the information you need, ask if you can come back with some suggestions (your "proposal") after having an opportunity to think about what you have learned. You are now poised for the last act before the close.

In closing this chapter, I want you to remember these final three rules when it comes to giving a first-class presentation:

**Be Bright.**
**Be Brief.**
**Be Gone.**

# CHAPTER 10

# WRITING WINNING PROPOSALS

Y ou have completed the interview, identified your prospect's needs and your ability to address them, and now you want to follow up with a proposal. First, some words of comfort. When putting thoughts in writing it is natural to experience what is commonly called "writer's block." (If this has ever happened to you, then I am glad to report that you show signs of being human.) I believe salespeople tend to complicate this skill far more than necessary. So, let's keep it simple.

I want you to become familiar with two types of proposals: (1) the requested proposal — when a company sends out a formal request (an RFP, or request for proposal to bid on their business); and (2) the informal, or "letter" proposal when the prospect asks you to send your response to his needs. The primary difference is that in the formal RFP, you answer the prospect's specific questions in a format defined by the prospect. You can embellish your answers and suggestions here and there, but the company that issues an RFP is looking for a structured response to a well-defined need. The letter proposal on the other hand is entirely up to you. This can be a one pager or a full 100 pages with attached graphics accompanied by a 3.5

inch disc and instructions on how to download more stuff from your web site.

Either way you go, and I say this with extreme caution, I believe based on my experience that eighty percent of companies requesting a proposal have already made up their mind who they will be working with.

Why? Because people tend to do business with people they like. And if an RFP is the only way a decision-maker gets to know you, well . . . you've lost the deal already. But if you initiate the relationship with direct mail, telephone follow up, personal interviews, and live face-to-face communications, the decision to do business with you is being established throughout the process. If I decide to do business with you, the details are not going to get in the way of that decision. We will find ways to deal with the details. If I decide that I do not want to do business with you, having all the details tightly tied up in neat rows on four color graphs will not change my decision.

That being said, you are still going to have to write your share of proposals before your sales career comes to an end. So, get used to the idea and comfortable with the process.

Let's discuss the letter proposal first.

## Writing Letter Proposals

Don't wait to be asked to submit a letter proposal. Many decision-makers spend most of their day reacting to problems created by others. Simply put, they are too busy putting out fires to acquire and apply the requisite flame retardant to their business.

This presents the perfect opportunity for you to take the initiative and come up with some well-thought out ideas and pass them in front of the decision maker in an easy-to-read, clear and concise letter proposal. You are helping organize his work. (Your thoughtful proposal in effect provides a service to the prospect.) I did just that recently. Here is the story.

I attended a national convention for speakers at significant cost. I had every intention of getting my money's worth, so I attended every event I could. I was a mad man as I ran from seminar to seminar, to dinner, to workshops. I went up and down every aisle at the trade show and met everyone I could. I was a man on a mission.

Well, on the plane ride home I got to thinking. If I felt this way when spending my money investing in my future, many other people would probably appreciate a chock-a-block schedule at their annual meetings.

Rather than compete with a hundred other public speakers for the 2:30 p.m. workshop slot at my prospect's conference, I wrote a proposal for a 6:30 a.m. sunrise seminar program. My rationale was to provide the motivated professionals with an opportunity to pick up a few more pointers during the "dead time" of the day.

I had an idea. I put it on paper and I sent it in. I got the job.

Back to the letter.

The elements of a letter proposal are:

- a need;

- specific objectives;

- recommended methods;

- your qualifications;

- a budget or time line; and

- future follow-up programs (optional).

Let's look at one element at a time.

• **Element #1: A Need.** Hopefully, you've had your face-to-face meeting with the prospect and have identified his need. However, if the prospect wasn't clear as to precisely what he needed, you may want to go the "idea" route rather than the "I know what your problem is and I can fix it" route.

The approach of your proposal is, "Hey, I have an idea," or "If you're like everyone else in your industry this is a major concern of yours."

• **Element #2: Pin-pointing Objectives** — "With this particular need, I envision your objectives to be a, b, c." Back to our travel agency example. The objectives might be to maximize your company's travel while decreasing your travel budget by ten percent over the next twelve months. Another objective might be to introduce a form of payment which will maximize your company's float.

• **Element #3: Recommended Methods** — "This is how we are going to achieve your specific objectives." The key to success in this section is to keep the recommendations focused and easy to read. Use bullet points for each recommendation, with a few words bold faced to capture the idea.

• **Element #4: Qualifications** — Here you tell why you are qualified to take up this much of the prospect's time. You can go into personnel, your experience in the industry, your experience with similar problems, your success addressing similar problems, etc.

• **Element #5: Budget and Time Line** — Every prospect wants to know "how much?" and "how long?" Keep it short and sweet. Supply a time line along with your fee. For example, "If we can begin the project by the end of the month, the program will be fully functioning by the first week of September. The cost is $10,000."

- **Element #6: Follow up Programs** — If the nature of the service calls for one or more service follow ups, then propose accordingly. You may wish to convert follow ups into on optional engagement for recurring services (at a fee).

Anything else you want to include should be an attachment. You want the letter proposal to be no more than three pages (unless the prospect's needs are many and complex). No one will read a term paper. If you have additional ideas not directly associated with your proposal, include these in an attachment on "optional initiatives."

## The Formal Proposal

An RFP is sent to you to solicit your response to specific services or needs the prospect has identified. This proposal takes a little less creativity than the letter proposal because you are primarily "reacting" or "responding" to directives.

RFPs usually request responses in five different areas, although the order and specifics vary with the particular assignment:

(1)  specific services required;

(2)  facilities;

(3)  staffing and organization;

(4)  management and control; and

(5)  administration, billing and payment.

Let's use an actual RFP for travel services and focus on each section.

- **Section 1: Specific Services Required** — The RFP may ask you to describe your hours of operation, telephone system, how you handle incoming calls, how you input the information with regard to frequent travelers, your VIP profiling system, how you propose to deliver tickets on time, if you have American Express or Diners Club credit card programs and benefits, how you handle last seat availability, how you deal with unused tickets or partially used flight transportation coupons, how you would enforce the company's travel policy, how you assist with passports, visas, health certificates and other international travel items.

The typical travel service RFP will go into trip planning — how you help pre-plan trips, including airline schedules, airport locations, terminal services, ground transportation, and so on. The RFP may ask how you handle airline reservations and whose computer system you work with. Do you handle hotel/motel reservations? Do you accept commissions from the hotel/motel reservations? Do you call a centralized toll-free number or do you call the properties directly? Do you have special programs with auto rental or limo companies?

You can now clearly see the difference between your letter proposal and a full-blown RFP. You will be asked questions that might appear to be mini-micro management. (Take heart: When multi-millionaire J. W. Woolworth was building what was at the time the world's tallest skyscraper in New York City he wrote to the architect complaining of a $2.50 phone charge!) Don't think that every company you deal with will be this microscopic. Our travel agency example is probably a worst case scenario.

- **Section 2: Facilities** — Most travel agencies can't say a lot about facilities. The prospect usually wants to know how many miles you are located away from his plant to get a comfort level regarding service. In my experience, most people really don't care where you are as long as the product or service is delivered on time.

- **Section 3: Staffing and Organization** — Most RFPs ask the respondent to identify who will work on their specific account. Some even ask how much you pay your people, to get a feel for whether your workforce is permanent or transient. The RFP will also want you to explain how the designated services fit into your organizational structure.

- **Section 4: Management and Control** — Closely related to organizational structure is how you intend to manage and monitor the quality of products or services your firm provides. How will you handle complaints and resolve problems? How frequently will you monitor the program? Evaluation and feedback systems which insure effective communication should be explained. You'll want to give the company reassurance about the security of any information you receive that the company would not want made public.

- **Section 5: Administration, Billing and Payment** — This section always appears in a RFP for travel services. You'll need to describe your reporting procedures and the reports you plan to deliver to the prospect on a regular basis. How do you plan to handle audits? How long will you retain the company's records?

  Finally, state the cost for your services along with any associated fees or reimbursements (e.g. lost ticket charges, fees connected with visas and foreign itineraries, passports, etc.).

As you can appreciate, you can't write a formal proposal in an hour or two. A great deal of time and effort is involved. Therefore, I suggest you feel pretty good about your chances of winning the business before agreeing to respond to a RFP. Know when to hold 'em, and know when to fold 'em.

## CHAPTER 11

# HOW TO KEEP YOUR ACCOUNTS
# SAFE FROM THE COMPETITION

U p to this point we have focused on finding new customers. But . . .

**The most important people in your business
are the customers you already have.**

One of the most common errors salespeople make is to pursue new business at the expense of the business they already have. Remember that the people you are now working with are paying your rent and salary. For that reason, I believe it is critical for you to solidify your current customer base *before* you go out looking for new customers.

An analogy will help orient your approach to this task. If I gave my twenty-three year old son advice to save him money, he would nod and, if I was lucky, think about it for a minute or two before deciding to ignore it. But if my neighbor told him the exact same thing, the odds are a whole lot better that the advice might be adopted. Here is one more example. I haven't seen my college fraternity brother, Jim Kleiber, in over fifteen years. If he walked into my house right now I would treat him exactly like I remembered him fifteen years ago. I would reminisce with him about war stories and pranks we committed.

Here is the point: Is my fraternity brother the same person he was fifteen years ago? No. Some of your customers have been your customers for a long time. There's a good chance that you are treating them like you remember them when you first started doing business together. There is a good chance that you are treating your children like you remember them, as dependents. But your next door neighbor treats your child like he sees him today, like a young adult.

Your competition is treating your customers the way they want to be treated today. But you may be treating them like you have always treated them even though their business and needs have changed.

So here is the plan. Begin at base zero and reintroduce yourself to everyone in your life. You want to size them up brand new in today's terms. Start with those closest to you. Look at them with a fresh pair of eyes. Then, turn to your customers . . . all of your customers. Schedule an appointment to get to know them, their business and their needs all over again. Find out what they like . . . today. Find out what they don't like . . . today. Make a new pact with them and follow through accordingly.

Here is how you might approach this with a customer.

**Salesperson:** *"Jim, I've recently been reviewing our customer base and I'm dumbfounded, but I think it's true. You and I haven't met in over a year. So, I'd like to come in, ask you a few questions, just to make sure we're delivering the service that you expect from us."*

When you do sit down and reintroduce yourselves, find out if your client is looking for other services (services that you may now offer that he is not aware exist). By doing this you re-establish your relationship and keep it on a firm foundation. At the end of the meeting, also request a referral.

## Putting Your Commercial Accounts "In The Vault"

Over the years I have developed a list of things you can do to protect your commercial accounts from the competition — to put your accounts "in the vault." I call these :

### Twelve Commandments for Preserving Clients

1.  Boost customer awareness among employees.

2.  Fuel customer service from the top.

3.  Ask your employees to complete the customer questionnaire.

4.  Enroll in the C.I.A.

5.  Put your best customers on the team.

6.  Demonstrate a long-term commitment.

7.  Attack sales-killing complaints.

8.  Become a partner in your customer's success.

9.  Use your small company competitive edge.

10.  Humanize the business relationship.

11.  Say thank you.

12.  Measure and improve customer satisfaction.

Let's look at each suggestion individually.

## #1: Boost Customer Awareness Among Employees

First, you need to understand the difference between a company run with a "marketing philosophy" and a company run with a "production philosophy." I've found that many small companies which do not know better have adopted a production philosophy. This philosophy says, "This is what we do. Are you interested or not?" Kind of a take it or leave it attitude.

In contrast, a company run on the marketing philosophy determines what the customer is interested in, what he needs and what he expects, and then delivers on the promise to satisfy these criteria.

A classic example of the production philosophy would be Ford's attitude during its early years. Ford said that customers could have any color Model T they would like . . . as long as it was black. General Motors was one of the first major companies which understood the economic sense of the marketing philosophy — of giving the customer a choice. GM built Buicks, Cadillacs and Chevrolets — each one in different colors with a myriad of options. (Interestingly, once they dominated the industry, GM apparently lost its marketing focus and created products based on what it felt consumers should have. GM did not listen to what the public wanted. The result: the rise of companies that did listen — Honda, Toyota, Volkswagen, etc.)

Success in business today requires total customer focus — provide choices and services that customers truly want. First, *you* need to embrace this philosophy. Then, you need to get it through to your people, especially to your outside salespeople. How do you pin-point your customer's specific wants and needs? You talk to them, listen and create mechanisms in your organization for the customer feedback to reach the decision-makers and product/service designers.

Believe it or not, I've been in companies at ten minutes of eight in the morning when I hear the phone ringing and nobody makes a move to answer it. If I ask, "How come you don't answer the telephone?", they say, "We don't open until eight o'clock." After spending thousands of dollars and countless hours doing everything under the sun to get customers to call, they decide that the phone is ringing four minutes too soon! The personnel are clearly operating with the attitude that if they answer the phone every time it rings they won't have time to "do their work." Teach them "their work" is servicing customers (and prospective customers).

From time to time, sharpen your employees sensitivity to customer service by having internal office contests. You might call it "Operation Customer." For example, every phone in the office must be answered within two rings or everyone must deposit a dollar into a kitty. The first employee who receives a glowing customer service letter gets the pot. Or, designate a certain major customer as the "Company of the Week." Or you can have a sales contest with a "We Care" theme.

Let your customers know about these internal programs and contests. It's a good way to show the customer that your people are focused on customer satisfaction. You emphasize that every customer contact is important. You preach that no customer problem is irrelevant or too small.

Draw up a rating system and rate yourself. Post the results on the wall. Challenge this month's results and try to do better the following month. Make a game out of servicing your customers.

Believe this. The most common reason why you lose a customer is because you stop paying attention to that customer and take the customer for granted. Perform with this mindset: You have an opportunity to service your customer for just thirty days. After thirty days you will lose that customer. But if you manage to bend over backwards for the customer, you will get another thirty days. Your company will find energies and perform magic like you never thought possible. Your response time will instantly improve.

One final idea: Beginning immediately, put all your major customers on a thirty-day customer service performance review. You will be very glad you took this advice.

## #2: Fuel Customer Service From The Top

As a president goes so does the company. Show me a squared away president and I'll show you a company which has its act together. As a president laughs, the people laugh. As a president gets nervous, staff gets nervous. If a president answers the phone quickly within three rings, the people will answer the phone within three rings. Employees usually adopt the personality of the company's management.

Therefore, the marketing philosophy which is so necessary today must be exhibited daily from the top. If that means you . . . enough said. But if you are not the Top Gun, the message still applies. All the people who report to you take their cues from you.

## #3: Ask Employees To Complete The Customer Satisfaction Questionnaire

Too many companies today contradict their mission statement. Companies are quick to send out questionnaires to find out if clients are pleased, but often fail to respond to criticism.

By all means, ask your customers regularly to evaluate the products or services you provide. But also use this different approach: Send a customer questionnaire to your own employees and ask how *they* think things are working . . . what is right and what is wrong with the current system. When your employees work in a system they feel is flawed, who do you think suffers? The customer takes the hit just before your wallet does. Customer service audit questionnaires take a little guts but are a good idea. They provide useful results and put your employees into the mind of a customer — a sure way to boost awareness.

## #4: Enroll In The C.I.A.

That stands for "Competitor Intelligence Acquisition." Everyone in your entire organization should be trained to keep their ears and eyes open to learn as much as they can about your competition. This market sleuthing involves your sales personnel, your customers, your suppliers, trade literature and advertising. Here is a hit list.

- **Present Customers** — Your salespeople should talk to present customers to find out who's soliciting their business. Salespeople should think of themselves as information sources and detectives finding out where their competition is trying to strike. Your better customers are an excellent source of information, and once the relationship is formed you can ask them, "Who's knocking on your door? And what are they offering to do for you? Anything we are not?" You can be as straightforward as that. (I've asked customers if they'd let me look at competitor's proposals. Sometimes they do. Sometimes they don't. There is no harm in asking, and customers never hold it against me. In fact, they feel that I am pretty aggressive . . . in a good way.)

- **Suppliers** — You can get information from any supplier's rep who comes into your office to sell you something. Remember, if they are calling on you, they are probably calling on your competition. Ask questions, and you'll be surprised how many times you get answers. Just be honest and up front with your questions.

- **Trade Literature** — Trade literature is another good source of information on competitors. Take a good look through your industry's trade magazines. Read the articles and the ads. See what your competition is up to. Funny thing about "trade secrets" and ideas, many people tell the press everything they are doing because they get a kick reading about themselves. Read the literature and you can often go the bank on other people's ideas.

Read your local papers, not for entertainment but for leads and ideas. Find out what the competition is advertising as "new" or "improved." Look in the Want Ads to find out if your competition is hiring people and what positions they are filling. Evaluate your competitions' ads to see how they are spending their money.

## #5: Put Your Best Customers On The Team

Getting your customer into the act is another good way to hold on to customers. Make them a part of the "team." Ask them to be on your customer "board of advisors" or a focus group. More and more companies are building their corporate brochures around identified major customers — complete with quotes and pictures of the customer's CEO.

## #6: Demonstrate A Long-Term Commitment

Going the extra mile with service is the fastest and the easiest way to demonstrate a long-term commitment. Let me give you a personal example. I was at a business meeting in Jamaica, and my client realized late Friday afternoon that he needed some 35 mm slides Monday morning which were currently hung up in customs. The problem: The Customs Office was closed over the weekend. I saw this "impossible" predicament as an opportunity to cement my relationship with the client.

I first tried phone calls and the hotel's leverage — both to no avail. So, I drove down to the Custom's Office, spent some time befriending the people on duty, got one to make a phone call to the home of the big cheese who finally came down to the customs area (cup of coffee in hand) and handed me the slides. To this day, that client thinks I walk on water.

Making an investment in your business which directly benefits the customer is also another way to show your long-term commitment. You can invest in a service clients may be looking for or train their internal personnel on a software program (like PowerPoint or Excel.) Use your imagination to find ways to show your sincere interest in helping your clients succeed.

Becoming an important business contact for your customer is another way to solidify a commitment. I use the term "bring something to the party." When you are invited to someone's house for dinner, you usually bring a bottle of wine or desert, or something. Do the same thing when you visit your customer. Bring information . . . or an invitation to a business event . . . or a book, audio or video that pertains to their industry. Every time you make a sales call do a little homework on the industry so you can say to your customer, "Did you know . . . ?" or "I thought you might be interested in learning that . . . ?" If your customer learns something useful each time you meet he will welcome your sales call.

Developing a personal relationship is always a good idea if you believe you have a natural affinity with the client. After you've done some business with a client whose personality you enjoy, ask him to join you for dinner, a show or a sports event. (It's a good idea to invite the client's spouse or significant other along.)

This may sound like hard work, and it is. This effort is suitable only if you want to get ahead and maintain sound business relationships with your good customers.

Top management involvement with customers also solidifies long-term commitment . Presidents and higher management should get out of the office and visit customers. You'd be surprised how many company owners have never met their best customers. Owners should occasionally call customers and get personally involved with complaints even when such involvement may not be necessary. When the top guy shows interest, this is proof positive to the customer that they care.

## #7: Attack Sales-Killing Complaints

The number one reason why service providers lose customers is by showing indifference. The perception that you are taking a customer for granted opens the door to your competition. And the motherload of indifference is failing to respond to complaints quickly and vigorously. That's the overwhelming reason why people go elsewhere with their business. Think of it this way:

**The customer's temperature is already up . . .
he is smoldering . . .
and the unresponsive salesperson
is dipping him in gasoline.**

You can prevent most of your customer service problems if you want to. There's no reason why you have to lose an account. Create a mechanism to handle complaints with these characteristics:

1.  All complaints get recorded and are passed up the line for review (not retribution);

2.  Empower the appropriate people to satisfy complaints on the spot;

3.  Collect frequent complaints and "fix the problem" permanently;

4.  Regularly test the system — call in with a complaint and see what happens.

## #8: Become A Partner In Your Customer's Success

Every chance you get, try to help your customers earn more money with cost, time and productivity improvements. Help your customers financially manage their accounts. Offer constructive ways of having them pay for services. Bring some information that will help customers run their companies.

Offer time-saving ideas to your customers. Sit down with your staff and the customer and see whether you can help save time on a project basis or an entire program basis.

Define what the "Ultimate Service" means to your customer. This doesn't mean that the ultimate service has to be free. People usually pay for services they value. If your customer wants something you can provide, put a price on it and let the customer decide whether to buy it or not.

## #9: Use Your Small Company Edge

Think big. Act small. This is what I call the "Small Company Edge." I don't care if your company is big . . . and I don't care if your company is small. You want to achieve the Small Company Edge.

Many prospects are concerned that they may lose personal attention with a big company. The big company emphatically says, "No, no, no . . . you won't get lost in the bigness of our company. We will dedicate three, four, or five people to work with you. We'll maintain that personal approach." Guess what? Your small company already has that personal approach.

Small companies have several advantages. One, obviously, is personalized service. The customer won't get lost in the shuffle. When customers call, you know their names, and customers like that.

Response time is also generally an advantage for the small company. The customer does not have to navigate red tape. You can respond to your customer's needs and problems (sometimes working "out of the box") without signatures from several different people. (This makes life more enjoyable in and of itself.) Small companies can be more efficiently managed. You can make decisions and break rules on the spot. Smaller companies have spontaneity on their side.

Small companies are used to a lean and mean approach to doing business. They don't have all kinds of money, so they have to hit projects, run and dodge, and get the job done any way they can. This is known as gorilla warfare, and small companies are the odds-on winners at this game.

Small companies must also practice niche marketing. (Pronounced "nitch" in my home state of New Jersey. If you pronounce it "neesh" I should have charged you $129 for this book, just so you'd feel sufficiently abused.) Niche marketing is an exercise in focus and self discipline. It runs contrary to the belief that you are good enough to be all things to all people. Niche marketing involves identifying your strengths *and* your weaknesses, and attacking the segment of the marketplace that makes the most sense to you. In niche marketing you don't try to sign your competitor's biggest customer . . . you find out who or what need that you can uniquely service is not being serviced properly in the market. Then you approach that opportunity with a vengeance.

## #10: Humanize The Business Relationship

If people aren't buying your act there's nothing you can do about it. Be natural. Be yourself. You can't be anything else, so why try? Believe in yourself. Believe in your product. Believe in your company.

With that mindset, follow these simple "humanizing" suggestions to help make prospect and customer contacts turn into lasting relationships.

- **Break a rule.** — Be a human being. Just get the job done. If that means you bend or break a non-essential rule to deliver what your customer needs . . . do it. (But let the higher ups know that you did so to "invest" in the relationship.)

- **Make a friend.** — When you go to make a presentation, go with the objective of making a friend. Be a nice, friendly, polite, up-front person who is receptive to meeting another business professional.

- **Customize your service.** — Don't exhibit tunnel vision. Find out what your customers are looking for, then do everything you can to satisfy those needs within the scope of your capabilities and resources.

- **Laugh at yourself.** — If you make a mistake, have a good laugh . . . when the mistake is non-critical. Hopefully, this kind of thing doesn't happen every day. But learn to accept and enjoy the side of you that is human. I assure you that most mistakes that put you in a blue funk are not as big a deal as you think. You can have a lot of laughs once you learn to take yourself a little less seriously.

## #11: Say Thank You

One of the easiest and most effective ways to convince customers you care is by saying "thank you" more than once every fifteen years. Let's face it, we get so busy day to day that we often fail to say thank you to the people who matter most.

You can say thank you the simple way and you can say thank you with a little more flare. I use both. Just last week I sent two American Express Gift Checks to a speaker's bureau that books me — a reminder that I know what side of the bread the butter is on. The bonus from a "thank you" campaign is that handing people small, unexpected gifts is pure joy. Try it, but don't be surprised if it becomes addictive.

## #12: Measure And Improve Customer Satisfaction

You should initiate a two-way dialogue with your customers to stay on top of customer satisfaction and head off problems that can cost you accounts. On-going customer research is imperative. Here are two practical ways to do it.

- **Dial for the "Un-smile"** — Call your best customers on a scheduled rotation and simply ask, "Is everything Okay? How are we doing?" Usually the answer is "Fine." You are off the phone inside a minute, but you remain inside your client's memory for a very long time.

- **Mail for the Fail** — Send your customers the old "How am I doing?" questionnaire from time to time. You might trigger some uneasiness and unrest early in the relationship, but that's exactly what you want to do. You want to flush out all problems and head the major complaints off at the pass.

If you tell your clients they are part of a "full client survey," few will fill out the questionnaire. So select a few individuals from time to time and tell them they are a "select" group you are asking for feedback.

Make the questionnaire simple to fill out. Let the customer circle an answer rather than comment in long hand. Expect a bunch of favorable returns — the "butterflies." These will give you the fuzzies, but they are not the ones that have much value. You are looking for the "bees" — the ones that sting you. These are providing the "wake-up call" that you want and need. Respond conscientiously to these stings, and your business will flow like honey.

## Conclusion

As you can see, there really is no secret agenda when it comes to protecting your customers from the competition. You've worked hard to land an account. You've determined that the account is very important to your future. Simply focus your energies toward keeping your account satisfied. Treat people properly. Identify what they want and need and show them you are serious about supplying it. At every opportunity that presents itself, thank them for the opportunity of calling them customers.

Make up your mind to service accounts the way that you said you would when your current customers were prospects. Customers are not easy to come by, so they are worth every effort to keep.

# SECTION

# 3

# MARCHEV'S RULES TO SELL BY

## Chapter 12

# Rule #1:
# Transcend Public Opinion

Over the years, the sales practice has appropriately earned a pretty poor reputation. To grasp the scope of the negative predicament salespeople have created for themselves, try this exercise: Put this book down, walk over to the person nearest to you (spouse, friend, co-worker, stranger . . . it doesn't matter) and ask what word immediately comes to mind when you say "salesman." Go ahead . . . I'll wait.

Did you hear any of these very predictable responses: Sleazy; crooked; fast talking; unscrupulous; dishonest; shifty; lacking trust; lacking ethics; liars; car lots; insurance; egotists; manipulative. I'm sure you can come up with a few thoughts of your own . . . perhaps even based on a previous personal experience.

I am aware that some of you salespeople will take exception to this exercise. The words that come to your mind might include honest, trustworthy, friendly, helpful, courteous, etc. Quite frankly, I envy your sunny disposition and self-esteem but I must respectfully inform you that you are an island in a sea of cynicism toward sales professionals.

The reason why these less-than-attractive labels of the sales profession persist results from a concept known as "easy entry." To become a salesperson all you need to do is to have a card printed identifying you as a salesperson. Good, bad or indifferent, this is how too many small companies create their sales force. They find people who can "fog a mirror", and they go out and print them calling cards. The sooner you acknowledge this reality, the more quickly you will combat it.

## A Story Worth Repeating

In 1987, I was teaching marketing courses to both graduate and undergraduate students at Fairleigh Dickinson University (FDU) in Madison, New Jersey. On the first day of a new marking period I asked an undergraduate class,

*"How many of you in this room, are interested in helping people after graduating?"*

Virtually every hand in the class went up. I asked a second question,

*"How many of you want to earn a lot of money as soon as you graduate?"*

For a second time, every hand in the class shot up. I followed with a third question,

*"How many of you upon graduation would like to be in a position where you can be your own boss?"*

99% of the students had their hand in the air. Then came the eye opener,

*"How many of you are planning on becoming salespeople?"*

Not one person in the class raised their hand. This response paints an accurate picture of the public perception of the sales profession today.

How could we have let this happen? Where did we go wrong? Is it that every consumer has been injured by a salesperson and is carrying a grudge? Do we owe this negative press to Al Bundy, the TV Sitcom shoe salesman on Married With Children? Or how about Herb on the old TV show WKRP in Cincinnati who was always wearing loud sports jackets that didn't match his pants?

If perception is reality, salespeople have a major obstacle to overcome. Right or wrong, salespeople have apparently earned themselves a less-than-glowing reputation over the years. Many people, in fact, still consider salespeople to be less than honorable, or simply people between "real jobs."

Frankly, I cast much of the blame on sales managers and sales trainers . . . especially those who have never actually "carried the bag." I take offense with a manager or trainer telling me it is my duty to "overcome" people's objections or to sell people "up," or to recite any phrase designed to take advantage of an individual's lack of knowledge, experience, or decision-making ability.

There will always be people in the world who are out to make a fast buck at the expense of others without a trace of guilt or a second thought. I can't change this. I can only remind you that the behavior of these few individuals does not have to prevent you from becoming a consummate professional.

Begin by asking yourself these questions:

- *"What am I doing here? In this job? In this company?"*

- *"Am I here to help people . . . .or would I prefer to harm them?"*

- *"Am I planning to be a sincere, honest and straightforward business professional . . . .or does lying, cheating and dishonest behavior fit into my plans?"*

- *"Am I eager, qualified and prepared to bring something of value to the party . . . or am I here looking for a free ride?"*

If your answers to the first parts of these questions are positive, then you have the fundamental attitude to change your life forever.

Sure not everyone is cut out to be a highly skilled sales professional. But those who are can literally write their own ticket in nearly any field they wish. Selling skills (which are nothing more than people skills after you isolate a few industry specific nuances) are easily transferable and cross most industry boundaries quite easily.

And for us commoners who haven't been gifted with multi-million-dollar athletic talents, sales is one of the remaining arenas where you can realistically make all the money you want. The ceiling you place on your earnings is self-imposed.

I want you to remember the one thing that virtually every salesperson forgets over time:

## A career in sales can be and should be fun.

Hunting for customers is fun. Calling people who don't know you from Adam and trying to schedule an appointment with them is challenging and fun. Addressing people's concerns and supplying the correct solution is fun. Having lunch, or dinner, or coffee with potential clients is fun. Helping people is fun. Meeting people is fun. Doing research on the web before calling your next person on your list is fun. Signing an order is fun. Travel is fun. (Although the travel part is fast becoming less fun all the time.) Getting paid for your hard work is fun. Spending the money you earn is fun. Sales is fun!

Never make the mistake of confusing selling with hard work. As I mentioned earlier, hard work is going out to State Highway 25 shortly after noon on a 95-degree, humid summer's day with a shovel in your hand and digging a trench while nursing an aching back. This can never be confused with sitting in an air conditioned car or office, a refreshing coke or cup of coffee in hand, and dialing for dollars . . . or editing a sales letter of introduction . . . or brainstorming your next sales strategy or plan of action. Making good things happen for your customers is fun and will always be a pretty cool way to run your life.

# CHAPTER 13

# RULE # 2: STOP TRYING TO SELL

F ew people enjoy the idea of "being sold." A key step toward becoming more successful in sales is to take a contrarian approach to what you are doing. Once you learn to do this you will immediately find yourself in a more natural and comfortable position and you will become more pleasant to be with. Your words will be received favorably while your recommendations will be treated with respect. When you approach sales from this contrarian position, your success is sure to follow.

What is this contrarian approach? To become more successful in sales you must,

## Stop trying to sell!

Notice I didn't say stop calling people . . . meeting people . . . questioning people or listening to what people have to say. I didn't say stop seeking opportunities to be of service to people or stop fine-tuning your product or service presentation. I didn't say stop writing to prospects or sending newsletters, postcards or press releases. I didn't say stop attending trade shows, seminars, workshops or conferences. I didn't say stop subscribing to trade papers, magazines or bulletins. I didn't suggest that you sleep late or hang out at Barsalloti's Bar & Grill on Tuesday afternoons. I recommended that you simply STOP TRYING TO SELL.

Most people don't like being around people who have "selling" on their minds. In fact, other than a few rare cases, I don't think you can sell anything to anybody. People today (consumers and purchasing agents) are pretty street-smart and are skeptical of "empty suits" (salespeople who don't have a clue and can't tell third base from the dugout). If somehow a salesperson does manage to finagle a buyer into spending some hard earned cash for an un-needed product or service, chances are it will be that salesperson's last victory . . . with that buyer or his organization.

Even the phrase "being sold" is a turn-off. I don't believe I was ever "sold" anything. I wasn't "sold" my car. I don't believe anyone "sold" me my house. Nope, I don't believe anyone has ever "sold" me anything.

Yet, I feel very natty and confident when I don a well-fitted, stylish business suit. I experience joy knowing my family is comfortable and safe while riding in a clean and practical automobile (which, I am quick to mention, I personally decided to buy). I have lived up to my responsibilities knowing that my life insurance policy is adequate. The last time I wandered into a men's shoe store and exited with three new pairs of shoes, it came as a direct result of my deciding to buy each pair. A salesman didn't sell me anything. I take great pride in having decided, without the unwanted pressure of a well intentioned salesperson, to adopt my two greyhound dogs, Jetta and Eddie. In short, I take pleasure and pride in the things I personally decide to own.

People enjoy owning things which they themselves decide to own. But the idea of being sold, on the other hand, conjures up feelings of manipulation and resentment. I don't like it. You don't like it. And your prospects don't (and won't) like it either.

So, it should come as no surprise when I tell you again in a voice just shy of shouting . . . STOP TRYING TO SELL THINGS!

Spend your time instead looking for, and isolating people like me, who find enjoyment in buying stuff . . . in ownership . . . in making sound financial decisions, and finding solutions to problems. Then (and here comes a blinding flash of the obvious):

## Help people make good buying decisions.

Plenty of people in your immediate universe need help. Your objective, and it is a challenging one, is to find them. But a formidable obstacle stands squarely in your path. People today, and for good reason, have a hard time trusting other people, especially when it comes to parting with their money. Once you learn how to focus on helping rather than selling, you will be on your way toward establishing this all-important level of trust. It won't come easily but its absolutely necessary to become an effective sales professional.

You reap several attractive and healthy upsides to my "no pressure" approach to making a living:

- When trying to help people make decisions that are right for them, you feel good about yourself and what you do for a living. You will never have to apologize for your actions, your thoughts or your intentions.

- You will experience minimum levels of stress. In this age of stressed-out, whacked-out, frazzled-out and burnt-out people, finding ways to lower your stress level is a pretty useful way to spend your time.

• You will never be accused of being manipulative or for double-talking your prospect in any way, shape or form. You won't experience guilt when trying to minimize or overcome legitimate concerns or objections, or for recommending higher priced products or services when it is appropriate. You are simply trying to help people help themselves by asking the right questions.

The beautiful thing about having this mindset is that you will maintain healthy eating and sleeping habits, while exhibiting a welcomed sense of humor.

## CHAPTER 14

# RULE #3:
# YOU'LL FIND JUST TWO KINDS OF
# PEOPLE IN THE ENTIRE WORLD

Your sales career will instantly blossom as soon as you embrace Rule #3 which states that there are only two types of people you will ever come in contact with regardless of your industry. Your mission is to find out as quickly as possible who is who. The two types are: (1) people you can help; and (2) the other kind.

If there is one overriding lesson that I would like you to internalize at the expense of all the others, this is it. This rule, when internalized, will place you in the driver's seat. You will become more effective, and your life will become less stressful (and more pleasurable). This rule is a real life saver.

Your job is to sort out suspects/prospects by determining the type of each new acquaintance as quickly as possible. If the prospect qualifies as someone who has a need for your professional help, you do your thing. If the person appears to be someone who cannot use or is not interested in what you can do for them, you bid them a pleasant "good day" while you promptly ease yourself on down the road.

I get chills when I hear skilled trainers tell their sales force, "This ain't no picnic. You have to push for the order." Or, "Don't take no for an answer." Or, "Go for the jugular!" Or, "You are the loser if you don't get the order."

These guys have been watching too many professional wrestling matches on channel 57. This is not a matter of who can beat up whom, how fast for what payout. Who, I ask with a modicum of indignity, do these managers/big shots think we are? Some Neanderthal rejects who just crawled out from under a rock? This "pound 'em into submission" approach may work at carnivals and football, but it certainly doesn't work in today's sophisticated marketplace when trying to establish long-term relationships with intelligent people. Yes, a number of less-than-squared-away individuals are floating around the world these days — people who skipped a few classes while hanging out at the corner candy store. But by and large, most folks today are both honest and up to speed.

Your task is to enter the marketplace to identify people who have a need for what you do. Then, you can provide a service or product that is both useful and appreciated.

It makes little sense trying to talk your way into helping people who don't need or want your help. This exercise of misguided competitive persistence regularly leads to unsuccessful, painful, unfulfilled dead-end, frustrating and bitter sales careers. And besides, while you are trying to push through these man-made "barriers", your stress level is spiking beyond the healthy zone. Who suffers beside you when this happens? Everybody. Your family suffers. Your friends suffer. Your associates and anyone else who comes into contact with you suffers.

My time proven, hold-no-punches, shoot-from-the-hip, candid advice is to stop trying to sell stuff and spend more time locating those individuals who have a genuine interest, need and want for you and what you represent.

# Chapter 15

# Rule # 4:
# One Impression — Three Outcomes

Only three things can happen when you come in contact with people:

(1) They feel better having met you;

(2) They feel worse having met you; or

(3) Having met you, they really couldn't care less about the experience one way or the other.

After years of observation, I've concluded very few people have a strategy when meeting strangers. Most people automatically stick out their hand, mumble their name while glancing around the room, utter something without much confidence, conviction or personality, and in general, wing their way through the often times uncomfortable introductory encounter.

If you believe the old saying that "first impressions are lasting," then you will find it logical to evaluate just how you score when it comes to making a first impression.

Do you leave new acquaintances feeling better, neutral, or worse? Those are the choices. And in virtually every instance, you are in control of the outcome.

Once you realize that the ball is in your court, you can easily establish an approach where people respond favorably to your presence. How? Don't try to make them feel *you* are important. Instead,

## Make the people you meet feel better about themselves.

Try this idea on for size. Picture everyone you meet wearing a giant sign around their neck that says, "Make me feel important!" Go ahead, try it. This actually does work to help you focus on this new goal.

Once you adopt this strategy, meeting people becomes an honest form of entertainment, and a challenge. You will start looking forward to mingling at cocktail parties, attending Bar Mitzvahs and even attending your boss's nephew-in-law's graduation party (which kills a whole day as it is scheduled for 3 pm on a Saturday).

The number one reason people shy away from public gatherings is their fear that people won't treat them well . . . that no one will take the time or have the interest to speak to them. You have this backwards. Make others feel important. When you become the facilitator or the host in your mind, good things will result.

Having a strategy when meeting new people, and saying and doing the right things in often uncomfortable environments, is not being wish-washy. It is being mature, polite, creative, bon-vivant and considerate. This approach is also a major part of being the consummate sales professional.

Your goal, from this page forward, is to enter the introductory stages of a relationship with the notion that you are going to do everything within reason to cause an "I liked that person" outcome.

Here are some key steps to insure your success.

## The Eyes Have It

Acknowledge the impact your "eyes" have. Few people get this one straight without a great deal of effort. By looking people in the eye you are saying two things: (1) you are confident in who you are; and (2) you are interested in, and not intimidated by, the person with whom you are speaking. Both of these are very positive signals.

The obvious danger of eye contact is when it is overdone and appears that you are staring. It is okay to allow your eyes to drift off your subject, just don't wander for too long. Be sure to reconnect within a few moments. This will tell your "audience" that you truly care about them. If you find looking people in the eye difficult (and some people do), try looking between their eyes, in the center of their forehead just above eye level. To them, it will look like you are indeed holding eye contact.

## Shake 'n Take

Next comes the handshake. This simple maneuver, if not deployed properly, can all but kill your successful first impression. Firm yet brief. There is nothing worse than having your fingers crushed by a Hulk Hogan wanna-be or having the right side of your body shaken half to death by some young, eager, over-ambitious glad hander. The handshake is a sign of peace . . . of trust . . . of welcome . . . and of safety.

On the other end of the spectrum is the wet fish handshake. The major consideration here is if the shake takes the mind of the person you are speaking with off of you and down to your finger-tips. You don't want people thinking: "Is this guy flat lining as I speak? Maybe I should spring for the phone right now and dial 911!"

If either of these responses cross your prospect's mind, even for a moment, he is unlikely to remember your name, the name of your company, or anything else about you for that matter.

So, follow good eye contact with a decent handshake. If you aren't sure how you come across, ask a friend or associate or family member for some honest criticism.

## The Name's The Game

Are you so busy thinking of what you are going to say that you never pick up the name of the person you are meeting, or you instantly forget it? If so, you are in good company. The good news is that this habit has an easy fix.

You can correct this less-than-attractive practice by repeating the prospect's name as soon as you hear it. Try to repeat the name of your new acquaintance again during the early stages of your first conversation. This will help cement the name in your mind. As soon as it is practical, add this new name along with a key reminder phrase to your Palm Pilot, address book or database for future retrieval. What works for me is to connect the person's name with something or someone else I am very familiar with — a TV personality or celebrity who looks similar, is in the same line of work, etc.

Don't sell this name thing short. People place trust in people they feel comfortable with. People take notice and are flattered when others remember their names. Call someone by their name after a period of separation and you will see that it truly does make a positive impression.

# Follow The Leader

The person who speaks first is in position to lead the conversation. All things considered, this is where you want to be. I strongly recommend when you do lead, lead with a question . . . and then wait for, and pay attention to, the answer.

People who get the question part right but aren't interested in who they are speaking with, often fail to hear the answer. People know when you aren't following along. And you can bet that they are resenting you for your lack of interest in what they have to say.

Cut this one off at the pass by actively listening to the answers to your questions. If you want to cement the relationship in the mind of your prospect, give them what I call the limp leg move early in the conversation. This is what you do: When you are following the conversation intently, politely interrupt them in mid sentence to confirm the fact that you are hanging on their every word. For example, here's what I might say:

**MM:** *"Whoa! Time out. Back up a minute. When I heard that appetizer tray coming I think I missed part of your point. Could you repeat that?"*

You can also try saying something like this if it comes more naturally:

**MM:** *"That is a very interesting point of view. Let me see if I am hearing you correctly. Are you saying that . . .?"*

Sometimes an interruption will kill the flow of an important message. Even though they may be totally lost, some people feel that it would be impolite to fess-up. So, they continue to stare, nod and grunt, not knowing what the speaker is talking about. They are not fooling the speaker. If this happens to you, just stop the speaker and get back into the conversation. If you don't, you will lose.

I can hear some of you saying, "This is beginning to sound like manipulatory audio antics." Quite the contrary. If you think so, you are missing my point. I'm suggesting that if you are interested in getting other people to like you, you had better learn to get into their world and move at their pace. I'm also saying that you must communicate in a way that is sincere, honest and appropriate. You accomplish this by doing your best to be genuinely interested in what other people have to say. There is nothing manipulative here. This is a key step in advancing from amateur to professional status.

# CHAPTER 16

# RULE # 5:
# THE PLATINUM RULE

People are not, never were, and never will be wired the same. They don't think the same or act the same. They don't appreciate the same things, and they don't dislike the same things. They don't laugh at the same jokes, and they don't watch the same TV programs. They don't vote the same ticket, and they don't all root for the Mets. Some play golf while others play mahjong. Some have higher morals than others. Some have a higher tolerance for things they don't understand. Some are loud while others speak just above a whisper. Some have pets while others dislike furry animals with a vengeance.

The key to establishing sound working relationships is to recognize the fact that people don't enjoy being treated the same way. They like to be treated as individuals. Once you manage to meet people on their own terms, in a way they find acceptable, you will be well on your way toward establishing a working relationship.

Years ago, we were all taught the Golden Rule: "Do unto others the way you would have them do unto you." The Rule is clearly an honorable strategy designed to help people get along with each other. At the time these twelve words were memorialized, they were universally accepted as the road map for success. The philosophy this rule endorsed was definitely worth a shot.

The harsh reality in today's fast-paced, what-have-you-done-for-me-lately world is that the Golden Rule needs a new coat of paint. To say it another way, the Golden Rule has become yesterday's news— mulch for the vegetable garden.

It is time for a new, updated slant to this guiding light. It is time for . . . The Platinum Rule. This rule will improve your relationships while minimizing unnecessary stress, and it will lead you to all sorts of new and interesting experiences.

---

## The Platinum Rule:

## Treat others the way THEY like to be treated.

---

The difference between these two doctrines is dramatic. The Golden Rule assumes that everyone thinks and acts the same as you do. It implies that if you like to be treated in a particular fashion, others will enjoy the same treatment.

This is not the way things work. The fact that you enjoy reading doesn't mean I enjoy reading. The fact that you find Roseanne reruns amusing doesn't mean that I have nothing better to do. My wife thinks Lucille Ball hung the moon. I don't.

What you think . . . what you believe . . . what you want in the big picture of interactive relationships doesn't matter. The only thing that matters is what your prospects and your customers think, believe, and want. If you treat others the way they like to be treated, you are hedging your bet in favor of better chemistry and you will be well on your way toward establishing relationships worth treasuring.

This lesson deserves a little more scrutiny. So let's take a closer look at the Platinum way of looking at things. Consider four individuals. I will give them numbers for identification purposes.

Person #1: the president of a Fortune 500 company;

Person #2: an engineer at Los Alamos National Laboratories;

Person #3: a salesman for a copier company;

Person #4: an office manager at a major insurance company.

All four individuals in our example are good, honest, hardworking people. The world needs each and every one of them to maintain a balanced spin on its axis. No one individual is more important than the other. Thank goodness for them all.

For the sake of argument, assume you are Person #3, the copier salesperson. Let's take a look at a few communication combinations so you can internalize the importance of this chapter.

## The Engineer

If you want to establish a level of rapport with the Los Alamos Engineer, you would be wise not to refer to the handle on the left side of the copier machine as the "what-cha-ma-callit," the "gizmo," or the "thing-a-ma-jig." A down-to-earth, fun loving salesperson would know exactly what you were talking about as long as you were pointing at it. But this would not hold true for the engineer. You, the salesperson, believe that if people know what you mean, then that is all that counts. Everything else is just semantics.

The engineering personality, however, spent many hours of schooling and study to learn exactly how the machine works and actually respects the nomenclature of each and every working part. The engineer is concerned with precision, details and practicality. He needs to make himself entirely clear at all times. You, on the other hand, are a little less disciplined. By nature, you don't enjoy the nitty gritty or the small print. After all, you have another appointment at 2 o'clock this afternoon on the other side of town. You could have personally beaten Richard Carlson to the punch and written *"Don't Sweat The Small Stuff"* with your hands tied behind your back, but you were pressing to make your 10 am tee time.

If you are not careful, your haste to get through your sales interview may be interpreted as lack of knowledge or disinterest coupled with a low tolerance level for engineers. You, on the other hand, feel certain that the engineer is tracking right along with you, and that he understands exactly where you are coming from. In fact, because you feel that you are so easy to get along with, you believe that most people can read your mind. Your thoughts are so basically fundamental that others must know exactly what you are thinking. This can be, and often is, a costly mistake made by many new (as well as seasoned) salespeople.

Engineer types can be very taxing, but thank the heavens above that we have them bobbing and weaving down the corridors. Engineers make things work, albeit very slowly and meticulously. They can be very frustrating at times due to their slow pace and thorough decision making processes. You, the salesperson, must learn to cool your jets and work with them at their speed while making every effort to address each question, doubt and concern.

## The President

What would happen if you, the copier salesperson, treated the Fortune 500 president the way you like to be treated? Major problem! Mr. Big, as a rule of thumb, expects your undivided attention and you would be wise to err on the side of respect. You are quick to invite Mr. Big to call you by your first name, or even your nickname. On the other hand, it is a good bet that he would prefer initially to be called "Mr. Big." Begin this relationship more formally.

In most cases, president types are fixated on the bottom line. Give them: (a) the facts; (b) the trends and a recommended solution with a back-up option; (c) the anticipated cost savings; and then (d) get out of their way.

When in the presence of a president type, practice the "3-B Strategy" I mentioned earlier: Be bright. Be brief. Be gone. These people are decision-makers. They are busy and are responsible for feeding many mouths. They are serious and mean business. In other words, net your story out and don't spend too much time getting comfortable in your chair. If you are asked if you would enjoy a cup of coffee, don't take it to heart. (This is like someone from Atlanta telling a Yankee salesperson "Y'all come back now . . . ya hear?") This is a polite something to say, not an invitation to move in. President types come with an ego. Treat them like the important people they are.

## The Salesperson

Salespeople, in general, enjoy a little more shmoozing. They have a reputation of being easy going . . . they enjoy being on stage . . . they enjoy the sound of their own voice and making other people laugh. They rarely find themselves in a situation they can't talk their way out of. (Or at least, so they believe.)

This isn't necessarily bad, and it is not necessarily good. Sometimes these characteristics are an indication of nervousness or a lack of self-esteem. Most sales types have a tendency to believe their own press. Someone, many years ago, told them they had the "gift of gab" and they decided to milk this trait for all it is worth.

Salespeople can be hard to read at times. They can shift from calm and interested to bored and antsy in the blink of a gnats eye. You must "stay tuned" and not overstay your welcome, as they can go from placid to hurried in a heartbeat. You must pay attention and carefully watch the depth and pace of their interest level. A good clue comes from their eyes. Key on their eyes. Once you notice them glancing off to the water cooler, you might as well pack your bags and head for the elevator.

Sales professionals are action people. At first, everything sounds like a good idea. They are quick with "one upsmanship." Get ready for the "yeah, buts" or "That certainly has merit, but I have a better idea." They often don't have a clue how things work. As a rule of thumb, don't sell them short. They are street savvy and not afraid to say or do the unexpected.

## The Office Manager

Office manager types are warm and security oriented. They need time to understand what's going on. If they trust you, you can make decisions for them. But don't guess wrong. Their memories are long . . . very long.

In essence, these occupations break down into the four types:

- detailed-oriented people;
- fact-oriented and bottom-line people willing to make quick decisions;
- action and personality-oriented types; and
- patient and caring "people" people.

Despite their distinct personality differences, the common denominator among all four types is that they are naturally drawn to people who exhibit similar characteristics and personalities as their own. People feel comfortable with people who think and behave like they do. Once you learn to identify the traits of each personality type and connect with and wholeheartedly embrace the Platinum Rule, you will be in the top 3.2% of relation-building aficionados.

For a more complete study of identifying and adapting to behavior styles, let me direct you to two valuable resources: Tony Allesandra's book, *The Platinum Rule*, and Target Training International's book, *The Universal Language*, by Bill Bontetter, Judy Suiter and Randy Widrick.

## The 60-Second Observation Exercise

This whole concept of knowing your individual style, recognizing other styles, and marrying the two in conversation is a critical skill if you want to enter the Big Leagues of Sales. Here is an exercise that will put you miles ahead of your competition when it comes to dealing with people.

The next time you are introduced to someone for the first time, I want you to ask yourself two questions and then observe the person closely for the answers.

- **Question #1: Does this person appear to be introverted, or extroverted?** Introverted people tend to keep to themselves and only speak when spoken to. Extroverted people are quick with a joke, a hello or an opinion. Extroverts readily introduce themselves. Introverts normally wait to be introduced.

- **Question #2: Does this person appear to be people oriented or task oriented?** Does the person in question appear to care about family, employees, prospects and customers, or is the prospect focused on the bottom line and the results of the deal. For signs of orientation, look for clues such as pictures of family and friends, or documents of achievement and certifications on the wall.

Here is how these orientations/personalities and the occupations we discussed cross-reference.

| Style | Type |
|---|---|
| Introverted and task oriented | Engineer |
| Introverted and people oriented | Office Manager |
| Extroverted and task oriented | Company President |
| Extroverted and people oriented | Salesperson |

Here are some other small clues to be looking for:

- How quickly does someone flash a picture of their wife, kids or dogs?

- How quickly does a smile appear?

- How is this person dressed — conservatively, or flamboyantly or in between?

- Is the handshake firm or not?

- How's the jewelry factor?

- Have they washed their car in the last five years, and what kind of ride are they driving?

- When was the last time they took a vacation?

There are clues just about everywhere. All you have to do is start tuning in and you will be able to identify who you are dealing with and what your best approach should be.

It also helps to remember that people like to socialize with people they like. And people have a tendency to like people who think and act like themselves.

Some people :

Like to be direct,

Like to have fun,

Like new products,

Like proven products,

Like a lot of data,

Get confused by data,

Like to be touched,

Like personal chit-chat,

Like time to think,

Like to negotiate,

Like showy products,

Like traditional products,

. . . and others are just the opposite

## Key Behaviors For Each Type

Here is a quick re-cap of the four types we covered in this chapter, along with some do's and don'ts for each.

- **When you are in the company of Engineer Types:** Provide lots of proof. They need time to absorb your information. Make it a point not to rush them.

- **When you are in the company of Office Manager Types:** Take it slow and easy. Be sure to answer all of their questions. Make it a point to earn their trust over time.

- **When you are in the company of Sales Types:** Do not spend much time on the details. Allow time for socializing. Make it a point to have fun.

- **When you are in the company of President Types:** Don't say or do anything that can be interpreted as a waste of their time. Be efficient and businesslike. Make it a point to get to the point. Acknowledge their position.

# CHAPTER 17

# RULE # 6:
# THE POWER OF NOW!

My college fraternity was known for its annual formal Christmas Party. Each year we hired a piano player by the name of Charlie Bradshaw to play our out-of-tune piano and lead the singing of Christmas carols well into the early morning hours. For reasons unclear to me, in 1968 I waited until the last minute to begin searching for a date to this "must-attend" occasion.

The day before the event I realized I would be singing solo if I didn't find someone to accompany me. It was time for some history making Marchev phone magic.

**MM:** *"Hi, this is Mike Marchev. Have I got an opportunity for you! Would you be interested in attending the Theta Chi Fraternity Christmas Bash with me? . . . Tomorrow night . . . Oh . . . Well, maybe next year . . . Bye."*

What? Me worry? I had a back up number. Doesn't everybody?

**MM:** *"Hi, this is Mike Marchev. Would you like to attend the Theta Chi Fraternity Christmas Party with me? . . . Tomorrow night . . . Oh . . . Well, maybe next year . . . Bye."*

0 for 2. But the University of Massachusetts was a big place. I once figured out that if the same guy asked a different girl out every night for 365 straight nights for four straight years, he would graduate not having the pleasure of knowing or dating about 85% of the 9,000 women who attended U. Mass. (That, I have come to learn, is known as market research.) Back to my dilemma . . .

**MM:** *"Hi, This is Mike Marchev. Would you . . . Hello!"*

0-3.

I really thought I had the next one . . . 0-4.

One day too late: 0-5. 0-6. 0-7. By this time, although I hated the thought of it, I began asking my fraternal brothers for a few leads. The next 6 "shoe-ins" became defeat numbers 8, 9, 10, 11, 12 and 13.

The word was quickly getting out. My loving frat brothers started to make side bets on my demise, wagering on when I'd hit ground zero. They were enjoying watching me go down in flames. But, I wasn't done yet . . . not by a long shot. I had an ace in the hole, good old Father Quigley.

My fraternity house was conveniently located next to the Catholic Newman Center, home of Father Quig who knew just about every nice girl on campus. He would save me from further embarrassment. Just as I expected. The good father gave me three more sure things.

0-14, 0-15 and 0-16. (I now understood why Father Quig had decided to become a priest.)

Joe Lang, my football teammate, fraternity pledge brother, and good and reliable friend, was doing everything humanly possible to avoid wetting his trousers while taking great delight in my lackluster performance. I hadn't put on a show like this since I busted my collar bone in the Rhode Island game inside a nano second of leaving my first varsity huddle. What idiot would wait until the last minute to get a date for the Theta Chi Annual Christmas Party? Answer: Marchev.

Then I called Mary Jane Watson (not her real name — why humiliate her in the unlikely event this book ends up on the New York Times Best Sellers List). When she said without much voice inflection, "Why not?" I felt the weight of the world lift off my shoulders. Marchev is back! That's right. The stud-muffin comes through again, pledge brothers! I had managed to find a date to the Christmas Party . . . and a very lovely young lady she was, I might add.

1-17! Lucky for me, she came with both self-esteem and a sense of humor.

The lessons I learned from this embarrassing episode were many. While attending the University of Massachusetts, in addition to learning all about the Battle of 1812, I learned the value of:

Planning — or the frustration of lack thereof.

Persistence — the fundamental ingredient for success.

Rejection — most things only hurt for a moment or two.

Sense of Humor — if you can't laugh at yourself, you're wrapped too tight.

Realism — after all, there is always next year.

Tenacity — kicks in when you have worn all the way through persistence.

Referrals — there is no such thing as a sure thing.

Sure things — see referrals.

The Power of NOW — versus later.

All of these lessons proved valuable when building a successful career in sales. The former New York Yankee Baseball Manager hit the nail right on the head when he said:

> *"If my pitcher would pitch at the beginning of the game*
> *the same way he pitches at the end of the game,*
> *once he realizes he is losing, he wouldn't be*
> *losing in the first place."*
> – Casey Stengel

For those of you who don't speak Stengelese, allow me to translate: Do important things now so you won't have to play catch up and sweat the entire ordeal later.

In the Christmas of '68, I made it more difficult than it had to be . . . but I made it. And in sales, a ratio of 1 for 17 may be very well on target.

One closing note on persistence: As I was writing the first draft of this chapter, the daytime television actress Susan Lucci won her first Emmy. As most people in the civilized world know, Susan Lucci was nominated a record 18 times before finally winning her first award in 1999. Susan beat my 0-17 and for this I wanted to publicly thank her for helping me put my rejection in perspective. Susan's annual loss became a perennial joke, yet she never appeared to lose her grace, her beauty or her sense of self-esteem. And Susan now owns one more Emmy than you or I. Congratulations, Susan. You are a model sales lesson.

## CHAPTER 18

# RULE # 7:
# FOCUS ON YOUR TARGET

Sometimes during my speeches, I walk up to an unsuspecting woman in an audience, take to a knee, and ask her to marry me. I usually get her attention along with a peculiar and startled look of disbelief. That's right, I propose to a stranger. I catch her by surprise, and she immediately says "No." (What did you expect?)

Then, I ask a woman sitting next to her if she would consider being my wife. "Not a chance!" I try a third time. "Fuhgedaboudit!" One after another after another. "No. No. No." is the inevitable response I get, and the response I expect.

I then return to my first "target-wife," and remind her that if I were sitting in her seat, I would not be flattered, as I immediately rebounded from her rejection and directed the same question to a fresh candidate. Then, to #3, #4, #5 and finally to #6.

By now, it is glaringly obvious to everyone in the room that "this guy is operating on an agenda that appears to be self serving." Based on his rapid-fire proposal trail, he really had no genuine interest in candidate #1 at all. His mission was to get married sometime before noon, and he really didn't care who his victim was. I then point out that if the first woman I asked accepted my proposal, then I would have good reason to be personally alarmed since she obviously was working on an agenda of her own.

After a brief pause, I shift from this fictitious marriage scenario to a more realistic example. Pointing toward an unsuspecting member of the group, I ask, "Can I have your business?" Without waiting for a response, I ask another guest, "Can I have your business?" And then on to a third in rapid succession, "How about your business? Can I do business with you?"

As with the marriage proposal it is clear that I don't genuinely care about any one individual business prospect. I just want to sign a new account for reasons of my own. Perhaps I want to make a lot of money so I can buy an expensive car and retire at an early age. This personal agenda is not only very transparent, but it also lacks any sign of sincerity. Sadly, this "style" is as common as it is unappealing.

Relationships, whether they are business relationships or personal relationships, take time and usually a plan to develop. Once upon a time, my wife, Barbara, was a perfect stranger. We lived in different areas of New Jersey for the first thirty-two years of our lives. We simply did not realize that the other person was alive . . . nor did we know enough to care.

But one day, upon initial visual sighting, I decided that it might be in my best interest to invest some time and effort in getting introduced to this woman. From that day forward, a series of individual steps unfolded which were all necessary in building a trusting relationship. It took a series of steps to break down the inhibitions she held for a stranger. I then attempted to establish, and then expand upon, her comfort level . . . one opportunity at a time. We sipped a coke. We viewed a movie. We sat through dinner. We enjoyed a day of skiing. I met her parents . . . and she met mine. Each step led to the next logical sequence in this relationship-building strategy. There was virtually no stress and no reason to question the process. The relationship matured, developed and evolved into a strong and healthy bond culminating in marriage . . . a quick three years later.

(By the way, since the "sale" was finalized, I have spent a good number of years fine-tuning my "customer service" skills with Barbara. But I'll cover that in my next book!)

A successful sales effort works the same way as personal relationship building. Nothing worthwhile is going to happen until the involved parties establish a mutual trust. Then, a number of additional events occur at their own pace. This happens usually by design, and depending on the service or product you are selling, over a period of days, weeks, months, or sometimes, years. Remember these seven words:

## Everything worthwhile takes longer than first imagined.

Until you take the first step, however, the meter doesn't begin to run. So here is my candid advice to you: Step out of your comfort zone and put things in motion.

Put yourself in gear.

Get the ball rolling.

Take a shot.

Make a move.

Fail.

Call.

Write.

Drive.

Attend.

Do.

Start the relationship building cycle.

Tune in.

Turn on.

Get jazzed!

Begin at once . . . today . . . now.

To be more specific:

1.  List those people, groups and companies you would like to do business with. (For this, all you will need is a pencil and a piece of paper, so no excuses please.)

2.  Determine three logical ways in which you can enter each prospect's universe . . . and make an initial connection with each one. (Here are some ideas: a postcard; a letter; an invitation; a telephone call; a personal referral; a visit at their trade show; walk up to someone, stick out your hand, and simply introduce yourself to them.)

3.  Make the connection. (Be Brief. Be Bright. Be Gone.)

4.  Keep building on the previous calls until a relationship built on trust develops. (The secret here is to stay visible. Don't give them the opportunity to forget who you are for more than eight weeks at a time.)

# CHAPTER 19

# RULE # 8:
# SOME DAYS YOU'RE THE WINDSHIELD,
# SOME DAYS YOU'RE THE BUG

Here are the realties: Bad things happen. They will happen to you. The world does not always play fair. When these realties strike, don't bother telling people your problems. Ninety percent won't care and the other ten percent will be glad you have them.

Let's add some perspective to these realties. As far as I know, I don't have an incurable disease. I know I have never been run over by a bus, and (knock on wood), I have never been in a bad car accident. All of my airplane rides have terminated in safe landings, and I have never had to call a lifeguard to pull me from fifteen foot waves off of Wailea. Therefore, this chapter will pale in comparison to some of my fellow authors who tie their lessons to some real doozies of disasters. Just the same, I'm here to tell you that some bad things are going to happen to you just as they have happened to me. The key is how you react. By whining? Or, by taking QVC President, Barry Diller's, mindset:

## *"They won. We lost. Who's next? (Bring him on!)"*

Feel free to skip this chapter if you are pressed for time. (I like to read it whenever I want to feel sorry for myself.) Compared to the possibilities of the Big Show, my "disasters" are really nickel and dime stuff. But I'm betting that most of your "troubles" in life probably amount to chump change. You be the judge.

## Dems Da Breaks

I didn't realize it at the time, but playing football while attending college on an athletic scholarship was a job. It was a real money saver for my family, but make no mistake about it, this was *work*.

The deal was this: The University of Massachusetts would pay for my books, board and tuition. It was entirely up to me if there was a degree at the end of my senior year. No guarantees here. In return, I would provide sweat, tears and what later would become a great deal of blood and broken bone tissue for a shot at a free education and a gray athletic T-shirt with matching shorts which read "Athletic Department." At the impressionable age of eighteen this sounded like a sweetheart of a deal.

When I arrived on campus, I thought (along with every other student-athlete) that I was something special. I was coming to U. Mass to show these athletes how the game of football was meant to be played.

The guy playing my position on the U. Mass team at the time was Greg Landry, who later would graduate and mold a pretty impressive twenty-year career in the National Football League. At the time I was not impressed. I was the new Broadway Joe Namath from New Jersey (call me "Main Street Mike"), and I was about to ply my trade.

Until . . . a mere eight days into my freshman season I very unceremoniously broke my ankle during a practice scrimmage. Bad break #1.

In the blink of an eye, Main Street Mike was crawling to the side of the practice field like a baby, without a single sign of sympathy from anybody. I became an early season casualty . . . expected . . . budgeted for . . . and dealt with on a business-as-usual basis at the college level of play. The terse response from the Head coach: "Who's next?"

I wasn't around long enough to get the showmanship part down and break the gul-dang thing during a game. I ended my freshman season on the practice field. No fans. No deathly silence from the standing-room-only crowd. No polite ovation as they carried me off the field. No nothing.

For the next thirteen weeks I spent most of my waking hours trying to coerce co-eds into signing my left foot. I learned a lot during those thirteen weeks but the two things that have always stayed with me were: (1) chemistry teachers don't give a hoot about football players on crutches ("Get to class on time Marchev or get an F"); and (2) playing the game was a lot more fun than watching from row 25. But as the popular saying goes, there was always next year.

I prided myself on being a quick study. I decided to learn from my freshman "mistake." So year two, I decided that if I was going to break anything from here on out, I would make sure it was during a game. I very wisely waited for a Saturday afternoon game in Rhode Island before I separated my shoulder, bringing my come-back season to an abrupt halt. Break #2.

At that point, my combined two year college offensive totals to date were: 3 yards rushing, 0 passing, 1 broken ankle and 1 separated shoulder. I realized right then and there that if I was ever going to win the Heisman Trophy, I needed a lot more yardage the following year and a little more playing time. Even my momma didn't tell me there would be days like these!

For those of you who believe that lightening doesn't strike twice in the same place, I have some information to share with you. I had to kiss year #2 good-bye as fast as you could say, "Who was that 270 pound lineman with the lightening bolt on his helmet?" Unknown to me at the time, my medical chart was just getting interesting.

I was outfitted with a shoulder harness which conveniently strapped my throwing wing tightly to my chest. For the second time in two years, I became a football statistic and an early season spectator. Two tries . . . two season-ending injuries.

But, I am one of those up-beat people who always looks for the silver lining in every rain cloud. The good news was that I never had the opportunity to play long enough in the first two years to prove to my coaches or to the student body that I wasn't any good. Smart thinking! As a result, I still enjoyed favorable press in the Daily Collegian campus newspaper and the glances of quite a few co-eds. Although I had only taken three snaps in two years, I was still the *quarterback.*

In the spring of my sophomore year I decided to try out for the baseball team . . . a sport a little less physical and one for which my delicate 175 pound frame was better suited. After all, baseball had always been my first true love. In fact, "bazeball had always been bedy, bedy good to me."

Prior to launching my record (and bone) shattering career at U. Mass football, I was in courtship with Oklahoma State University and their varsity baseball team, the Cowboys of OSU, which earned its way to the College World Series in Omaha every year. I had always dreamed about jacking one out of the park in the seventh game of the College World Series in Nebraska. But a partial scholarship to OSU didn't fuel my ego at the time, so I opted for the full boat to U. Mass.

I was known as a "walk-on" on the baseball team at U. Mass. That is someone who was not recruited to play and who asked for permission to audition his talents. The odds of a walk-on making the team are always quite slim. But to everyone's surprise but my own, the cocky kid from New Jersey made the team and waited for the opportunity to squeeze into the starting line up.

One evening, after practice, I reminded the coach that I was not only eager but was prepared to help the team at a number of positions. This might be a good story to place in a chapter entitled "The Power of Asking" because the very next week I was called to play right field during a game at Williams College.

"Marchev is back!" I chanted to myself as I trotted out to assume my position next to my good friend and fraternity brother Mitch Salnick, who was in my eyes the great Willie Mays incarnated. I was ready. I was poised. I was well-trained and correctly positioned. When . . . Crack! A soft fly ball to right field. This ball is a can of corn . . . an easy out. No, maybe not. It is sinking fast. I better quicken my step. Dive Marchev! Diiivvve . . . Craaaaaack!

"UH-OH!"

The first crack was the sound of ball meeting bat. The second crack was the sound of New Jersey bone tissue breaking in half. (I obviously still lacked the showmanship part. I didn't even make the catch. And quite frankly, at the point of impact, I really didn't much care that the guy was jogging into third with an uncontested stand up three-bagger.)

It was April 28th, and I was finished competing at the collegiate varsity level . . . for the third time in two years. Main Street Mike was Marchev the Mutt. Mr. Big Shot Athlete from New Jersey and his athletic career were going down the tubes in a blazing streak, complete with thrown objects and abundant profanities. I came to college as a high school success story, and I was going to compete in two sports. Then I was dealt a triple dose of how cruel and unbiased life can be to people with nothing but good intentions. I remember like it was yesterday, lying in a bed at the university infirmary, with warm tears streaming down the side of my face . . . asking no one in particular . . .

### *"Why did this have to happen to me? Why me?"*

Have you ever heard yourself muttering these same words?

The final blow came a few weeks later, when I saw the headlines: "U. Mass to play in College World Series in Omaha." My team earned a berth at the National College World Series. They were going to the big show . . . without Main Street Mike.

I know now that in the scheme of things my setbacks were just a drop in the bucket of life's small disappointments. But just the same, I learned two valuable lessons from my university breakdowns.

First, life doesn't unwind in a carefully written script. Life is a day-to-day adventure, and you had better be prepared for both the ups and the downs. My lessons were gentle compared with the litany of curve balls life can throw at most people — loss of family . . . loss of limb . . . loss of reputation . . . loss of a loved one.

Second, regardless of the apparent severity of the situation, the crisis shall pass. And hopefully, if you don't keep your head between your hands for too long, you become a tad stronger from each negative experience you're introduced to. As long as you keep your sights on the horizon and keep on keeping on, you will look back at these lessons and see some humor or hope in it all.

Face it! There is little logic in living in the past, lamenting life's unfair situations. Life is sometimes unfair. Go with it. For most of us, our "big hurts" are nothing more than small blisters. The key to a healthy existence is to accept life as it unfolds.

Ann Lamott, the author of *Bird by Bird*, said it very nicely when she wrote, "Bad things happen to good people." Today, thirty years after my "break dance," I have matured and seasoned enough to categorize these experiences as little "inconveniences."

## It's Deja Vu All Over Again

Here's one of life's comic post-scripts. While out on a training ride getting ready for the 1997 Ironman competition, my bike's steering mechanism loosened up and I went over the handle bars and landed shoulder first. CRAAAACK! "I recognize that sound," I immediately said to myself. But this time the feeling was not new to me. I had been there before. Fifteen weeks later, and a few sleepless nights, I was back in the saddle. I finished the Ironman in the allotted time in 8th place . . . counting from the back.

## CHAPTER 20

# RULE # 9:
# USE THE "SEVEN SEE'S" STRATEGY

I don't particularly like the word "aggressive" when used to define a sales professional's behavior. I consider myself a professional, yet I don't want to be thought of as an aggressive person. If I don't enjoy being around aggressive people, why would I want to be one?

Being recognized as professionally conscientious and persistent, on the other hand, is a reputation I could learn to live with. "Persistence" connotes a non-quitter, a go-getter, a person who sticks with a task until it is completed. People who don't pack up their tent at the first sign of discomfort are always welcome and appreciated. Persistence is a flattering label. So, let's put persistence to work.

The first step to get someone comfortable enough to do business with you is to have them realize that you exist. You must tell your target audience that you are both "in the game" and "qualified to play." Telling people you are alive, just once, won't cut it. Having introduced yourself, you must proceed with a planned campaign of timely reminders. Think of this maneuver as a battle for the mind.

Once your prospect realizes that (1) you appear to be a qualified supplier, and (2) you are available, the next step is to get the prospect to feel comfortable with you. A meaningful business relationship is, and always has been, based on trust. But, breaking into a prospect's guarded "comfort zone" takes more time than most salespeople budget for. Prospects will move the relationship at their own pace. You can't rush them any more than you can cook a steak in one minute by turning up the heat. The result is the same for both endeavors: a scorched failure.

By implementing the Seven See's Strategy, you will position yourself in your prospect's eyes as a good person — a thrifty, brave, clean, reverent, courteous and persistent team member who is prepared, interested and able to contribute to solving the prospect's problems. The Seven See's Strategy also cuts through the clutter and daily noise created by the big boys' promotional budgets. Here it is:

---

## The Seven See's Strategy
### Contact each qualified prospect seven times during the next eighteen months.

---

You don't have to "see" the prospect each time although at least one or two personal visits are advisable. Sincere phone calls and correspondence count, too. What is so magical about eighteen months? Why not three months or six months? The answer has to do with "spaced repetition." This time frame prevents you from appearing too pushy while helping the prospect view you as a true ally. At the same time, your name passes in front of your prospects often enough to serve as a non-threatening reminder.

To make this strategy work you need to provide your target audience with something useful with each contact — i.e. information, tips, mistakes to avoid, directions, heads-up alerts, etc. You also need to set up a tickler system that reminds you every six weeks to send something of value to your target audience. Follow with an E-mail or phone call now and then . . . very matter of fact . . . very brief. Less is more when it comes to reminding people you are alive. You can even simply send a postcard with your web address and the words "Pay Us An E-Visit for Information" stamped into the message area. This simple communication device passes your name in front of the prospect and gives a location (www.you.com) where the prospect can find more information if he has an inclination to check you out or learn more about your available products and services.

The key to this system is consistency. Consistency works miracles. Your objective is to keep your name and the name of your company fresh in the prospect's mind . . . and to show the prospect that you want his business. (This is really courtship without the romance.)

You are probably saying to yourself at this very moment, *"I'll never have the time to do this for each prospect."* Be smart. Don't begin to implement the Seven See's Strategy for your entire prospect list. I said in an earlier Rule that there are only two types of people in the world — those we can help, and those we can't. Use your persistence (and limited time) only for those prospects who you firmly believe belong on your A list or the top of your B list. You also probably want to be convinced that the Seven See's works before committing yourself to the strategy. I don't blame you. So try this. Pick out at random thirty prospects and split them into two groups. One group of fifteen prospects will get the Seven See's treatment; the remainder will receive your customary sales approach. (You don't like thirty? Pick a number!)

Keep track of your sales from each group for the next eighteen months. If you like computer generated visuals, make a graph for the sales from each group. As the months unfold, the "normal" group's graph will look like a freeway on ramp; the Seven See's group's graph will look like the road to Pike's Peak. Over time, many prospects exposed to the Seven See's treatment will turn into long-term business relationships.

## Why The Seven See's Always Works (Well Almost Always)

As I observed in an earlier chapter, approximately 80% of sales happen after multiple contacts with a qualified potential buyer. The research indicates that most business transactions happen after the fifth contact. I personally think the number is closer to the seventh.

Despite this documented fact, 50% of all salespeople still quit after the first contact with a prospect. They lob in some unrehearsed sales banter and give up after the painful rejection. Another 25% of salespeople stop trying after their second contact. So 75% of your competition has packed up and gone home after two at bats . . . at least three at bats short of getting a hit.

Your amateur competition, those who have no idea how the process works, successfully eliminate themselves long before the sale becomes as easy as smackin' a slow, floating lob into the bleachers. Use the Seven See's Strategy and you'll suspend that ball over home plate waiting for your bat.

## CHAPTER 21

# RULE #10:
# PHONIES, LIKE OIL SLICKS,
# INEVITABLY SURFACE

I originally tagged this chapter for men only, but after giving it some thought, I think that women will benefit from knowing that most of them have an extraordinary skill that men can't match.

Among the unique assets God bestowed on the female gender, which includes longer life spans and . . . well . . . let's leave it at that . . . , was a built-in "Creep-o-meter." Just as a dog can sense when a human is frightened, a woman can sense when a person has a serious character flaw. Women, can spot creeps across a room, down the block or at the "next exit" (a New Jersey phrase). These built-in creep-o-meters have advanced pentium chips. After over thirty years of study, I know this to be true.

Envision this scenario: Two women are on the 17th floor of an office building taking a coffee break. One goes over to the window to take in the view. Out in parking lot #3, a good 500 yards from their current vantage point, a salesman is gently nosing his car into an open parking space. He gets out of the car, opens the rear door, and retrieves his suit coat which was neatly hanging behind the driver's seat. He puts the jacket on, buttons the top button of a newly pressed white dress shirt, slides his tie up snugly into position and reaches for his briefcase. He closes the doors and locks the car. Just as he turns to head toward the building, the woman says, "Hey Susan, come quick. See that guy? I think he's a creep!"

How does she know? How can she tell? She can tell because women have a built in creep-o-meter. Woman can eyeball men within a few heartbeats, position them as good guys or slime balls and be right far more often than they are wrong. (The fact that some woman stay with losers for so long has nothing to do with them knowing or not knowing that these men are losers. These women pretend that their creep-o-meters are out of alignment or think that they can "fix" guys. This is perhaps a good topic for another book for another day . . . by another author. )

What does this have to do with selling? Simple. Regardless of how masterfully you may pretend you are somebody you are not, people (especially women) can spot a phony from 700 yards away. So always be real. Be you . . . for better and for worse. As soon as you arrive for a scheduled appointment, remember that people are watching you from behind the smoked glass window or from the other side of the Schefflera plant. The receptionist is watching. People in the elevator are watching. Cashiers are watching. People you pass in the hall are watching. Security guards are watching. They are all making judgments. No matter how great the temptation, don't fake it. I'm not smiling. The creep-o-meter is not a figment of my imagination. It is alive, well, hooked up and residing in most every person walking the face of the earth. Believe it. And act accordingly. Consider yourself warned!

# CORRECTING AND AVOIDING COMMON MARKETING AND SALES MISTAKES

# CHAPTER 22

# SET THE TABLE
# BEFORE YOU EAT THE MEAL

To lots of people the concept of marketing is still very much a mystery. Most people don't know what marketing is and don't know how marketing works. Marketing is not sales; and selling is not marketing. It is important that I clarify the two concepts before helping you identify and cure the most common mistakes that are made in each discipline.

Marketing can be thought of as setting the table, or properly preparing the meal for the dinner. It involves identifying and qualifying prospects, finding out what people are looking for, researching a market to understand how to best address the needs of its prospects, and preparing those prospects to accept your message. Marketing is done before selling can begin. The reasons why many "salespeople" are not more successful at marketing is because the process takes time and shows no immediate positive results.

Selling, on the other hand, is enjoying the meal . . . holding interesting and worthwhile conversations while you eat . . . delivering the goods. Selling happens during the final face-to-face contact when you are looking to close the deal. Looking at it from a different angle, selling can be thought of as transaction based while marketing is a knowledge-based discipline.

Selling involves the way you communicate and listen in the meeting and the attitudes you convey to the prospect as you seek to establish a business relationship. Here, you either savor the taste of victory from all your prospecting and preparation, or you poke yourself in the eye with the fork.

In this section we'll address some common marketing mistakes and I'll offer avoidance techniques and a cure for each one. The errors that salespeople typically make when setting the table relate to two areas of marketing: (1) the process of prospecting; and (2) preparation for the face-to-face meeting.

The common pitfalls to avoid during the selling process (the face-to-face meeting) can also be grouped into two categories: (1) your attitude (both internal and communicated to the prospect); and (2) your conduct of the meeting. We'll look at each of these four areas in the following chapters, and help you avoid the common mistakes associated with what happens after the sales meeting.

166

# CHAPTER 23

# COMMON PROSPECTING MISTAKES

Although we have dealt at length with the art and science of prospecting in prior chapters, let's take a moment to identify some of the mistakes I commonly see among the sales staff when I consult for companies. These errors do not usually relate to misuse of some high-powered prospecting tool or process. More often they relate to orientation and basics. Remarkable, but true. Here they are.

## Underestimating The Importance Of Prospecting

Some call it farming. Some call it mining. Others consider it more like a seeding process. Regardless of what you call it, failure to prospect *on a regular basis* is a malady among sales professionals which you can forecast and count on contracting. You may catch the bug for a few days or weeks after you land the Moby Dick of accounts or you may get it from fatigue induced by the perception of rejection. One way or another, we all get it now and then.

But if you don't consistently identify new sources of business, you will ultimately find yourself needing only your fingers and toes when it comes time to count your take home pay.

The overused old saying sums it up: "Nothing ventured, nothing gained." For something good to happen tomorrow, you must do some intelligent prospecting today.

Prospecting is 90% of a successful sales campaign. Identifying logical candidates to pursue, educate and relate with is the name of the game. Once you set the dominoes up and space them properly, one little push is all it takes to have them fall into place.

If you insist that prospecting leaves scars (even after reading this book) then repeat this workout Mantra of professional athletes:

## No Pain . . . No Gain

## Quitting Or Changing A Successful Program

Every once in a while a marketing gambit surfaces and works to perfection — perhaps by sheer accident or the position of the stars. Who cares? When one works it's time to celebrate. Then, after the celebration a strange thing happens. The "marketing genius" stops doing what he/she just did. He tries something new, something innovative, something creative.

Suppose you administer a successful direct mail campaign. The return requests for information are more than you expected. Orders resulted which surpassed your best case scenario. So . . . at the next marketing meeting, you suggest switching from direct mail to seminar marketing. This is what I am talking about.

Quitting a successful prospecting approach too soon is a common mistake. Realize that you are likely to grow tired of your marketing message/program long before others do. Once you find something that works, I am not suggesting you marry the idea until the end of time. But I am suggesting that you continue to "work it" until the facts indicate that a modification is in order.

Decide for yourself which of the following approaches makes the most sense when you've found a program that works:

- *"If it isn't broke, don't fix it."* (Old Proverb)

- *"If it isn't broke, break it."* (The Three Stooges)

- *"If it isn't broke, and it worked a moment ago, tweak it ever so gently but be careful you don't screw the entire project up."* (Mike Marchev)

## Walking An Inch In Your Prospect's Shoes

If you fail to think like your prospect, you are going to come in second place — and only one person gets the business. What *you* like doesn't matter. What *you* think, doesn't matter. What your prospect thinks and likes is what matters.

If you don't know what your prospects (or customers) want from you and your product, it is time you found out. How? Simply ask them.

In every opportunity that presents itself, ask your customers:

*"What would you need if . . . ?"*

*"What is listed on your all time dream list?"*

*"What would you eliminate or change if it was up to you?"*

I like to compare this customer inquisition to tea with Columbo. You remember Detective Columbo. He was the sleuth whose clothes looked like they came from the Salvation Army grab bag and whose car was powered by cats. He wasn't flashy, but he always managed to apprehend the culprit in the end.

The secret to Columbo's success was that he asked questions. One after another. Plodding question after question. He got others to speak while he listened intently and took notes on the corner of a piece of paper torn from an old scratch pad. Playing Columbo is good advice for salespeople who want success.

You'll be amazed what you learn once you get a prospect to talk. The key is not to predict your prospect's feelings. The information, at times, may sting a bit. But if it is the truth, it will remain a fact whether you are privy to it or not. You are better off knowing what is going on.

Once you learn what turns your target audience "on," the exercise becomes academic. Either you can satisfy their needs or you can't. (By the way, if you can't provide an appropriate solution but know who can, I want you to point your prospect toward the immediate fix. If you find this to be poor advice, you may not be where you need to be on the professional game board yet.)

## Relying On "Name Recognition" Promotions

I'll assume that most people reading this book are not part of the gigantic marketing machines of IBM, Merck or General Motors. Therefore, you probably don't have an eight-figure promotional budget. (In the beginning of my startup business, I had a "figure-eight" promo budget — $8. But that was per month!)

You probably need your precious advertising dollars to pay big dividends for you. If so, you better not think about placing large space ads in an attempt to build "name recognition." You can't afford this luxury, now or ever.

Your single objective when investing promotional dollars is to identify people who have a genuine interest in learning more about what you do, get them to raise their hand and eventually, send you a check. Your best strategy:

# Wave something of value in front of your audience and get them to reach for it.

I believe a two step approach is the best way to do this effectively and economically for most small enterprises. The quality of the leads generated is vastly more important than quantity. The most effective carrot you can dangle in front of would-be customers in this information age is useful, timely and meaningful "intelligence." This is something your future customers can't get too much of. I suggest that you send your prospects a letter, email or postcard on a somewhat regular basis (once every six to eight weeks) offering some form of free information on a subject that will ring their bell.

For example, a response from people who want to receive a copy of your latest "How To" booklet on "Mushroom Farming" is a clear indication that: (1) each respondent is interested in fungus (at least the edible kind), and (2) each is willing to give you his name and address for more intelligence. (I'll refrain from making a crack about I.Q.)

Here is a brief blueprint for building a direct mail campaign: First, mail a professional business letter introducing the How To piece. This letter must be easy to read and jam-packed with reasons why the prospect should ask for a personal copy of the "intelligence." Include what the pros call a bounce back device. (Postcards and self-addressed envelopes are the most common, but include a blank space for a daytime telephone number.) Once your audience asks for the free information, you must send it at once. (Notice I didn't say when you get around to it.)

When you send out the How To piece, include a second letter reminding the prospect/suspect how valuable the information is. Also, include an invitation for the prospect/suspect to contact you directly with any questions concerning the material, or to schedule an appointment with you to explore the topic further.

The next step is to follow up with a personal phone call. (That's why you requested the phone number in the bounce-back piece.) Your objective is to make a connection with the prospect by politely inquiring whether or not he received the information he asked for. During this brief call, make it a point to ask if you can help in any other way.

For those people on your list who did not ask for your How To booklet (the majority of the list), listen carefully to what I am about to tell you. Send these people the same letter a second time (that is, assuming the letter got a decent overall response on the first go around.) Yes, send the exact same letter to those prospects/suspects on your list who did not respond to your first letter. Based on my experience, you will get a good response.

Expect that most of the people you contact on the phone will not be enthusiastic once they figure out who you are and why you are calling. Don't take this personally. As Bruce Hornsbee sang: "That's just the way it is." One or two will hit it off with you, and a budding business relationship will be forthcoming. That's success . . . and you'll get a heap more per promotional dollar than you will by throwing bucks at institutional advertising. You may as well toss those presidential pictures on the "barbie."

## Stumped On The Question "Why You?"

Here is a sample of Q & A I typically have with participants in my seminars:

**MM:** *"Why should I do business with you?"*

**Participant #1:** *"We provide more service."*

**Participant #2:** *"We are faster."*

**Participant #3:** *"We are better."*

**Participant #4:** *"We care."*

These are all unpolished, store-bought answers — we . . . I . . . first . . . less . . . quicker . . . care . . . service . . . yada, yada, yada! All quite meaningless and irrelevant. The truth is the majority of business people today don't really know compelling reasons why anyone should do business with them. So when asked, they resort to a knee-jerk response and wing their way with an answer they feel sounds logical and maybe believable.

I want you to be the exception. Do a little work on the speedbag before jumping into the ring. Think about how to favorably position yourself with future customers. Having an answer — a well thought out, meaningful, believable answer — to the very intelligent and fair question: "Why should I do business with you?" is vital to your future success. (Amazingly, very few salespeople take the time to develop this key response!) Consider framing your answer along the lines of the following example.

**Prospect:** *"Mike, considering all of my options, why should I do business with you?"*

**MM:** *"That's a very intelligent question. (Pause) I'm glad you asked that. The last three meeting planners who chose me to speak at their annual convention chose me because . . ."*

This response accomplishes a couple of things. It congratulates the person who asked the question as being knowledgeable. (*"That's a very intelligent question."*) People like to feel they are smart rather than feeling like they just asked a dumb question.

Second, your response gives instant credibility to your superior competitive position in the marketplace. You are passing along a few documented reasons why *other leading companies* have chosen you as a trusted business partner. What you think of yourself is not relevant at this point, other than to boost your PEQ (personal ego quotient). But what other people (clients) think of you and your organization is compelling to prospective clients.

Key Point: Although you may be more knowledgeable about the specifics, the views of your customers will always be more believable when selling the benefits of your services to prospects. Use your customer's words, thoughts and experiences whenever possible. Your prospects will place significant faith in this type of communication.

Don't be embarrassed at first if you don't know why your customers choose to do business with you. Just make it a point to find out by asking them the next time an opportunity presents itself. Plus, when you get it straight from your customers (versus surveys) you will sound more believable when relaying the information to others. You may even want to provide the prospect with the opportunity to contact a few selected clients directly. (Just make sure you have permission from your clients before handing out their name and phone number as references.)

## Forgetting Former Prospects And Clients

You will typically invest a lot of hours and probably some money trying to identify, qualify and then schedule face time with a prospect. You finally say and do what it takes to establish some degree of rapport. But for any one of a million reasons, the prospect chooses not to do business with you, and you drop them like a hot potato. Not much logic here folks.

I recently received a phone call from a woman who I used to do business with years ago. She was responding to a postcard I sent to her a week earlier. I was just keeping in touch, but my timing was perfect. She called and gave me the name of the person I should be speaking with if I was interested in earning some money. Is this the only time a random postcard has worked some magic for me? Not on your life. I can't count the occasions where my touching base with former clients and prospects has resulted in a solid lead for new business.

I don't want to bang my fist on the table too many times in this book, but this deserves a "knuckle numbing,"

## Don't give up on past prospects and clients.

Contact them. Don't quit on them and don't quit on yourself. Persistence works when administered with patience.

## Not Using "People Proof"

What you say about yourself and your company is, or will be perceived as, biased. No one is particularly impressed with what you say. The secret to gaining credibility and respect rapidly is to get others to sing from the praise book for you. Think testimonials.

Many sales professionals fail to use this high-caliber weapon. In fact, they fail to even obtain the bullets — which are *free* for the asking. The next time you blow one of your customers away with high-quality service, position the customer as a spokesperson for your program. Be careful; this can be a tricky deal. You want the customer to show appreciation for working with you but you don't ever want to place him in a compromising position.

So, always request a testimonial letter from satisfied customers. (You can never have too many.) Then, and this may come as news to some, make it your business to get those letters in the hands of inquisitive prospects. I can't tell you how many copies of beautiful, well crafted, Mike Marchev- oriented letters I had in my files, doing absolutely no good for me whatsoever — until I uncovered their power.

175

First, get those testimonials written. Second, get them out.

Final proof: Tell the truth. Honestly. Weren't you impressed and motivated to read this book when you read the awesome Mike Marchev stories and testimonials on page 270 from such pitchmen, sales superstars and executives as H. Ross Perot, Bill Gates, Steven Jobs, Michael Jordan and Tiger Woods?

Testimonials work like a charm.

# CHAPTER 24

# COMMON MISTAKES OF PREPARATION

A large portion of this book relates to preparation, as do a large number of all career success stories. Preparation is a necessary prerequisite for virtually all aspects of an effective system of selling — from prospecting and qualifying to making presentations, handling objections, sealing the deal and following through with service. Rather than overwhelm you with the many ways you can fail to be prepared, let's just look at some of the most common areas of preparation failure.

## Not Developing Your "USP"

We've all heard of "ESP" — extra sensory perception — and its paranormal cousin telekinesis. If you are the kind of salesperson who can make money slide across the table and into your pocket without touching it, you've definitely got a paranormal gift. But if you are one of the rest of us sales mortals, there is still some good news. You definitely have "USP," and if you develop this "gift" as part of your sales preparation, you will definitely close more sales.

USP is your "Unique Selling Proposition" — your competitive advantage. Trying to compete without identifying your competitive advantage is about as smart as a Superbowl coach sending his team into the big game with no plays. To prepare for the "game" you need to identify your USP and consistently articulate it over and over again to your target audience.

Think about this. There are probably a number of competitors in your immediate market who provide the same basic product or service you do. If you don't know what you are bringing to the party that they are not, then why should your prospect care? Establishing a Unique Selling Proposition will distance you from the competition faster than by competing head to head over price.

So, you owe it to yourself to give the following question a considerable amount of reflection.

### What is it about you that makes you different, unique and more valuable to your customers?

Here are some broad competitive factors to help jog your thought process. Use these as a springboard to identify those specific advantages you offer.

- Hours of operation

- Locations

- Skill level

- Experience

- Delivery Policy

- Return Policy

- Service Policy

- Price Points

- Unusual Services

- Special product training/knowledge

- Industry contacts/connections

Once you have identified the specific factors that separate you from the pack, you need to get this information to your prospects on a recurrent basis.

## Random Exposures

Another common error salespeople make is failing to prepare a system to promote their businesses repeatedly to the target prospects. Banging the drum over and over again, even in a modest way, is very effective in getting people's attention.

Here is a three-part system that works very effectively:

- **Postcards** — Think of postcards as mini-billboards. The postage is affordable and the message gets read. The content should be useful information to your prospect, or tips on where he might find such information or intelligence. Postcards are easy and fun.

- **Articles** — Sending articles is also an effective way of keeping your name in front of people. While writing this book, I was talking with a client and mentioned my book in progress. Around a week later I received a note from him saying, "For your book project" with a New York Times article attached. Short, sweet, and of interest to me. Perfect. Sending articles of interest to your prospects is simple if you tear the article out of a magazine and attach your calling card with a written note saying; "Thought you might find this article of interest. Let me know how I can help!"

I try to highlight a sentence or two within the article that makes an immediate point or can stand on its own. Without exception, this highlighted area gets read, even if your prospect does not read the entire story. Quite frankly, you really don't care if the prospect reads the article or not. Your job is simply to pass on meaningful information.

- **Industry Reminders** — Reminders are used like articles. Simply identify an industry event coming up in your area and remind your prospect to mark their calendar as they deem appropriate.

## Going With Your Gut

Going with your "gut feeling" rather than testing your assumptions can be a costly error. This mistake more often than not involves a shortage of discipline rather than time or money. For some reason, many entrepreneurs believe they have a mystical knowledge of the precise thoughts and needs of their market — a sophisticated camouflage that amounts to guessing and winging. They fail to test assumptions which would actually put them in the know, and resultingly, in the "green."

Things like market . . . price . . . size . . . timing . . . color . . . offers . . . and policies can and should be tested to arrive at accurate answers. Some business people mistakenly believe that if the test market doesn't consist of 500,000 people, the results will be skewed. ("Skewed" for you non-market research aficionados means "screwed up due to lousy information.")

Do you know how big the test market is for surveys of such inconsequential questions as "Should the President be impeached?" or "Should we send ground troops into Bosnia?" Usually it's 600 to 1,200 people. You don't need a cast of thousands to get your hand on the pulse and pointed in the right direction. Most businesses can get good direction from surveys, direct mail, or test marketing with far smaller samples. Another approach is to utilize focus groups. Setting them up with participants is easier for consumer products than business products. One approach you can try with business people who are pressed for time includes organizing the group around the time/place of an industry event.

By testing and paying attention to the answers you hear, you will cultivate a true advantage over the "I think therefore it must be true" mentality prevalent with many of your competitors.

## Not Keeping Up-To-Date

With today's technology literally pouring tidal waves of data and information right onto the top of our desks, there is no excuse for you to not keep up to date in your industry's news. I'm not here to sell magazine subscriptions or newspapers or Internet providers. But you have, at your finger tips, a zillion ways to keep in touch and informed. Pick one and use it. Do your homework. Ask inquiring questions of those in the know. Stay in the game.

## Not Planning Your Day

Your success will come as a direct outcome of how well you plan. You may already practice strategic or even tactical planning in your business. But I am talking about the hand-to-hand combat of your normal workday.

If you hit your desk in the morning and dive vigorously into tackling every project on your desk, you will prove your energy and dedication while wasting a good chunk of it.

Instead, plan your day around the acronym W-I-N. Win stands for:

### What's Important Now

Regardless of the tasks at hand, you need to start each day by asking yourself, "What is the most important use of my time today?" Your answer will undoubtedly change from day to day or week to week. But this technique keeps you focused on the tasks most critical to your success.

Here's what I do. Each day I simply write out a list of my "to do's," preferably in order of priority. No need to computerize the list, engrave it, or otherwise make it look pretty and permanent. It isn't. This is just your check sheet. Throughout the day as you knock off tasks, just put a checkmark next to what you've done. At the end of the day, pull out the sheet and assess your productivity. Sometimes you'll get the psychic reward of seeing all you accomplished that day; sometimes you'll wonder if you were abducted by extraterrestrials who erased your memory of a large chunk of the day. Either way, you are ahead of the game because you are focused, and you have the first few items to put on tomorrow's list.

Your old lists (I keep mine) are also useful to assess how you spend your time over extended periods. If the tasks you list and do first are the one's you feel most comfortable with or one's which truly keep you from the sometimes intimidating work of actually putting yourself in front of prospects, the old lists won't lie. Take the cue accordingly.

## Not Keeping Sales Tools Organized

You can't afford to lose time hunting down a tool from your selling arsenal, especially when you are on the phone or preparing to dash out to an important meeting. A professional salesperson needs to know how to "stash" (i.e. file) things in a fashion that is conducive to easy retrieval.

I recently found a low-cost software filing system that I can recommend for someone who wants a very simple system. It is called Paper Tiger and costs about $50. If finding things within the four walls of your house and/or office is giving you fits, take a look at the Paper Tiger system. It has made a wonderful contribution to my peace of mind, not to mention speed of paper retrieval.

182

# Taking Detailed Notes

Relying on memory can be fatal to your prospecting and selling system. Here is the long and short of it: Write everything down. Take notes. Memories can be short. And nights are for sleeping, not tossing and turning trying to remember if you have forgotten some important issue for tomorrow's sales presentation.

The master at this is a friend of mine, Paul Moskowitz. This man runs a $150-million company and forgets nothing. Paul has a mind like a steel trap. He never drops a ball while juggling a great many of them simultaneously. His secret? He writes *everything* down. And he doesn't throw the note away until he feels that he has received complete satisfaction. Once the task is appropriately addressed, completed or formally delegated, he takes the piece of paper and rips it into tiny shreds before throwing it away — which apparently clears his mind for the next task. When this guy crosses something off his list, it stays crossed off.

Do a Moskowitz. Write things down, give your memory a much needed rest, and never disappoint a prospect, client, or associate again.

# CHAPTER 25

# ATTITUDE ADJUSTMENTS

One of the medical miracles that I find most amazing is not a new discovery. The recent sequencing of the human genome, the discovery of new disease markers and antigens, the clinical applications of gene splicing and recombinant DNA are all mindboggling. But, frankly, the one that bowls me over every time is the good old "placebo effect." This is where, say, 100 patients are given a white pill to cure a medical problem. Fifty get the real medicine and fifty get nothing more than white powder (the "placebo"). Yet, some significant percentage of the placebo group (sometimes well more than half) will show symptom relief or even get cured.

This proves beyond any doubt the staggering importance of the mind and a person's attitude. If a positive attitude can cure a medical problem without medicine, what can it do for a "sales" problem?

So, let's tackle some of the more common problems relating to attitudes which I find among salespeople today ... attitudes which can have unintended destructive consequences on your sales effort and client relationships. (Note: I do not like to dwell on negatives, and sometimes in this chapter it may seem like I am unduly focused on negatives. Unfortunately, that comes with the territory when pointing out problems. Remember, we are trying to deal constructively with mental processes which may need some adjustment and realignment for the sake of a sales career. We are not judging people.)

## Thinking The Mission Is To Change Other's Attitudes

Have you noticed any associates or prospects who walk around day in and day out looking as if they have just lost their best friend? These people seem to communicate to the world that life is and will continue to be an unfair experience. Daily existence appears to be a total drag to them — life offers nothing to them in return for their "showing up."

If you happen to know one or more of these people (and I'm betting that you do) let me suggest that you avoid trying to improve the lot of anyone engaged in a continuous exercise in self-pity.

Don't think for a minute your job is to get these people singing from the right side of the page. Your job is to get *your* thinking straight, in gear and firmly positioned for greater things to come. Here is a thought that I have grown quite fond of:

### You can't change the world, but you can change YOUR world.

Your job is to light a fire under your own backside and make certain that you don't come across looking like you are marking time between now and the hereafter. People are attracted to people who are alive, energetic, and happy — who have ideas and crazy notions about life — who have kind things to say about others. So, if you truly want to be the exception, pick a game . . . any game . . . and then get into the game. Become a player . . . today!

185

## Not Permitting Mistakes

What stops most people from identifying and pursuing what they want to achieve? The answer: Fear. Fear of what? Fear of failure, or on a more incremental basis, the fear of making mistakes.

Here's how you can completely reverse that psychology:

### Give yourself permission to make mistakes.

You heard me right. I'm not suggesting that you commit flagrant fouls. I'm simply asking you to allow yourself to experiment and make the mistakes that come with trying to stretch beyond your current comfort zone. Mistakes are visible signs that you are trying to do something new.

Here is a corollary: Allowing yourself to make mistakes will actually make you, and your life, more interesting. The words "mistake" and "boring" do not work well together. Mistakes are never boring. Quite the contrary, mistakes can be catalysts for adrenaline surges. Some may be dangerous and others may be stupid. Some mistakes will be costly while others will be painfully embarrassing. But without exception, they will never be boring. Plus, people are drawn to people who are not afraid to make mistakes and find it delightfully amusing to laugh at themselves. So stick your neck out now and then. Stretch a little. Make a mistake.

## Not Taking Responsibility

If you don't make it happen, chances are nobody will. You must make it *your* business to grow your business. Not assuming responsibility for what happens in your career, week, day or sales call is a mistake.

The outcome of your sales career is entirely up to you. That is one of the beautiful things about sales. Your hands are on the controls. Your future, for the most part, lies entirely within your power. You set the pace. You plan your day. You make the calls. You take the credit. You take the hits.

Take responsibility for your success and for your failures. No excuses. During the Nagano Olympics, Alberto Tomba, the reigning downhill skiing superstar, was expected to take the Gold. His style was to pull out all the stops and "go for it." (He was most definitely never boring.) But at Nagano he didn't make it to the Gold; he didn't make it down the mountain. When asked by a commentator what happened, the interview was short, sweet and to the point — no excuses: "*I* fell." (No, the mountain did not push him.) He didn't win the Gold but I remember Tomba's reply and not the guy who did win.

## Too Little Competitive Spirit

If we were to play tennis and just short of taking your first serve I declared you the winner, you would feel somewhat unfulfilled. Likewise, if we were going to play golf and I declared you the winner on the practice putting green, I don't think you would relish the victory.

Then why do salespeople want to accept victory before they have had a chance to earn it? Competition is what makes "the game" worth playing.

I am reminded here of another interview. This one was between Howard Cosell (the lawyer turned commentator) and Jimmy "the Greek" Snyder (the famous odds maker). Howard asked Jimmy what he enjoyed best in life. Jimmy quickly responded, *"Howard, I like to win."* When Howard followed with what the Greek one liked second best, Jimmy answered just as quickly and said, *"Howard, that's an easy one. I like to lose."*

Here was a man who took pleasure in playing the game . . . who enjoyed the action. Win or lose it was the competition that brought Jimmy the Greek to the game.

Here's the winning competitive mindset for you to cultivate. Know the rules of the game. Know that you honestly can't win them all. But learn to enjoy the process of selling. This will insure a healthy competitive spirit.

## Not Seeking Success For Your Clients

If you want to get to the top of the sales profession, you have to focus on helping others, not on "selling." When you try to sell, it appears to everyone that you are selling, and nobody I know enjoys being "sold." But, when you are legitimately, openly and sincerely interested in helping people, you will have their undivided attention, and eventually, the combination to their check book.

Zig Ziglar is a famous sales trainer who began his career selling pots and pans and is now an icon. Zig said it well:

**"You will get everything in life you want if you first try to help others get what it is they want in life."**

Look at it from a slightly different angle. Make it your business to make other people successful. That's your new mission in life . . . to make your prospects, clients (and associates) successful. If your product or service can help make others successful, then you will soon be in high cotton.

Bottom Line: Get out of you and into others. Focus on trying to help other people succeed. Use what you know and who you know for a single purpose, and that is to help others.

## Seeing The Prospect As An Adversary

As bizarre as this sounds, a "me against you" mentality is a common mistake among salespeople. Maybe this is a misdirected competitive spirit that pits the salesperson against the prospect. Sales should not and cannot happen this way.

Let's see . . . prospects will only become customers if treated properly. Customers pay our bills and are responsible for feeding our families. No customers . . . no business. So here's a brainstorm: Let's bad mouth our customers and show them what a lousy attitude looks and sounds like every opportunity we get. (I hate this phrase, but it seems to fit perfectly right about now — HELLOOOWWW!!!!!!!!)

Let's get something clear. Prospects, having passed from the suspect stage, are good things. Talk to them as if they were good things. Treat them with respect as if they were good things. Behave in public as if they were good things. THEY ARE GOOD THINGS.

## Corollary: Underestimating The Prospect's Intelligence

A counter-productive attitude that often accompanies looking at the prospect as an adversary is underestimating the prospect's intelligence. I suppose doing this can soften the blow of "rejection." After all, the guy who just turned down your supremely perfect proposal must be a dummy, right? But all this does is insure rejection.

Most people are smarter than you give them credit for. They may not be book smart or school smart. But people usually know which end is up, particularly when it comes to their businesses. Don't make the mistake of selling people short. Deal with them on a level playing field with respect and sincerity. You will not only enjoy the results, but you'll find more pleasure in what you are doing for a living.

## Not Taking Pride In Your Job

What you do for a living is important. And it affects more people than you will ever know. If you haven't already, it is about time for you to adopt this mindset.

Maybe your immediate supervisors are so busy with their own problems that they fail to reinforce the importance of your contributions. An amateur can easily get bent out of shape when this happens. A professional knows the importance of his or her contribution and doesn't need to hear it from others on an hourly basis. (But they do need to hear it from time to time, just like everyone else.) Sure we enjoy the sound of others applauding our work, but we don't depend on it to do our jobs. We know that we add value to our company and to our customers. You are a professional. Take pride in that fact.

## Taking Rejection Personally

As I mentioned in Section I, the notion that rejection comes with the territory is a myth. But if you insist on interpreting events as a rejection, then please absorb this advise. Taking rejection personally is an enormous waste of time. Sales comes with a whole bunch of "No's" attached to this profession. These usually have nothing to do with you. Sales, my friends, is not about you. Sales never has been about you. Sales will never be about you.

Sales is about a buyer with a *pre-existing* need for a service or product. You are the conduit, the middle person. You are the mailman, the purveyor of information. You simply can't take this thing personally, either good or bad. A decision to pass up the chance to buy probably would have occurred with you or in your absence. You can only help those in a buying mode. Don't waste your time and the time of anyone else within earshot by taking rejection personally.

## Focusing On Negatives

It's human to sometimes focus on negatives. Heaven knows there are enough negative things going on in this world to provide plenty of opportunities to succumb to the Dark Side. There isn't much you can do to change this fact or what people do. But you can decide to change your response to the world's stimuli. You absolutely do not have to follow the pack and become a negative person. Being positive is an option.

It confuses me when people decide to re-orient their lives toward the positive immediately after a catastrophe whacks their lives into a ball of unfortunate turmoil. Death of a loved one has a tendency to straighten people out. Disease has straightened people out. Fires and even tornadoes have straightened people out.

Let me save you some time, money and hurt. Straighten yourself out. Don't wait for nature to serve as a catalyst. Begin to see the positive side of things on your own and the benefits of feeling positive versus negative.

In a previous chapter I quoted Barry Diller, QVC's president. The situation surrounding that quote is an excellent example of the way I want you to begin to see things as professional salespeople. Mr. Diller learned that his bid to take over Paramount Pictures fell short. This billion dollar bonanza fell as flat as Wiley Coyote after the Road Runner runs him down with a steamroller. If there ever was a good reason to become negged out, this failure would qualify as Numero Uno. But when asked how he felt upon learning of this failure, Diller very casually responded, "They won. We lost. Whose next?"

What a great way of looking at "the game." When approaching any business opportunity, the professional knows that a number of things can spoil the sale. In fact, in the majority of cases, the sale does not materialize for one reason or another. This isn't negative thinking. It is a fact. True professionals refuse to spend much time focusing on bad news. There isn't enough time in the day and there is too much to accomplish.

"Whose next?" should be your only response. If you insist on feeling bad after a disappointment, that is understandable. Just don't get used to feeling sorry for yourself. Take a few minutes to shed a tear or punch a wall (depending on your personality type) then get back to business. You have work to do.

# CHAPTER 26

# MISTAKES TO AVOID IN FACE-TO-FACE MEETINGS

I f prospecting and preparation set the table and decide the menu, and attitude sets the ambience, then face-to-face meetings are where your fork hits the meat. This is where marketing goes bottom line and becomes selling. But don't let that fact deceive you. Many of the common mistakes in face-to-face meetings originate with the subconscious mindset that *"selling"* means *"forcing"* the process to a close and to a result that serves the salesperson's agenda. Trying to force a result is like trying to pick a lock with a noodle. Can't be done.

Here are some mistakes commonly made in face-to-face meetings and how to avoid them.

## Selling Up

In 1995, while visiting Egypt, I had the pleasure of meeting an elderly British couple in the lobby of a Sheraton Hotel, just north of Aswan. Upon recognizing my accent, the couple approached my wife and I, introduced themselves, and announced that they were eagerly awaiting their first trip to the United States later that fall. Their excitement was contagious, and I asked where they were planning to visit during their stay in the United States.

"We are going to Staten Island," giggled the 85-year old couple from England, like two high school sweethearts. Here was a couple who some people would write off as fossils-in-process, but who really were fun to be around. (Note: Being around enthusiastic people — regardless of their country of origin, age, religious or political preference, or the color of their hair — is measurably more fun than being around duds of any rank, serial number or political persuasion. My recommendation, given the choice, lose the duds.)

"Besides Staten Island," I asked, "where else are you going?" They said, "We are going to visit New York City." I surmised that their limited itinerary was due to budgetary constraints. "How long will you be in the United States?" I asked. "Three weeks," they said. I gasped for a lung-full of fresh Egyptian air (an exercise in futility). "What do you plan on seeing?" I asked to mask my growing concern. "We are going to ride the Staten Island Ferry."

Now, I may be a bit jaded having been raised so near the Jewel of The East River, but spending three weeks in Staten Island after waiting 85 years to visit the red, white and blue, is not my idea of a major league slice of the "Big Apple". . . Staten Island Ferry ride or no Staten Island Ferry ride.

Knowing it was none of my business, I asked, "May I suggest a few ideas?" (As I suggested previously, always ask permission before asking questions. It immediately and effectively eliminates any chance of your interest being interpreted as an unwanted and unappreciated interrogation.)

"Why not fly into Boston where you can check out the freedom trail and Paul Revere's contribution to our dissing the Motherland? You can then take a scenic train ride down to

New York City where you can spend a week to ten days sightseeing the greatest city in the world." I recommended a few of the many sights that I would want to see if I was visiting the Big Apple for the first (and probably the last) time . . . the Empire State Building, the World Trade Towers, Times Square, the Guggenheim, a Broadway Play, breakfast at Tiffany's and of course Jimmy Joe Bob's Famous Swap Shop just south of Canal Street. I suggested they continue their journey with another short train ride to a third history-laden city, Philadelphia, where they could snap a few pictures of the Liberty Bell after taking a stroll through the fascinating Franklin Museum. In another short two-hour train ride they could be chugging into Washington D.C. where they could experience the Capitol Building in all its splendor, the Smithsonian, a couple of bazillion monuments, a tour of a bona-fide mint, and the White House, home to some of our nation's most photogenic and charismatic characters.

In three weeks they would catch the entire northeast corridor without having to rush ... and they would be experiencing so much more of our beautiful country. I did acknowledge the fact that they would be logging a few more miles, but any travel-related inconvenience seemed well worth the experience. As long as they traveled at their own, slow and leisurely pace, they would be fine.

That was over two years ago and I will never know if they heeded my advice or if they ever even made it to the States. But I ask you this . . . Was I *"selling this couple up"* or was I simply recommending what I believed to be in their best interest? I think the answer was obvious to them judging by the sincerity in my voice and the enthusiasm and animation of my recommendations.

Many sales books I have read include a lengthy chapter telling how you should sell people up. "If the prospect says this . . . you say that. If they do that . . . you do this. When the prospect finally does buy this, you slide in a few that's." Sounds pretty manipulative if you ask me. I feel strongly that you should think less of yourself if you ever find yourself trying these tactics. Selling people up is not a good thing, unless, of course, it is in their best interest for you to do so. The moral. Don't sell up. Sell right.

Think about it. I didn't sell the English couple anything . . . up, down, over or under. I simply recommended what I truly considered a more exciting and memorable itinerary. It was easy for me to do so, and I didn't feel that I owed them an apology. I did what was right . . . as I interpreted the picture at that moment. No hesitation. No mumbling or stammering. No queasy stomach or sweaty palms. No raised or fluctuating blood pressure. No negative feelings whatsoever. Just good, old fashioned, shoot-from-the-hip communication.

Would my recommendation cost them more money? I think it would. Would their travel agent enjoy a higher commission? I think she would. Did I feel that I owed them an apology for attempting to alter their original course? I did not.

You are the expert, the specialist. So, tell your prospect what he needs to know. If he doesn't ask the right questions, tell him what he should be asking. If it cost more, so be it. If it cost less, learn to live with that as well. On occasion, you will feel that the right thing to do is to "sell down," or recommend a less costly item. Sometimes it will be correct to make no recommendation at all. Other times you may find yourself pointing your would-be clients toward the competition. If you need a slogan to live by, here it is.

## *"Do what's right for the prospect."*

A sale for a sale's sake is short-sighted. Your primary objective is to establish a long-term relationship with your steadily growing customer group based on *trust*. This requires honesty, straightforwardness, and time. If you or your boss find it difficult to swallow this advice, you are probably running your sales program from a script hand written by monks on parchment. Unfortunately, you still have company — salespeople who are proud to proclaim their well-traveled tongues can, in a lizard-like fashion, jet out from their mouths, reach across a desk, and nab the wallet of a prospect who has a difficult time saying "No." I call a person with this prehistorical approach a Saleosaurus (literally, a "sales lizard").

What turns many people away from a career in sales is the misguided mind-set that they must learn how to present ideas and solutions that border on fiction or shear nonsense. Nothing is further from the truth. To become successful in sales you must speak the truth in a clear, slow and orderly fashion while encouraging the customer to candidly voice their concerns.

One of the most successful salespeople I know is so laid back you are tempted to check him for a pulse every few minutes. His sincerity simply pre-empts any need to tap dance through a high-energy sales presentation.

## Trying To Convince Rather Than Convey

If you try too hard to sell something, prospects will question why you feel that you have to sell so hard. They will begin to doubt the quality of your product or service. All you need to do (assuming you have a quality product or service) is to tell your story to people interested in listening. Period. No manipulation is required. No overcoming tough objections. Communicate the facts of your product and address your prospect's concerns in a matter-of-fact conversational tone.

You sell . . . you lose. You talk to me, take interest in me and try to help me . . . you come out smelling like a rose.

196

# Not Listening To The Prospect

You have undoubtedly heard the real estate mantra that the three most important determinants of value are: location, location, location. In sales, the three most important determinants of your value to the prospect are: listening skills, listening skills, listening skills.

Not listening to what others are saying (and not saying) is remarkably common in our profession. One reason may be that many salsepeople anticipate "objections" they have to stomp out and work from a script designed to crush opposition and sell up. So, at the first sign of resistance from a prospect ("But what about . . . ?") they spring into respond mode before they understand exactly what the prospect has in mind.

No prospect really cares what you want or think . . . unless it ties directly to what the prospect is concerned about. But once you allow the customer to speak freely about their needs and concerns, and the prospect perceives that you are truly listening, you are bound to witness a sale unfold before your very eyes. You'll become a spectator and won't have to say or do very much more.

Ask and then listen. Repeat back to the speaker what it is you think you heard and then listen some more. Remember: People who are in the market to buy stuff will buy if you simply act as a guide, as a sounding board, and as a source for information and confirmation.

# Corollary: Not Empathizing With The Prospect

This mistake is a kissing cousin to not listening. Empathizing is listening with our mind and emotion simultaneously. More specifically, you must learn to see your offer through the eyes of your prospects. Being truly empathetic in a sales context takes practice, because a motivated salesperson is naturally focused intensely on his own objective and viewpoint of the product or service he is selling.

When you want a distinctive edge, start envisioning the world from your customer's side of the table. Once you learn to tie your point of view to your customer's primary interest, fears and concerns, you will be well on your way toward establishing a working relationship.

The next time you begin your sales presentation, pause and reflect on the person you are speaking with. Think about what is important to him. Think about his current working environment . . . the problems he might be dealing with. Only true professionals can perform this improvisational meditation during a face-to-face meeting. Adopt this practice and you will multiply the fruits of your labors ten-fold.

Recently I was dealing with a personal issue over the phone with a bureaucratic bank representative, when the mis-communication escalated, as did our voices. I, being the international instructor of customer service, suggested that the bank representative, just for a moment, put herself on my side of the phone and think how she might respond to such lunacy. She did just that and instantly became miss congenial customer service rep extraordinaire. Quickly and painlessly I became a very happy customer once again.

When agreement with the prospect appears headed for a premature deep-six, resurrect the deal with a shot of empathy.

## Becoming Distracted

Amazingly, becoming distracted in sales meetings occurs more frequently than we care to admit. A few reasons:

- You are moving ahead of the conversation to prepare a response;

- You are focusing on yourself and how you appear to the prospect;

- You feel a threat of rejection and emotionally you want to bail out;

- You naturally have a short attention span.

Reality and my personal experience say your mind will inevitably wander at times during some meetings. Accepting this fact is 99% of the battle.

Once your prospect interprets your wandering mind as a sign of disinterest on your part, your sale is a definite, un-resurrectable D.O.A. (dead on arrival). So, stay focused on your prospect. Concentrate. Resist the temptation to head back to the future before the prospect gets there.

This especially is true when you are not within direct eye sight . . . like when you are on the telephone. Resist the temptation to plug the phone into your shoulder while opening envelopes, fingering memos, clicking through computer screens, etc. People on the other end of the line can often hear this activity or sense it even if you leave no audible trace.

You might want to try standing while speaking. I do this regularly.

## Not Checking Your "Look"

A book is sometimes judged by its cover, but people always are. So,

### Dress and look "2 under."

That's golfing lingo for 2 strokes under par (which means pretty darn good). Some otherwise lousy golfers dress like the pro's (hence the booming clothing business at the pro shop). A couple of things can result from looking pretty nifty on a golf course: (1) your mental state might very well elevate your game; or (2) you still will play a lousy game of golf but you will *"looook mahvelous."*

You can't afford to take the chance that your prospect might not approve of your "packaging." I'm not talking about the price of your wardrobe. I'm referring to the condition of it. Sometimes it is helpful to have your spouse, secretary or associate you trust give you a final viewing before you head out the door to the big pow wow. Sound basic? It is. But I can't count how many "professionals" show up to my conferences, with a room filled with associates and competitors, looking like Kramer (on the Seinfeld Show) did their hair and selected their wardrobe.

A few other useful checks:

- Loose the seventeen-inch (wide) tie with the picture of Bill Clinton pointing his finger in apparent denial.

- Update your belts now and then (loose the giant EXXON buckle).

- When using cologne, remember this guideline: If bees swarm on you after application, lighten the dosage.

- Remove old tattoos (especially any referencing Hells Angels or acquaintances you made while in the Navy).

- If your handkerchief is stuck to your suit when you try to pull it from your pocket, odds are it's time for a clean one.

With that last observation, I can confidently proclaim *"'Nuf said!"*

# Rushing The Sale

Hard driving, highly motivated salespeople tend to make this mistake. It's like a great basketball point guard bringing the ball down the court and trying to make the play happen too soon. The result is often a big, fat air ball.

People make decisions when they are ready to make decisions. Don't become impatient and expect that something you say or do will speed up the decision process. Rushing the sale is bad business.

Everything takes more time than first expected. There is always more information to learn and competition to contend with than you initially anticipate. The prospect's fear of making a mistake (a.k.a. "losing money") comes into play in every decision. And finally, buying decisions often involve more than one person today, which adds to the selling cycle.

These four points make it unrealistic to rush a sale today. Get your records in order, stay close, and let people make up their minds at their pace. Anything else could result in bad karma or even worse, doubt and mistrust in the relationship. Learn to "cool your jets" and allow time to work for you.

# Buzz Lingo — To Infinity And Beyond

People will see right through any attempt you make to be a fancy linguistic impresario. Drop from your vocabulary outdated phrases and jargon designed to impress. They conjure doubt in your prospects and divert their attention from your message to somewhere else in their galaxy of competing priorities.

Besides purging the buzz, I suggest you lose four words which I describe as "Meeting Muggers." Words to avoid . . . according to me:

- **Pitch** (as in sales pitch) — Drop this word from your vocabulary like a hot potato. I welcome people who have a sincere interest in me, and I enjoy a two-way conversation. But try "pitching" me with your tightly rehearsed song and dance and I'll show you the exit door. The word "pitch" immediately conjures up negative pictures of a packaged, insincere spiel designed to pull the wool over the prospect's unsuspecting head. You don't pitch your deal, you present solutions to your customer's valid concerns. Lose the word "pitch" with prospects and associates.

- **Schtick** — A "schtick" is a bit — a show — a canned performance with a planned outcome. How would you feel if after your presentation, a prospect said to you, "Nice schtick." Not very flattering is it? Reverse the direction of the communication and imagine how your prospect or fellow sales professionals will react.

- **Problem** (as in "The problem with that is . . .") — Yes, this word is legitimate, but it conjures up negativity and is a bona fide balloon buster. In America, it seems that having reached the age of twenty empowers one to burst another person's balloon. You share your brainstorm or good idea with an associate, he tells you what's wrong with it. You recommend something that goes a bit against the grain, and most people will poke holes in it faster than you can say "Dunkin Donut Munchkins!"

  The truth is that in all probability, the idea, brainstorm or clever thought is going to be less than front page material. But, that doesn't give someone the license to blow it away in a single breath.

Begin practicing the following response. The next time someone tells you his or her gem of an idea (good, bad, or otherwise), listen attentively and then say,

## *"That sounds like an interesting idea. What are you going to do to make that work?"*

Then prepare for a genuine (but silent) belly laugh, because the speaker won't be ready to respond intelligently to your question. Chances are, he (or she) will mumble something semi-incoherent in response. By asking, you will be doing him a favor by motivating him to think through the full implications of his idea. You will not be demonstrating a belligerent or a contrarian position. Instead, you will have shown a sincere interest, laced with compassion and support. This alone will make you pretty unique.

If the idea really does "pose a problem," substitute the word "concern" whenever you can. We all have concerns, and it's healthy to voice concerns when appropriate. We all face obstacles and challenges from time to time. The word problem seems to turn off the constructive search for a solution to the "challenge" or "concern."

- **But** (as in "That is a good idea, but . . .") — Remember this: To your prospect the word "but" negates everything that comes before it and paves the way for the message from on high.

## When you say "but," your client hears "BEHOLD ULTIMATE TRUTH."

Here is an example.

**Sales Rookie:** *"I understand where you are coming from about delivery problems, but . . ."*

**Prospect Hears:** (*"You are too stupid to realize that the delivery timing you want is totally unrealistic."* )

Work on removing the words "pitch," "schtick," "problem" and "but" from your vocabulary. You will be better off once you do.

203

## CHAPTER 27

# COMMON MISTAKES OF
# FOLLOW THROUGH

Congratulations. The face-to-face meeting went great. You firmly believe that the prospect is now a client. It's Miller Time . . . or is it?

## Being Fooled By "Sure Things"

Thinking positively is admirable. But banking on soft commitments or being fooled by "sure things" is a dangerous mistake. Don't spend your commission until the check clears the bank.

There are no sure things. Seasoned sales professionals get together at annual conventions and take turns outdoing one another by telling stories about the sure things that weren't so sure after all. At the time the business was lost I am sure they weren't laughing, but over time these catastrophes soon become coveted war stories. It seems like the more money you end up losing, the more interesting the story becomes. Yuk. Yuk. Yuk.

My advice to you is that when you catch yourself counting a chicken or two before it hatches . . . DON'T. Instead, get a cup of black coffee, put a brand new light bulb in your desk lamp, and begin dotting each and every one of your i's over and over again. Don't let up until the order is chiseled in a stone tablet which has been Fed Ex'd to your office, put in a Number 10 hotel size mayonnaise jar, and placed in a high-tech burglar and competitor proof vault on Funk and Wagnall's front porch.

## Corollary: Failing To Follow Through

One key to closing a higher percentage of sales than your associates or competitors is follow through. Everyone says they know this . . . very few people to do it.

> **Talk is cheap, so . . .**
> **after all is said and done,**
> **more is said than done.**

If you want to distance yourself from the competition, simply do what you tell prospects you are going to do.

- Show up or call if you say you will — on time;

- Deliver what you said you'd deliver.

- Provide the information requested.

That's it. The Big Three. Do each sooner than promised.

Everyone is quick with a promise today. Most of us have good intentions. But, prospects' experience tells them that few people can really be counted on to follow through consistently. Become the exception.

## Riding The Trojan Techno-Horse

Consumers and business buyers today have a myriad of eager-to-please suppliers for just about everything. Therefore, you need to eliminate anything and everything that might get in the way of a working relationship. The good news is that most of your competition has gone to great lengths over the past few years to build a major league obstacle to new customers . . . and its your Trojan Horse to ride into your competitor's stable of customers. It's called . . . the electronic voice mail system.

Simply make certain that calling your company and getting to the right person is not a Lewis and Clark exploration of techno-garble. Here's what I mean.

## Voice Mail System Greeting Of Prospect

*"Thanks for calling us rather than the other 10,000 people you could have called to get the same level of stress. If you would like to raise your blood pressure a few notches and check your memory quotient while taxing your patience, then indicate your interest by punching the #1 key on your telephone and standing by for some more information . . ."*

*"If you know the middle name of the brother-in-law of the person you would like to finally leave a message for — due to the fact that nobody in this company answers their own phone, no way, no how, no matter what you thought to the contrary — punch #2 and get ready for the telephone ride of your life. If you need CPR, stay on the line and a live operator will assist you as soon as we hire one."*

The above example of today's phone "service" is an invitation to your success. Simply make working with you and your company easy. Take the burden off the shoulders of your customers as quickly and painlessly as possible. Try calling your phone mail system to see how tough it is to get through. (A friend of mine in the financial services industry recently tried this and on the third option menu heard such non-financial options as "concierge" and "room service." He discovered the phone system they had for two years was designed for resort hotels.)

I'm not suggesting you necessarily relegate your voice mail system to the junk heap, but be sure you streamline it. Leave your customers feeling happy they called . . . happy they had the good fortune of speaking with you . . . and looking forward to doing business with an organization that makes communication with decision-makers easy.

## Losing Customer Focus

Cutting through the noise and clutter in today's marketplace while remaining focused is a skill. The customer . . . a customer . . . your customer is the person who delivers the cash necessary to keep your business in business. Therefore, it should come as no surprise when I tell you to never stop focusing on the most important person in your business . . . your customer (existing and prospective).

This may sound absurdly simple to do, but I assure you it isn't. You have so many things competing for your attention that it's easy to have your focus stray from the prospect you have psychologically moved into your trophy case. The staff is asking you to decide the color of the new rug, quantity of paper towels to order, whether to buy the color printer or the black and white model, negotiate the lease of the new phone mail system, proof read the 148-page letter proposal you wrote before reading Chapter 10.

I know what you are faced with. Believe me, I know. But, let me make the point. Without customers, you don't have one more blessed thing to worry about. Think customers first. Think customers second. Think customers third. If you still have time, call a meeting to talk about your customers. Then, in the few moments remaining at the end of the day, you can flip a coin to decide what color the new rug should be.

Customer focus is a constant, and you'll find lots of suggestions for maintaining this vital orientation for yourself and your firm throughout this book.

# SECTION

# MORE STRATEGIES FOR MULTIPLYING YOUR BUSINESS OPPORTUNITIES

# CHAPTER 28

# LEARNING TO RECOGNIZE OPPORTUNITIES
## (WHERE'S WALDO?)

If you have children you are probably familiar with the "Where's Waldo?" books. The name of the game here is to find one brightly clothed Waldo in an ocean of people, animals, toys and things. Each scene is cram packed with all sorts of stimuli, but Waldo is always there if you look for him. What's amazing is that I can stare at a scene for an hour and never find that little bugger, but my young niece will walk by, notice the new book, stop and say, "Oh, that's a new scene . . . let me see where Waldo is . . . that's him!!" Whack . . . bam . . . boom. Back to the toys!! She has clearly learned how to zero in on the look of Waldo.

The analogy holds true for business opportunities. Like Waldo, they are in just about every scene in your life (or certainly every day of it), if you know how to spot them. So the good news is: (i) learn how to spot business opportunities and you will find they are everywhere; and (ii) you competitors probably have not learned this skill yet.

My famous "F" routine has received countless chuckles, has induced a fair share of embarrassment and has demanded the attention of lots of "know-it-alls" since I first began using it in training sessions over fifteen years ago. It visually conveys an extremely important message. Take a look.

---

**FINISHED FILES ARE THE RE-SULT OF YEARS OF SCIENTIF-IC STUDY COMBINED WITH THE EXPERIENCE OF MANY YEARS.**

---

Here's the drill. How many F's do you count in the preceding box? This is not a trick. Just count the number of F's you see in this box. To make it interesting let's assume you'll earn $10,000 for each "F" you identify.

Heck, let's not make it an "essay" question where you have to write down the number, let's keep it easy as pie by making it a multiple choice question. Circle the correct answer below (in No. 2 pencil . . . just kidding).

---

| 1 | 2 | 3 | 4 | 5 | 6 |

---

The vast majority of you will count three, with a few spotting four. A couple of you may see five. One problem: You are all wrong. Look at the box again, and take another count. This time I will give you a hint: the word finished begins with an "F."

Did you stick to your original number or have you changed your answer after a second try? (Get out your pencil again.)

---

Change_____        Stick_____

---

If you still insist on seeing three, congratulations — you are in a large, if not very observant, group. If you changed from 3 to 4, congratulations — you are making progress. If you changed from 4 to 5, congratulations — you are almost there. Trouble is: You are still wrong.

The one and only correct answer can be found below, but don't look yet. F's are found in the words finished, files, scientific. These will satisfy those of you who are sticking with three as you answer. But in addition to these big words, the letter F can be found in three little words . . . "of." The answer is six. There are six F's.

Some of you have probably just said to yourself,

## *"How did I miss that?"*

After all these years I still find this an illuminating exercise. Why can't we pick up all the "F's" in the first pass? Because we aren't tuned in to the guises an "F" can take — i.e. hiding in plain view behind the "o" at the end of the word "of". Try it again. Now that you know how to search, you can easily spot the "F's" — and you will with any other sentence I give you.

This exercise is obviously not about counting F's. It is about the skill and importance of learning to spot opportunities. The "F" in the exercise represents a business opportunity. And business opportunities present themselves and are right in front of our eyes . . . every day . . . undisguised. Yet most of us fail to spot them, or at best see only a few of them.

Here's one more example of something hiding in plain view. One of America's oldest and most elegant resorts is the

Greenbriar in White Sulfur Springs, West Virginia — a few hours drive from Washington, D.C. For years (in fact decades), attendees at corporate conferences would take the elevator to the second floor of the conference center, walk down a hall and through the ballroom doors and enter an exhibition hall to view various vendors of their industry. What no one knew from the 1960s until 1998 was that the exhibit hall was actually underground, the doorways to the hall were fake and camouflaged fifteen-foot high 25-ton steel doors, and that the two conference rooms off the exhibit hall (with capacities of 100 and roughly 500 seats each) were sized for a very specific purpose — to hold members of the U.S. House of Representatives and the Senate. The exhibit hall was part of a top secret underground installation to house up to 1,200 members of the government in the case of nuclear war. (You can tour this "bunker" and I recommend it.)

You are probably wondering how the facility could be underground when the meeting attendees took an elevator up to the second floor to walk into the exhibit hall. The answer is that the facility was subtly built into the side of a hill. The facility was perfectly hidden "in plain view" and remained a secret for over thirty years. But once you were tipped off to it, you could easily understand that it was underground, and you could spot telltale signs that gave away the huge doors and, of course, the reason for the seating capacity of the meeting rooms. Just like the F's, you would proclaim,

### *"How did I miss that.... for thirty years?"*

This is a phrase you do no want to say in your sales career.

Yet, this hidden in plain site phenomenon also holds true in your business. Once you know what your opportunities look like, they will jump out at you. The good news is that your competition hasn't taken the time or made the effort to identify the exact outward appearance of an opportunity. They do, and will, continue to miss most of them. Advantage you.

One reason opportunities are missed is because they often come disguised as problems or screw-ups or with a little camouflage. But with practice, you can learn to see through the camouflage and spot them quickly. Let's look at a few more examples.

## Waldo #1:   Phone Messages

You come back from lunch to find fifteen message pink slips on your desk. Some say "urgent"; some are problems you know you'll have to sort out. What is your knee-jerk response? "Man, doesn't that phone ever stop ringing? Don't these people know anyone else's number?"

- **Opportunity:** Someone believes in your ability enough (now) to try to contact you to help him. If you call the prospect or client back (now) it will not only surprise the willies out of him but will be a sure sign that you are interested in him. If you don't have the information needed by your caller, call back anyway and inform him that you need more time. By acknowledging the call, you are positioning yourself as someone he can depend on.

## Waldo #2:   A Casual Letter Or A Post Card

A normal response would be to read it, feel good for a moment, and get back to doing what you were doing.

- **Opportunity:** Use the card as an excuse to call the sender. Perhaps you can bring up a topic of interest, which you have been postponing. Always be on the lookout for reasons to call people to say "thanks for thinking of me."

## Waldo #3: Phone Chit Chat

When speaking on the phone this morning, the caller said she had a very nice experience at a recent industry conference. She mentioned the president's name and said she had a nice conversation with him.

- **Opportunity:** Since conferences hire speakers (and I am a speaker) I write that man a letter (today) referencing my caller and the conversation he had with her. I will also be sure to mention how delighted she was with the conference. Then I will invite the man to place my name on his list for future speaking candidates.

## Waldo #4: The Morning Paper

At breakfast you read about a local promotion, accomplishment, or honor to be bestowed.

- **Opportunity:** You jot off a quick letter to the recipient and include the article. (A common error we all make is that we feel the subject of the published piece must already have a copy of the article. This is often not the case.) You applaud people who deserve applause and in so doing open a brand new set of opportunities.

## Waldo #5: Your Sister-In-Law's Barbeque

Her back yard is filled with about twenty-five to thirty adults. You are there to have a good time and are in social mode.

- **Opportunity:** You don't like to hit on people for business at social functions, and that is fine. But you have a chance to let everyone know through polite conversation what business you are involved in. And you can easily and cordially ask what business they are in. Make a mental (or covert physical) note of who they are and their job and follow up with a friendly call later in the week to see if they need travel services or if they know someone who does.

## Waldo #6: Radio News Flash

You hear on the radio that there are massive delays at the local airport due to weather or an airline strike. Lots of business and vacation travelers are stranded.

- **Opportunity:** Call the home office of your major local corporate travel accounts and offer your help for any stranded executives — booking hotels, rental cars, alternative flights, rail, etc. What's better, call your prospects or those accounts your competitor has locked up and offer to be the "fixer". You will be remembered the next time someone needs travel services.

## Waldo #7: Price Increases

The airlines (or any other industry supplier) have just announced a pending price increase.

- **Opportunity:** Call your clients and prospects and offer to book any travel plans they have in advance of the increase, or offer to do a cost analysis of the impact of the increase on their travel budget. (Added benefit: You may get great intelligence into the firm's travel volume and needs.) As with all of the above examples, you are using this opportunity to show the client and prospect that you, indeed, are The Exception. That inevitably will translate into more business.

Although these examples are travel industry related, the list is almost limitless for any industry. Take the time to sit down and think about how the opportunities in your industry can be hidden in plain view, and you will create a list of "trigger events" that warrant your response and lead to new business.

So, what do opportunities look like? They look like post-cards, junk mail, advertisements, wrong numbers, old databases, new databases, smiles, frowns, complaints, bad news, good news, kind words.

They come disguised sometimes as friends, relatives, negative remarks and positive remarks.

They can be found at tradeshows, airports, water coolers, hotels, churches, reunions, and in all forms of print or communication.

Be receptive to the commonplace and peculiarities of everyday living. You will not only spot more opportunities, but you will find yourself having more fun in the process.

# CHAPTER 29

# HOW TO INCREASE YOUR VISIBILITY

Another key to growing your business is to increase your visibility — your awareness factor among prospects and clients. You do this through repetition. (Jim Stampoulos) I have given you some ideas for increasing the awareness factor in my Basic Sales System (Section II) and Marchev's Rules To Sell By (Section III), but let's visit this topic one more time because it is fundamental for building a bulging book of business.

Let's play a word association game. I will mention the first name of a few individuals and I want you to let your mind do the rest. (Break out the 'ole #2 pencil again.)

| When I Say: | You See: |
|-------------|----------|
| Mick | _____ |
| Madonna | _____ |
| Tiger | _____ |
| Bing | _____ |
| Billy | _____ |
| Liberace | _____ |
| Andre' | _____ |
| Jim | _____ |

Without claiming to be clairvoyant, I'm betting you wrote Mick Jagger or Mickey Mantle. Then you wrote "Madonna" because you don't know her last name (but a blond singer with a reputation for being more than a little flamboyant). Tiger probably prompted "Woods" (or perhaps, "Tony the"). Bing Crosby shot into your imagination followed by either Billy Joel, Billy Martin or Billy Crystal. Liberace (again no last name) brought to your imagination a piano player with candelabra and lots of rhinestones and jewelry. With Andre' you either saw the tennis player (Agase), the musician (Watts) or maybe a bubbling glass of champagne. For Jim, you probably had to think of someone you knew personally. Nothing shot into your mind's eye when I said Jim, right? Maybe Jim Croce. Jimmy might have been Durante.

Did you think of my brother in law, Jim Stampoulos? I don't think so. But you will when I get through with you. Pronounced "Stam-Poo-Lus." Watch how this thing works.

How do you go about getting this kind of name recognition — at least in your own small corner of the world? If I ask a stranger who Mike is, I am quite certain that very few would respond with my last name, Marchev. Some might say Mike Wallace, or Mike Tyson. This wouldn't come as a surprise to me. I am not well known. And neither are you.

But, if people don't know we exist, how in the world can you expect them to decide to trust us enough to do business with us? (Jim Stampoulus owns an incredible restaurant in Stirling, New Jersey. He is my brother-in-law. Pronounced "Stam-Poo-Lus.")

Let's agree that simple awareness is the first step toward building a relationship. Then, every prospect in your marketing area should have a rudimentary idea of who you are. (Remember Jim Stampoulus? He graduated from Millburn High School in 1972. He owns a restaurant in New Jersey. He is my brother-in-law.)

This is worth repeating. How can anyone decide to try your services if they don't know that you are alive? Here is a fundamental strategy to increase your visibility that is worth every minute of your attention.

## Awareness Strategy 101

First, let's benchmark the here and now. Call up five or ten prospects you have never contacted before and ask them to name the three providers of goods or services similar to the ones you provide. Keep this exercise local if your market is local or if it is consumer, as opposed to business, oriented.

Don't get depressed if all ten fail to recognize you or your company as one of the candidates. They often can only name one (the one they use) for the simple reason that they know of no other proven alternative. (Thinking of Jim Stampoulus? Now you are.)

Here's your challenge:

**Everyone in your local market
who you want to recognize your name
will know who you are
one year from today.**

How can you make this happen? By bombarding the marketplace with you, your employees, your company and lots of information. Here are some near -, and far -, fetched ideas, to name a few:

- Call people and introduce yourself. ("Hi. I'm Jim Stampoulus." Remember him? He is my brother-in-law, the restaurateur.)

- Go to functions and be visible.

- Rent a blimp balloon with your name on it.

- Paint your company's name on your car.

- Appear in 2,132 consecutive baseball games (or at least some local chamber of commerce athletic outings).

- Leave your business cards everywhere.

- Sponsor events — youth, charitable, educational.

- Adopt three greyhounds and parade them around town with your company's logo imprinted on their warm up coats.

- Write editorials.

- Write an article.

- Go somewhere strange on vacation and submit it as an article in your local newspaper.

- Press release or advertise hirings, promotions, or employee honors in your company.

- Send duplicate copies of publications which reference you (besides the local "Police Blotter" column) to everyone and everywhere.

- Have golf shirts printed.

- Give a couple of plane tickets away at a well attended local function and make sure that you are the one who gets to present them at the awards banquet.

- Buy a hole-in-one insurance policy and donate it at the local hospital golf outing.

- Get mugged at a charity ball and go on the local 10 o'clock news. (Use this one only as a last resort.)

These are just a few of the ways for you to begin improving your visibility. Ask your employees for more ideas. Then give yourself one year to make it happen. I guarantee you'll get amazing results from this simple promotional campaign.

We know who Mick, Madonna, Tiger, Bing, Billy, Liberace, Andre' and Jim are because we have heard their names over and over and over again. Simply copy what works. Right, Jim? Who? Why Jim Stampoulus of course. (I don't have to tell you who he is or what he does, you are already "aware.")

# CHAPTER 30

# FISH WHERE THE FISH ARE

On Tuesday, any Tuesday, at around 10 o'clock in the morning, you can probably be found at your desk in your office. Let's assume again that you are a travel agent. Perhaps you will be speaking on the phone, or drinking a cup of coffee, or perusing a memo or trade publication. In any event, you are where you are supposed to be on any given day, Monday through Friday — at least by the working standards we were taught when we were growing up.

Each Tuesday, while you are at the office, an aerobics class is being conducted down at the local health club. Furthermore, this class is very likely filled — most likely with women who choose not to work for one of many reasons. It is probably safe to assume that these women care about their health and are pro-active. These are the kind of women who go on skiing vacations or who would love to take a cruise to Bermuda or visit a spa in northern California.

Where are you while the Tuesday aerobics class is being conducted? At the office sharing your thoughts about the lack of business you are currently experiencing. Where are rooms full of prime prospects? At the gym working up a sweat sharing with each other their excitement about taking their next trip.

If you were in the travel business my suggestion would be to get yourself or one of your associates down to the gym. I'm betting that the aerobics classes on Monday and Wednesday are filled with some more action-oriented people. One agent per day makes good sense to me. (This is a classic example of thinking "outside of the box" — a creative term meaning "doing whatever it takes to get the job done.")

If you or your agents do not have a social flaw, chances are incredibly good that after a week or two of sweating to the oldies, you might share a post workout glass of orange juice with a few of these people and find yourself with an opportunity to introduce your services and lend your professional assistance the next time they begin globe trotting.

The upside: You develop another profitable client and a possible stream of referral business from a new social network you've penetrated.

The downside: If nothing comes of this "crap shoot," at least you will get yourself in some semblance of shape — something you have been promising yourself since the first beach day in 1993.

These kind of "out-of-the-box" prospecting hot spots exist for every service and product. You simply need to brainstorm and be willing to let go of old prejudices about the "right" places to generate business opportunities.

I dislike the title of this chapter because it seems too obvious . . . so axiomatic. It's painfully apparent that you won't meet too many world class surfers waxing their boogie boards in Des Moines, Iowa. You need to creatively discover new places where the prospect action is. If you spend less than two hours per month brainstorming these locations, you are leaving prospects and money for the competition.

# CHAPTER 31

# DIG A HOLE

Tom Peters struck it rich when he co-authored *In Search Of Excellence* with Bob Waterman. Today, Mr. Peters is a contributing writer for FAST Magazine, an interesting bi-monthly I recommend. Peters has followers and detractors, but who doesn't? (When I make my first bazillion dollars, I am sure a few of you will turn against me as well. The good news is that probably won't happen this year.)

I got the idea for this chapter from Tom himself. No need to get permission. (If I'm wrong about that permission thing, my next book could come to you via the Big House.) Tom once said:

**"It consistently amazes me how many people in the oil business fail to get the message that in order to strike oil, you have to dig a hole."**

I love this message.

Even in Texas, holes like many other things in life, come in just two varieties: (1) those that produce oil; and (2) those that don't. The sooner JR Ewing dug a hole, the sooner he learned unequivocally which kind he had going and whether he would cash in . . . or not — in which case he would cheat somebody out of their hole which did produce oil. The intelligent approach for JR, of course, would be to avoid randomly digging in places far removed from known oil deposits. (As a resident, I might observe that the only place you are likely to strike oil in New Jersey is at Jim Stampoulus's pizzeria.)

This oil well analogy has three important and related messages about building your book of business successfully.

(1)  You have got to sink the old drill bit into the telephone system and prospect if you want to get clients. You have about as much chance of them coming to you as JR has of finding oil by turning on the tap in his bathroom.

(2)  I tell salespeople all the time that there are only two kinds of people in our world: People you can help . . . and the other kind. Your job becomes non-threatening once you begin to view life from this clear point of view. All you need to do is look for people who are receptive to your help.

Likewise, as I have said throughout this book, you have to target your prospecting efforts to maximize you chances for success. "Drilling" for sales of travel services by attending Agorophobics Anonymous Meetings is an exercise in futility. (For those of you who have not been exposed to this sad condition, Agorophobia is the fear of being in open places — i.e. like leaving the safe surroundings of your home.)

(3)  You don't need to pour a lot of psychic energy into why a hole turned up dry. It just was that other kind of hole. Same with prospects. If they don't want your services or product no need to dwell on it. Just find another promising field and sink your drill again.

## Marchev's Million Dollar Earn-A-Break Strategy

So how do you set up a good drilling program? I gave you some guidelines in Section II: A Basic Sales System That Works.

But here's another strategy for systematically finding oil in your prospecting. If you give this strategy an honest try for four months, you will increase your business by as much as 30%. Guaranteed.

Chances are you enjoy a morning cup of coffee upon arriving at work. A few short hours later, you break for lunch. You find your way back to the shop after lunch, take a ten-minute afternoon break, and again, in a few hours, you head home.

Here is a strategy that is as close to a sure thing as there is. Just like always, I want you to show up at work, hit the java, break for lunch, return from lunch, and at the appropriate time, head for home. But here comes the twist. I want you to "earn" each of these "rights." To paraphrase old professor Kingsfield on the Smith Barney commercials, "Do it the old fashioned way . . . e-a-r-n it."

Before pouring your morning cup of coffee, make one prospecting phone call. No phone call? No coffee. Before heading for lunch, make one prospecting phone call. No phone call? No Big Mac. Upon returning from lunch, make one prospecting phone call, otherwise no afternoon break. And before you call it a day, make one more phone call you ordinarily would not have made. No phone call? No slamming the door behind you.

On day one, you will have made four phone calls which you ordinarily would not have made. Watch how the numbers work. With just four calls a day, you will be making twenty new calls per week, and eighty a month. These four daily phone calls will add up to more than nine hundred calls per year. (Multiply nine hundred phone calls by the number of employees in your organization, and the prospecting volume, and profit potential, become dramatic.) I can guarantee that if you make nine hundred extra phone calls within the year, a lot of things will happen that would not have happened if you had not made this effort.

To make this strategy work like a fine tuned watch, maintain a list of prospects and clients to contact with a specific purpose . . . literature follow up, request for an annual report, a congratulatory remark, etc.

Try this strategy. You will be happy you did. But don't just go with programmed prospecting. Besides being pro-active, you also need to be re-active to the next opportunity that is beamed into your vicinity.

# WINNING OVER YOUR PROSPECTS AND CLIENTS

# CHAPTER 32

# BECOME A FIXER

D oes it often seem that the only time people contact you is when they are in a jam? When they have a problem? When they need help? Never when things are going smoothly? Congratulations. That is exactly how you want it to be.

Although I am a better than average swimmer I am comforted when I see a lifeguard present and on alert. I don't remember ever approaching one to "shoot the breeze." In most cases, lifeguards are only summoned when something goes wrong, and usually without advance notice. Then, a highly trained professional springs into action with an efficient, thorough and polished display of expertise — and without an attitude.

The same analogy pertains to firefighters. They are on active duty for long and often boring shifts. And like the lifeguard, they are only asked to participate when there is a problem. But once a problem surfaces, they too respond with great alacrity, and never appear disinterested or put out.

Firefighters are professionals who are comfortable with the associated stresses, frustrations and demands placed on them from the public . . . for this is what they have been trained to do.

They do not appear to resent having to watch over us, while remaining prepared and braced for an unexpected emergency. For the most part, firefighters take great pride in "watching and waiting" for the opportunity to be of service.

The common denominator is that lifeguards and firefighters clearly understand the purpose for their existence. Their job is to help when help is required.

So what does all this have to do with you and your career? Just about everything. You, too, are in the business of helping people. Nothing more and nothing less. Think of your role as that of a lifeguard or firefighter . . . to offer your talents, skills and experience in time of need . . . whenever called upon.

Being the one clients and prospects call on when the going gets tough — what I call being the "Fixer" — is a compliment of the highest order, and how you perform when called upon will determine whether you win clients and prospects over for life or whether your tenure with them will be relatively fleeting. That performance boils down to two dimensions: (i) your attitude when the "fire alarm" is pulled, and (ii) whether you actually put out the fire or just hose it down a little, while your prospect/client slowly chokes on the smoke you are blowing his way.

## Drop Those Cards And Slide Down That Pole

When a prospect comes to a service provider with a problem, the sad reality in many businesses is that he often is given the feeling that he is bothering that provider . . . that he is rocking the provider's comfort zone and perhaps should apologize for taking Mr. Busy away from what he was doing. Often, the "fire" comes in the form of a complaint, the need for last minute or rush service, or some other special requirement. The attitude your firm conveys to the person pulling the alarm is critical. (Try calling in to your company with a couple of complaints and get a sense of the vibes you receive over the phone.)

Give me the individual who is eager to assist in time of difficulty. These are the people I want on my Rolodex.

## Talkin' Or Walkin'?

I often start my marketing seminars with this slide:

**"There is nothing in the world as accessible as people, professors and consultants who are ready to give advice."**

This quote supports the axiom that talk is cheap. Yet talk is often what prospects or clients get when they have a problem, or what employees get when they come to the higher-ups with company or customer problems — real problems which inhibit their ability to get the job done. Committees are formed, memos are sent, "I'll look into that is uttered" — all to no avail.

Will you or your firm just talk the talk, or can you walk the walk? You should assess how prepared you and your firm are to handle customer emergencies. Think of it like the firefighter's dry run to test response time when the bell goes off. You want to test response time and quality. Your system should enable you or your firm to respond to all complaints and special requests — written, e-mail, and telephonic — within a set period of time (preferably on the spot).

If you have a company employee handling complaints or special requests, be sure that employee is thoroughly schooled in the appropriate response to most common problems he or she is likely to encounter. Also, be sure the employee has the requisite authority to make on-the-spot customer service decisions to fix whatever went wrong or provide what is needed. (This is perhaps one of the most common failures in business today.) Again, test run your system by making a few requests and complaints in the guise of a customer. You'll know within three tries whether or not your team members are fixers.

Finally, if necessary always be prepared to step in yourself. Remember, being a fixer means not only helping your prospects and clients, but also fixing what needs to be fixed to enable the people in your firm to provide the highest level of performance and customer service.

Here's a great example that I personally witnessed early in my working career while employed in an electronics manufacturing plant in Bloomfield, New Jersey. The name of the company was GORDOS, which means "fat" in Spanish. (I don't want you to spend the next hour wondering where a stupid name like GORDOS came from, so let me nip that one in the bud. We manufactured tungar bulbs for film projection equipment which appeared rather fat. One of our largest customers hailed from South America, and they used to ask for the "fat" bulb — the "gordos bulb." The owner thought that GORDOS was a pretty neat sounding six letter word — probably after a few cold ones.)

The president was escorting a group of Japanese guests through the plant one day showing how switches were manufactured in America. The manufacturing process involved open flame burners and the shop floor often got very hot in the summer. A new ceiling recently had been hung which prevented the old-styled, swing-out windows from opening. No cool summer breezes were passing over our very talented, but hot operators.

Well, on this scorching hot, August afternoon, one of the more out-going operators approached the president and informed him that it was virtually impossible to work under such conditions. The Pres, in sincere concern for the well being of his people and in full agreement, suggested that the floor foreman follow protocol and contact the maintenance department to remedy the problem.

Two weeks later Pres was once again passing through the area. Lo and behold, the same operator approached and said, "Mr. Big Shot, I thought you were going to do something about this heat?" Mr. Big responded, "Are you telling me that the maintenance department didn't fix it yet?"

"Does it feel fixed to you?" shot back this very street-smart, shoot-from-the-hip employee who was probably thinking that unemployment was better than slow roasting.

"Well he is going to wish he had," the Pres said. With that, he wrapped his hand in an old towel, picked up a hammer, and proceeded to bash out each and every window . . . first on one side of the room and then on the other.

You could have heard a pin drop after the last shroud of shattered glass hit the old warped wooden floor. The operators didn't know whether to laugh, cheer, or run for the old freight elevator screaming. The Pres unwrapped his hand, calmly placed the hammer back down on the work bench, approached the shop spokesperson of cool, and said, "Now, you have cross ventilation, and the maintenance guy has a little project to sort out."

True story! This guy meant business. He realized that no one was more important to his organization than his employees. He knew what was right and fair, and he had given the proper department the first opportunity to deal with the problem. After that failed, he took control and fixed the problem himself. No red tape. No bogus excuses. No phony baloney. Just plain, simple old fashion ACTION. The lesson: When you come across a problem, fix it and get on with your life. You'll earn the admiration of all your co-workers and clients.

You can bet your last dollar that everyone on the shop floor that day is still telling this story (as I am nearly twenty years later). You can also bet that whenever the President asked these very same employees to go the extra mile for the good of the organization, they gave him a fair shake, a little more respect, and lots more effort.

By the way, just so you don't get the impression that the Pres coddled the employees, particularly the sales staff, let me share this motivational line which was frequently heard in the hallway whenever the president walked by the regional sales manager:

*"Hey, Angelo! Why don't you try selling something so you can tell me what it feels like?"*

Ahh . . . the sweet sound of gentle motivational persuasion. Ain't it grand?!

## CHAPTER 33

# THE LAGNIAPPE PRINCIPLE

Have you ever taken an airline flight where they plunk the tray of food in front of you, you check your briefcase for the Alka-Seltzer, and when you confirm your supply, cautiously dip your fork in, only to exclaim to yourself: "Hey, this stuff isn't half bad!" Would the meal score five stars from Zagat's? Hardly. But when you expect, well, "airline" quality food, you react favorably when the chow exceeds your expectations.

Here's another example. You've just bought an electronic toy (a computer, VCR, camcorder) and you need to call the manufacturer's customer hot line for help. You've seen these customer service hot lines in action before. In fact you watched one day when your Aunt Nell's body temperature slowly sank to 78 degrees as she went into a catatonic state while on hold listening to the elevator music. You feel your body stiffening up as you prepare to play the infinite number punch game with a recorded computerized voice.

In short, we have been programmed to expect less than excellent service even with all the fancy book titles shouting *The Nordstrom Way* and *Customers For Life*.

Here lies an enormous opportunity. Your customers may not be expecting much from salespeople in your field because they have grown accustomed to, and have learned to accept, mediocre service as a way of life. To position yourself as something special, and win by that Golden Millimeter we spoke of earlier, begin to use the Lagniappe Principle.

## What's A Lagniappe?

My step-son Brian was once the best in the business when it came to detailing cars — not to be confused with de-tailing certain breeds of dogs! Detailing is when you clean the vehicle from front to back, from top to bottom. You clean in places you never knew existed and make the car look and smell showroom new.

Shortly after completing one of his $70 jobs (detailing when properly executed takes about seven hours and is worth every penny of the price) I approached, examined the car and asked if he thought his work was completed to his satisfaction. He smiled at his latest example of fine-tune cleanliness and beamed with satisfaction. He told me he had just completed the finishing touches. Yes. He was done.

I applauded his meticulous work before I threw him a bit of a curve ball. "What are you planning on doing next for your customer?" I asked. He didn't know what I was talking about. He repeated that he had just finished. I said, "I know you're finished, so what are you going to do now?"

Performing the service as advertised should be expected. Quality should be a given. What you do after you have completed the job, that little something extra, is what will favorably position you in your customer's mind. That was the message I was trying to get across to my step-son . . . the need to "blow his customers away" if he wanted to own their business for the rest of his detailing career.

In Scotland, the term for delivering something extra is Lagniappe (pronounced "lan yap"). It is the cherry on the top of the sundae.

Ask yourself:

**"*After completing another first-rate job, what else can I do for my customer to insure that I have an uncluttered corner reserved in his memory?*"**

I remember reading about a car dealership which placed a picnic basket filed with fruit in the trunk of all new cars sold, only to reveal the gift during the walk-around after the deal had been consummated and all the customer's paperwork was signed and completed. This gesture always caught the buyer by surprise . . . and created a customer loyalty which significantly enhanced repeat business.

Your lagniappe doesn't have to be expensive. A few ideas that come to mind (depending on your industry) are:

- car wash coupons
- free drink coupons on airline flights
- small plants or flowers
- a box of candy
- a meaningful "thank you" card
- an electronic toy (there are millions of these in catalogues nowadays)
- tickets to a small, inexpensive event for your clients to attend with their children
- copies of a great new book which hasn't made the NY Times Best Seller list but is sure to help your client Become The Exception. (Do I have no shame?)

A little creativity is all it takes. Why not brainstorm this one with your troops on a Friday afternoon. A New York Travel Agency came up with the idea of giving to customers a few foreign coins apropos to the country being visited — enough to pay for a luggage cart at the foreign destination.

## A Constructive Addiction

Here is a corollary to the Lagniappe Principle: Get into the lagniappe habit. At the risk of sounding like a tree hugging, social psychology degree lugging remnant of Woodstock, I respectfully suggest:

### Make it your business to do something unexpectedly nice for a stranger once a day.

Not long ago I was dressed in business attire and walking to my car from the train station after a meeting in New York. Two men were digging up the sidewalk. As I detoured into the street, I caught the attention of one of the men and said "Hey fellas!" He returned a pleasant greeting and commented on what a pleasant day it was. I began to focus on what just happened. Two men laboring hard with shovels in the dirt, and me, Mr. Clean, sashaying down the avenue in wool tweed and highly polished wing tips, holding a nappy brief case filled with some very important "stuff."

Upon reaching my car, I shifted into gear and headed for Dunkin Donuts to pick up a small cup of Jo. I bought two extra cups of coffee and returned to the scene of the sidewalk demolition. I pulled up to the digging duo and reached out of the car window and said, "I hate to drink alone. I thought you guys might enjoy a cup of coffee." By the look on their astonished faces, they were both very appreciative of this small gesture. I must admit, I felt good for doing something nice for two hard working strangers.

Each day practice the Lagniappe Principle on some un-suspecting individual. For example, if you pass a parking meter which has expired, drop a coin in the meter and go on your merry way. If time allows at airports, try to offer a little help to women who are struggling with their bags or men who have bitten off more than they could chew. When you spot a woman pushing a stroller heading for an escalator, ask if you can be of assistance. When passing a couple staring blankly at a map, pause long enough to see if you might be able to point them in the right direction.

People don't expect unsolicited gestures of kindness today. It is really fun to watch their surprised (and sometimes suspect-ing) faces. Perhaps of more significance, such acts of kindness always seem to put a little more bounce in your step as you head for the departure gate. Try it the next time an opportunity pre-sents itself. I'm betting that it just may become habit forming.

## Put Some Lagniappe In Your Face-To-Face Meetings

While I am suggesting that you always add the Lagniappe Principle to your completed service for your customers, you can carry the concept over to all direct prospect and customer contacts and face-to-face meetings. Here, the "something ex-tra" is not necessarily a material item but rather a "gift" of extraordinary respect. People today, by and large, are not used to receiving special and sincere signs of respect in their per-sonal business dealings. By providing such simple but important signs, you will be winning over prospects and clients in a quiet, yet highly effective way.

Here are a few suggestions intended to "grease your men-tal skids" that won't cost you in time or money.

- **Answer the phone like you are genuinely pleased to get the call.** Sounds basic? It is. But so is a "thank you for your business" note. Become favorably programmed by the buzzer on your phone. Before picking up the receiver, stop and imagine that the caller is either (i) a prospect who has just heard you are the friendliest person in town to work with; or (ii) an existing customer who has reported to his superior that your company is the one to call when it comes to doing the impossible. Answer the phone with enthusiasm before the second ring.

• **Call people back promptly (always on the same day).** This is easy to do and makes a world of difference in establishing a relationship. You are clearly telling the person that he or she is important to you.

• **Stand up and warmly greet any prospect or customer entering your space . . .** be it a spacious office, a cubicle or a counter. On the flip side, escort the prospect to the door once your meeting has ended. Better yet, walk out the door with your customer or prospect to the elevator or the parking lot. This clearly indicates that the person is important to you.

• **Introduce prospects to the people in your immediate area, office or division.** You naturally perform this act of courtesy in your home when a guest arrives at your doorstep. But at the shop, this behavior sometimes becomes unfashionable for some unknown reason. If you make it a point to introduce your fellow workers, a loud and clear message is delivered. "We are proud of our entire organization, and it pleases me immensely to have this opportunity to introduce you to each and every one of our fine staff."

• **Call your customer within a week after your service was delivered to inquire how things went.** The key to making this work is to actually be interested in the answer. You've probably witnessed a non-sincere rendition of this strategy backfire at restaurants when the waiter or waitress asks, in cyborg style, "How was everything?" (You think, "Do you mean before or after we finally gang tackled you near the bar and got you to bring out these cold, Cajun-style catfish fajitas instead of the grilled chicken we ordered?!") You can tell the waiter was simply mouthing a company policy his boss mandated after reading a chapter on customer satisfaction in Bon Appetite magazine. Just the other day I encountered a woman behind the counter who said in a monotone, uncaring way, "Thanks for shopping Robots R Us. Come again." This obviously scripted sign of disinterest was more of a turn-off than if she had said nothing. (I did ever so politely observe that she had a brilliant future waiting for her in the funeral industry!)

There are many other small, seemingly unimportant signs of respect you can practice to capture the attention and loyalty of prospects and customers. Add this to your Friday afternoon Lagniappe brainstorm session.

# CHAPTER 34

# MOMENTS OF TRUTH

Jan Carlson, the head honcho at Scandinavian Airways, turned the one-time troubled company around from operating in the red to highly profitable. How? By focusing on those specific moments when a customer could make a judgement call about his company. He called these instances "Moments of Truth." I like this concept and refer to it often as a fundamental element of winning over prospects and clients. It takes discipline to effectively cash in on this idea, but it is time well spent.

Where and what constitutes a moment of truth in business? Here is an example. If you are fortunate (or unfortunate) enough to travel for business and frequently stay at hotels, I want you to check the answer to this question (number 2 pencil, Ho!). Who is more important to you:

____ A. The President of the hotel chain;

____ B. The associate manager who mans the registration counters; or

____ C. The person who makes your bed and sets your room straight each and every morning?

I don't think I have to tell you that it is almost never choice A and rarely B. The chamber maid dressed in black and white work clothes humbly slinks through the hallways with her head bowed in fear that she may make eye contact with one of the guests. Yet she and her work are the most frequent Moment of Truth in the hotel.

## Jump To The Pump

New Jersey and Oregon are still the only two states in the entire U S of A who believe that their citizens aren't quite squared away enough to pump their own gasoline. (I suppose New Jersey's Governor supports this law to insure that dumb Jersey guys like me don't stick the gas hose into the exhaust pipe and ruin the meticulous balance of nature we enjoy in the Garden State.)

The truth is, who in their right mind wants to step out into the cold and rain while inhaling noxious fumes (from the gas, not the Jersey air!) while "filling er up." I find it quite civilized to roll into an establishment built for refueling automobiles and simply say, "To the top if you please!" This requirement to "use an attendant" creates a Moment of Truth and an opportunity that station owners in pump-it-yourself states do not have. The trouble is, the owners in attendant states usually miss the opportunity.

More often than not, the hired "gasser uppers" are minimum wagers, take-me-as-you-see me, "customer? . . . what's a customer?" types. The owners of the station can usually be found where the real profits are made . . . back in the bay polishing a number 6 hex wrench.

From the safe vantage point of my cozy and ergonomically correct driver's seat, here is how I interpret this Moment of Truth:

- Owners in the back . . . new guys in the front.

- Customers in the back . . .prospects in the front.

- Polite knowledgeable customer service guy (a potential closer) in the back . . . guy without a clue ignoring prospects at the pumps.

If it were my gas station, I would hire a good mechanic to take care of repairing my customers' cars — the best mechanic money could buy. Meanwhile, I (the guy who cares most about the business and knows how to make people feel comfortable) would man the pumps and gently persuade the prospects to eventually trust me with their cars and their pocketbooks when it came to expensive fix-it jobs.

## Truth Or Consequences

Moments of Truth are everywhere . . . each time the phone rings . . . when someone enters your place of business . . . when you or your staff provide any information or assistance to prospects or customers. Each and every time an outsider can make a judgement about you and your company is a Moment of Truth.

Since these Moments are critical in converting prospects into customers (and retaining them as customers) then we better begin polishing our image where the rubber meets the road . . . at first contact.

Here is what I want you to do. Starting right here, from now on, recognize and pay homage to those individuals in your company who actually touch the customer. Don't miss a single opportunity to help sensitize these "goodwill ambassadors" to the Moments of Truth they will confront each day. Get them feeling good about themselves by reminding them of the importance of the work they do.

Who are the most important (based on first impression) people in your company? And what are the most common Moments of Truth? You need to ask and answer these questions.

One often overlooked Moment of Truth occurs with your switchboard operator or receptionist. This is your company's first line of communication. The receptionist/operator's actions and reactions communicate and advertise the caliber of your firm. They speak volumes for and about the company's personality, its care of personnel and its overall style of doing business. These key people are usually the most modestly paid professionals, on the lowest rung of the corporate ladder, and get the least marketing training. Yet, they are in fact, among the most important people on the food chain. Where managers often go wrong is to treat receptionists/operators as "entry level" personnel (whatever that means).

Employees, if trained to understand the importance of their Moment of Truth, can be among your greatest competitive advantages in this day of price discounting and impersonal technology. Every employee is in a position to do the company good . . . or harm.

One Final Point: The people who care most about the business, and know most about the business, are often the hardest people for customers to speak with. The lowest paid and newest employees are always the easiest people to speak with.

So, if you aren't doing so now, immerse *yourself* in direct prospect and customer contact. Learn to identify those hidden Moments of Truth, evaluate how you and your firm perform at those moments, and work toward a five-star rating.

# CHAPTER 35

# THE ASK FACTOR

There are three primary aspects to winning over prospects and clients and achieving personal success. After you ask what they are, you must keep on ASKing. This pneumonic, ASK, stands for Attitude, Skills and Knowledge.

I don't know if there is a correct order to these success keys, but I do know that without the proper attitude you might as well hang it up. Salespeople's self-assessment of attitude is very similar to most firm's assessment of their customer service. Everybody says they do it well but in reality it is often poorly administered. Likewise, everyone prides himself or herself with having the correct attitude toward customers, but in reality very few do.

The concept of attitude in sales is similar to the concept of attitude in aviation. In flying, "attitude" is the position of the nose of your airplane in relation to the horizon. When the nose is above the horizon, you are exhibiting positive attitude; when below, negative. The movement of the wings through the air creates "lift" which is the result of the two different pressures being created as air flows over and under the wing. Lift elevates the airplane.

With the right attitude the two vectors, lift and gravity, are balanced, and you move toward your destination in level flight. With a positive attitude you are gaining altitude. A negative attitude means you are losing altitude. Obviously, you can't keep going up forever. Likewise, you don't want to keep going down. So, I like to think that the correct attitude is when you are balanced and in straight and level flight.

Likewise, if you "position" your clients correctly in the hierarchy of priorities in your daily business life, you will fly straight toward your destination. No bumps, lifts and drops to scare the "passengers" of your business — just level and confidence-building progress. When you do hit choppy air (prospect problems, etc.) your job, as pilot of your own craft, is to respond by making the appropriate adjustments.

## Skills

You obviously want to get good at what you do for a living — for your customer's sake and for your own self-confidence and pleasure. We all must invest the time and effort to acquire the necessary skills. Skill development comes with practicing the right maneuvers and techniques (like the ones in this book) over and over and over again.

Practice alone does not make perfect. Perfect practice makes perfect. If we practice the wrong things, we will postpone our success. So, identify the skills that are important for your progress, and practice these skills *correctly* until you want to scream.

Here is a checklist you can use to evaluate the skills I believe are important for a sales professional. (Pencils out.)

## SALES SKILLS SELF-EVALUATION

| SKILL: | Excellent | Good | Fair | Poor |
|---|---|---|---|---|
| Decisiveness | ____ | ____ | ____ | ____ |
| Sense Of Urgency | ____ | ____ | ____ | ____ |
| Clear Vision For Your Future | ____ | ____ | ____ | ____ |
| Self Motivation | ____ | ____ | ____ | ____ |
| Self Confidence | ____ | ____ | ____ | ____ |
| Customer/Employee Interface | ____ | ____ | ____ | ____ |
| Listening Skills | ____ | ____ | ____ | ____ |
| Follow Up & Follow Through | ____ | ____ | ____ | ____ |
| Consistency | ____ | ____ | ____ | ____ |
| Paperwork/Organization | ____ | ____ | ____ | ____ |
| Attention To Detail | ____ | ____ | ____ | ____ |
| Following Procedures & Policies | ____ | ____ | ____ | ____ |
| Computer Intelligence (Moderate) | ____ | ____ | ____ | ____ |
| Writing Skills | ____ | ____ | ____ | ____ |
| Speaking Skills | ____ | ____ | ____ | ____ |
| Empathy | ____ | ____ | ____ | ____ |
| **TOTALS:** | ____ | ____ | ____ | ____ |

Now, multiply the total number of "excellent" scores by "4," the number of "goods" by "2," and the number of "fairs" by "1". (Poors get no points.) Then add the numbers together. If you scored more than 45, congratulations — you either have worked to develop excellent skills, or you get an A+ in self-esteem. Scores between 30 and 45 are good; 20 to 30 is fair; below 20 . . . well, you've got to go into training and you probably aren't eating very well as a result of your paycheck . . . yet.

You should do one more thing with this evaluation. Ask a trusted co-worker or associate to evaluate you. Then see if your self-perception conforms to a more objective party's view of your real traits. Good luck.

## Knowledge

Knowledge is not only what you know, its recognizing what you don't know. But never be intimidated by what you don't know. As long as someone helps you identify what you need to know, you can and will find the answers. The important point here is that product knowledge and sales knowledge are only acquired through the process of actually contacting prospects and attempting to make sales.

Ultimately, the way to enhance your knowledge and attitude and skills is to "ask."

- Ask yourself or trusted friends and colleagues what makes you unique and gives you an advantage over the competition . . . that builds positive attitude.

- Ask yourself what skills you have, and honestly identify those you need more of.

- Ask successful professionals the techniques and skills they have developed to achieve success.

- And don't forget, the ultimate expression of your attitude, skills and knowledge is to honestly and sincerely ask the prospect how you can help — i.e. to play the game with the correct objective.

# CHAPTER 36

# PERFORM WHEN IT'S SHOWTIME

I f you have attended a Broadway play, I am sure you enjoyed the experience. The play worked. You left feeling glad . . . or sad . . . or mad . . . or whatever the playwright had in mind when he wrote the play. If you were supposed to cry . . . you cried. If you were supposed to sing . . . you sang.

Based on the caliber of the performance, it could have been opening night, even though you might have seen the 300th performance. Actors know how the Broadway game is played. If theater goers don't feel they are getting value for their $100 investment (the approximate price of today's Broadway ticket), they will speak unfavorably about their experience, and the show will close sooner than later. Satisfy the public . . . or else!

Don't think for a moment that actors don't experience the same daily challenges as you and I. They get head colds that make them feel like going home early. They have family disputes that make them feel like throwing in the towel. They have cars they want to sell or drive into the East River . . . perhaps with the neighbor in Apartment 26F tightly fastened into the rear seat.

Problems in America play no favorites. They do not exhibit racism or bypass lefties, ex-jocks, the erudite, or the famous. The people on stage have the same problems that we do. And yet, the actors manage somehow quite miraculously to leave their problems behind the curtain, out of eyesight and earshot of their paying customers. Once the clock strikes eight, and the curtain goes up, it is Showtime. The actors perform to the expected professional standards (and the audience appreciates their ability to entertain).

With this picture in mind, I ask this: Are you satisfying the needs and wants of your "audiences" day in and day out? When your curtain goes up (i.e. whenever you are at a Moment of Truth with a prospect, client or fellow employee), do you perform like it is your Showtime, regardless of how you feel at the moment? Do you say and do what is necessary so your audience feels they can leave their burdens checked at your door — every time they come into your theater of operations?

My guess is that you probably need a little work in this area . . . that you can perform to the highest level — when you feel like it. When you are on a roll, I bet you are pretty good at what you do. When the stars are aligned perfectly, I can picture you as a real show stopper. But when things are not going well, on the job or in your personal life, do you *ever* put out negative vibes? If the answer is "No," you are the one in 100,000 who can stop reading this chapter. (You can sit in the front seat of a Don Rickles routine with no fear.) If the answer is "Yes," here are some simple observations.

## A Dose Of Reality

The nasty truth is, and please don't take this as a personal assault, people don't care about you, your problems, or the injustices which confront you on a daily basis. People are too wrapped up in their own unfair situations and spilt milk. Since no one (outside of your immediate family) cares about you like you think they should, avoid the temptation to succumb to self-pity and get back to focusing on your personal game plan.

Write down these two words and post them in a number of places where you are bound to see them throughout your day:

## It's Showtime!

Of course you will get tired, slide into a bad mood, or ache from time to time. You will get depressed and feel dejected. You will question your talent and your position in the overall picture. You wouldn't be human if you didn't.

But, the fact remains, no one will care like you do. More accurately, 90% won't care and 10% will be glad you have problems.

So when you feel burdened by life's dark side — when you hear the hoarse breath of Darth Vader (the Emperor's VP of Sales) in your ear — don't jeopardize your professionalism. Call a time out. Rest during intermission. Rant and rave in the solitude of your dressing room. Just don't do it in front of a customer, because until there is a major overhaul of the system, they still pay the bills. And until they tell you otherwise, they really don't care about your discomfort. To paraphrase the Billy Joel song:

### *"Don't let your customer see the stranger in yourself."*

# CHAPTER 37

# BE AN IDEA RESCUER

For the sake of argument, let's agree that the word "love" is the most powerful word in the English language. If it is not the most powerful, it surely is somewhere near the top. To prove this point, I can guarantee that if you randomly approach the next stranger you encounter and say that you "love" him or her, you will get unwavering attention (and maybe a subpoena).

Another word near the top of all-time attention getters is the word "idea." People love to hear about ideas. If you walk up to someone you know and say, "Hey, I have an idea!" and they respond with, "Ah, that's too bad," you are playing on a different game board than I am.

In virtually every case, people eagerly want to hear more about your idea. People like to hear ideas, and they like to have ideas. Time Magazine's Man of the Millennium was, quite simply, the ultimate human idea machine — Thomas Edison.

## Enter The KGB

Unfortunately, people also can be pretty negative when it comes to *other people's* ideas. Some people feel it's their birthright to blow away other people's brainstorms. I call these people agents of the KGB — Killers of Germinating Brainstorms. You, at times, may be one. It doesn't make you a bad person. You just have a bad habit.

If you think I'm stuck in a cold war time warp with this KGB notion, try this test. Approach somebody you care about, cold turkey, and pretend that a bolt of inspiration just jolted you. (Play act a little here.) You must look and sound excited . . . and eager to share your news. (If you really want to get into it, slap the side of your head a couple of times and jump up and down until you have everyone's attention in the room.) Say with emphasis,

## "I just got a GREAAAAAT IDEA!
## Who wants to hear it?"

Rest assured that everyone within earshot, without exception, will want to hear your brain child.

Then with uncontrollable excitement in your voice, tell them what you are planning to do. Start a new business. Go to Tahiti. Start a dating service. Learn to fly a blimp. Anything will do as long as you sound sincerely juiced. Cap your explanation with these four words: *"What do you think?"*

They in turn, without exception, will immediately enlist in the KGB with these five words:

(#1) The

(#2) problem

(#3) with

(#4) that

(#5) is . . .

The answer you will hear (and you can take this to the bank) is: *"The problem with that is . . ."*

You think I'm exaggerating? Here's a very brief excerpt from the long list of people whose ideas have been bombed:

| Person | Dumb Idea |
| --- | --- |
| • Copernicus | The Earth revolves around the sun |
| • Christopher Columbus | You won't fall off Earth sailing West |
| • Jesus Christ | The Kingdom of God On Earth |
| • Isaac Newton | Gravity, Laws of Motion |
| • Darwin | Evolution, natural selection |
| • Einstein | Theory of relatively |
| • Bill Gates | People will want personal computers and need software |
| • FedEx | You can actually deliver a package anywhere in the U.S. overnight |
| • Steve Jobs | Not everybody will want IBM computers |
| • Billy Joel | I can be a star |
| • Thomas Edison | Everything else (e.g. electric lights, audio recording, motion pictures, etc.) |

All of these people had great ideas or ambitions but very few people gave them much of a chance to succeed. Most people tried to punch holes in their balloons.

There are always exceptions. Take my Uncle Alfred. If you go up to Al and say "Hey Al, I have an idea." Al will quickly respond with "Count me in!" as opposed to the reverse-spin response, "Include me out!" Al is truly an exception to the rule.

(Alfred is an exception to just about everything.) Others will take great pleasure in tossing a series of darts at your unprotected balloon. Once you understand this to be true, it shouldn't bother you any further.

## Crush The Negative-niks

My message here is simply: Don't be one of these people. When a prospect, client or co-worker tosses out an idea, be positive. Be up. Be interested in their ideas, and seek out more information on how they plan on fulfilling the idea. Be supportive, a coach, a dream weaver. Be anything but a negative, pessimistic, dime-a-dozen, critic. You can help them think through ideas, just don't crush them.

Be the exception! Position yourself as the person decision-makers call when they need a lift, a breath of fresh air, and a positive sounding board. You'll become an indispensable member of their inner circle, plus every now and then you may help launch a major new trend or business direction.

# CHAPTER 38

# ETHICS

A recent edition of *Sales & Marketing Management Magazine* included a special article focusing on sales ethics. Call me naive, but my knee jerk reaction was, "Does this topic warrant a great deal of ink in this day and age?" The unfortunate answer is an unqualified "Yes, it does!"

Here are six headings from the article along with my personal remarks:

- **49% of surveyed managers say their reps have lied on a sales call.** A popular misconception underlies many sales campaigns: To be effective at selling, you must be less than honest and/or be skilled in thp e art of deception.

Call me old fashioned, but I was taught, and still believe, that passing along information to others that you know to be false is not cool — and not conducive to career success. Yet, for reasons probably stemming from too much sugar in their coffee, some salespeople believe that everybody but themselves are idiots. In fact, most people are pretty street-smart and can tell when you are slinging shovels of blarney. The day such salespeople get caught, and they do ultimately get caught, is one of the most costly, embarrassing, and painful days of their lives.

- **34% of managers say they have heard reps make unrealistic promises.** You are probably aware of the practice of "raising the bar" . . . the notion that it is both healthy and desirable to stretch beyond one's current comfort zone to improve individual performance — or, in the case of sales, customer service. I recognize this practice . . . and in fact, I endorse raising the bar. But, the operative word here is realistic. You must be realistic. Not only will you enjoy living with yourself more, but those in your immediate environment will appreciate the fact.

- **22% say their reps have sold products their customers didn't need.** Whoa!!! Sometimes people don't want (or realize they need) what you know as the product specialist is in their best interest. For example, I don't particularly want to buy more life insurance, thereby betting on my own demise. But you, as the insurance specialist and knowing my personal situation, might recognize that I am dangerously under insured. You are doing me and my family a favor upgrading my coverage. The key here involves determining what is right for the prospect. Don't risk being labeled dishonest. It's usually a bad career move. (Ask Nixon or Clinton.)

- **30% say customers have demanded a kickback for buying a product or service.** This one can get me in some hot water so, please, read my words very carefully. If someone requests a favor from me, I would consider one of two responses.

(1) I would take a declarative stance and offer to deliver what was asked for to the person's boss or supervisor. As long as our "arrangement" was visible for everyone to see and interpret, and the small favor was not the reason for

the purchase, I might agree to the request.

(2) My second option would be to thank the person for their time, and move on to my next sales opportunity.

If I provide you with a "finder's fee" or a "thank you" gift, I would like it to be my idea. When confronted with anything that remotely sounds like a kickback, #2 would get the nod 99.99 times out of a hundred.

- **54% say the drive to meet sales goals does a disservice to customers.** I'm surprised this percentage is not higher given the hurry-up, get-in, get-out business environment we operate in much of the time.

I remember an instance at the famous Boston Fish Market one Sunday morning when I heard a fellow hawking his daily catch from a wooden wagon. He kept hollering, "How many . . . what else . . . whose next?" as he adroitly wrapped a customer's purchase in waxed paper. He would shout this three-part question over and over again every few seconds. There was no attempt to bond with his customers. No sincerity. No attempt to establish a relationship with anybody. Here was a perfect example of a guy flogging his wares while racing against the clock.

I suppose if your product rots with each minute the sun climbs, this would be acceptable behavior. In the world of business as I know it (devoid of rotting catch or produce) this example of commerce falls short of my idea of what a client-seller relationship should look and sound like.

While I believe salespeople have more going for them than the above statistics indicate, I have found that due to easy entry and poor training the sales community does have these problems.

Sadly, a few salespeople know the difference between right and wrong, yet conscientiously practice the art of deception.

They brag about it. They make jokes about it. They actually take pride in allegedly "out-foxing" the prospect. My suggestion: Steer clear of these types.

## Dogs Have The Gift

If you ask people if they believe if dogs can detect fear in humans, virtually everyone nods in agreement. Dogs can sense when humans are frightened — maybe it's the scent. The dog takes a "read" on you each time you approach . . . and so do people. The human corollary is that most people have the ability to sense when people are being less than honest. This power is multiplied by ten when a salesperson enters the room. In short,

### *People intuitively know when a salesperson is full of baloney.*

The odds of fooling anyone today are about the same as . . . well, Presidential Impeachment! (We are two for six in the last few decades.) Younger sales wannabes need to understand this lesson fast. Seasoned professionals who think their gift of gab has gotten them where they are today, need to consider which Hawaiian Island they would now be retired on if they had simply shot from the hip for the past twenty years. People can sense when you don't believe in your company. People can sense when you don't believe in your service. People can sense when you don't believe in yourself.

Transmit positive vibes, be relaxed with yourself and your environment, believe in your company, your service, and yourself, and you will exude confidence and attract all the potential buyers you will be able to service.

As for the highly touted salesman's "gift of gab," let me suggest you follow an old New Jersey proverb:

### *Fuhgedaboudit!*

# POSTSCRIPT

# YOU ARE EXCEPTIONAL

As I look back at the previous (and what was intended to be the final) chapter, I realize that having the last words in my first book be "Fuhgedaboudit" is probably not where I want to leave you and your career. So, I decided to write this postscript.

There is absolutely no question about it — this is probably one of the best times in decades to be a skilled practitioner of the art of sales. Master this trade and apply it in today's marketplace and you stand to profit immensely in terms of material success and quality of your professional lifestyle. Why? Four reasons:

1. The U.S. and world economies are on a roll. Wealth creation, prosperity, spending, employment, production and consumption are at all time highs. Employers crave skilled sales professionals so their company can claim its fair share of the pie. Potential buyers have money to spend. This is the optimal environment for a salesperson to operate in.

2. At the same time, consumer perception of the quality of services available in the marketplace is relatively low. Your potential customers have been taught by adverse experience that outstanding products and services are the

exception rather than the rule — that personalized service is a cherished commodity. Provide that service — go the extra Golden Millimeter — and you will lay claim to an amazing number of loyal customers.

3. Since the sales profession suffers from a widespread adverse perception, many high quality people who might otherwise become your competitors in sales are drifting toward other (and frankly, less rewarding) professions. That leaves the playing field more open for you to score — score good employment, score high sales volumes, score success.

4. Commerce in America stands at the threshold of a new business model. The advent of e-business and web-based products and services provides an incredible array of opportunities for the creative small business owner. From information gathering, to product/service distribution, to customer research, to marketing, the web has created a modern day commercial gold rush of unprecedented proportions. Yes, web-based commerce creates challenges and potential threats for those who persist in doing business the "pre-e" way. But traditional companies are already proving that integrating this technology into their business creates new and rapidly growing revenue sources.

Under these conditions, the current opportunities for you to excel as a salesperson, regardless of the industry in which you operate, are enormous. To capitalize on those opportunities you simply need to follow the blueprint in this book to Become The Exception.

Here is more good news: You have already proven that you are exceptional. Simply by reading this book from cover to cover positions you as someone special — someone who is inquisitive, coachable and eager to learn and excel. Combine your high level of motivation with the opportunities available in the current business environment, add a little work on your part to perfect the strategies, tactics, and techniques I have provided in this book, and throw in some real world trial and error with prospects, and you will find yourself among the elite of the sales profession. (And you will add a few more digits to your brokerage and bank account statements.)

The truth is that I am pulling for you. I want you to achieve success beyond your wildest dreams. That is the reward I will harvest from writing this book and continuing to speak to professionals like yourself all over the world. But the fact that I believe that you are capable of achieving success means very little. As soon as you believe that you *can* do it and make up your mind that you *will* do it, then you will make your mark. Get it done, and then send me a note and let me know how wonderful it feels to have Become The Exception.

Okay, I lied. But weren't you impressed?

# Other Sales and Career Building Resources Available From Mike Marchev

In addition to *Become The Exception*, Mike Marchev offers a variety of sales and career building tools to organizations, businesses, and individuals — from print publications, to audio tapes and video tapes. Mike Marchev also organizes and speaks at industry and association events, conferences, seminars, and training retreats and motivational meetings for executives, sales teams, customer service front-liners, and other employee groups.

Among the topics of such resources and speaking engagements are:

## Sales
- How to Double Your Business Without Selling Anything
- Sales 101: First You Learn .. Then You Earn
- Sales 201: Sales Is Easier Than You Think

## Motivation
- TGIT - Thank Goodness It's Today!
- Making Things Happen
- Become the Exception

## Customer Service
- From Lip Service To Customer Service
- Shaking the Hand That Feeds You
- You Want It When? Fuhgedaboudit!

For more information on these resources or to arrange for a speaking engagement contact

**Michael Marchev Associates**
40 Autumn Court
Colonia, New Jersey 07067
800-508-1364; Email MikeM@Marchev.com;
or visit www.marchev.com.

献给所有受尽呵护，
但不得不独立面对未来的年轻人

励志珍藏

CHAOYUE ZIJI

# 超越自己

刘墉◎著

接力出版社
Publishing House

桂图登字：20-2009-153

原出版者：台湾水云斋文化事业有限公司

**图书在版编目（CIP）数据**

超越自己：励志珍藏／（美）刘墉著．—2版．— 南宁：接力出版社，2013.7
ISBN 978-7-5448-3009-6

Ⅰ.①超… Ⅱ.①刘… Ⅲ.①散文集-美国-现代 Ⅳ.①I712.65

中国版本图书馆CIP数据核字（2013）第139755号

责任编辑：车 颖 袁怡黄 楚亚男 美术编辑：严 冬 封面设计：门乃婷工作室
责任校对：刘会乔 责任监印：刘 冬 版权联络：董秋香
社长：黄 俭 总编辑：白 冰
出版发行：接力出版社 社址：广西南宁市园湖南路9号 邮编：530022
电话：010-65546561（发行部） 传真：010-65545210（发行部）
http://www.jielibj.com E-mail：jieli@jielibook.com
经销：新华书店 印制：北京鑫丰华彩印有限公司
开本：880毫米×1250毫米 1/32 印张：7.375 字数：170千字
版次：2010年2月第1版 2013年7月第2版 印次：2019年4月第21次印刷
印数：208 001—214 000册 定价：29.80元

# 目 录
Contents

# 前　言

人生在世，最大的敌人不一定是外来的，而可能是我们自己！

我们难以把握机会，因为犹疑、拖延的毛病；我们容易满足于现状，因为没有更高的理想；我们不敢面对未来，因为缺乏信心；我们未能突破，因为不想去突破；我们无法发挥潜能，因为不能超越自己！

其实每个人都有超越自己的经验，在幼儿期，没有人逼我们学走路，我们却试着自己站立，不断跌倒，不断站起，不断试步，终于能从爬的阶段，进入走的时期。然后，我们对走也不满足，又要学习跑。问题是为什么在我们能跑、能跳、能说、能写之后，那原先所具有的，不断超越自己的冲力，竟渐渐消失了呢？

因为这是上天设计的，让我们有了谋生的能力之后，就少有那继续超越的想法。也就是这样，我们才会安安静静地做一个"凡人"。

只有少数的人会说："我不要做一个普通人，我要超越！超越我那看来有限的自己。"于是在这种不信自己办不到的愤懑和努力下，他们将自己提升了。且随着不断地提升、不断地超越，为人类的历史创造出更辉煌的成就!

这本书里没有什么了不得的经天纬地,却充满一个父亲殷切的叮咛,通过书信的模式,教导他那走向成年的孩子,如何战胜自己的惰性和童年时期的依赖心,在龙蛇混杂的纽约市和充满竞争的明星学校里,找到生存自保之道,并寻求进一步的突破。

书中年轻人所遭遇的问题,岂止是那纽约史岱文森高中的学生所专有,其实也可能包括了你自己!

请以这本书作为激励的火种,在熊熊的火焰中,使你超越铁,成为钢!

# 原版自序

一九七三年，我写成了第一本《萤窗小语》，由于当时不过二十四岁，自己才离开校门，所以《萤窗小语》虽说是写给学生的，实际上等于为同一辈的人说话，也因此很能获得年轻读者的共鸣。

但是随着年龄的增长、生活体验的多样化，许多观点都不再像初出校园那么单纯，整个社会也产生了巨大的变化，为了表达新的认知，也由于许多老读者的催促，我又在一九八六年出版了《点一盏心灯》，试图通过趣味性的小故事，引起读者各自的感触，进而有所启发，算是为不同年龄的人，所写的一本书。出版两年多来，居然也印到了十几版。

可是就在这两年间，我发现自己的生活又有了极大的变化。过去听我使唤的儿子，突然长大了，声音似乎在一夜之间变粗，身高则一下子比我多出了半个拳头。过去我对他是低头训斥，而今不得不变成仰面教诲；以前常"叫"他陪我打球，现下则难得有"聚首"的机会。

我发觉家中唯我独尊的时代过去了，尤其在孩子进入纽约史岱文森高中之后，由我一人发言的时代也过去了，孩子开始有了他的价值观、人生观，不再是父母的财产，而是这社会的财产，更不是父母的影子，而是他自己！

当然，孩子的转型期，也是父母的头痛期，像是接力赛，上一代将棒子交下去，交不好，就可能掉在地上。也因此，我不定时地配合身边有关的事情，写信给他，其中的内容可能是我已经耳提面命的，也可能是不便在语言中表达的，写下的目的，是希望他能有多看两遍的机会，并加强他阅读中文的能力。

《超越自己》就是在这种情况下累积而成的。由于写作时，我尚未超过四十岁，不但在大学任教，常与青年朋友相处，又兼任电视新闻工作，所以许多理念都是较新的，但也因为我从事中国绘画理论和文史的研究，且有强烈的中国文化自尊心，所以其间必然也有较传统的一面。

史岱文森是美国最著名的高中，今年"西门子西屋科学奖"的第一、二名都是那里的学生，在全美入围决赛的三百人中，该校就占了四十七名。我在此介绍史岱文森，不是为了凸显自己孩子的优秀，正如我在书中不曾提到他的名字一般，而是因为我觉得台湾升学的压力、社会的变迁，可能远非美国一般城镇能比，却正与这纽约曼哈顿的顶尖学校类似。

史岱文森的学生，功课常要做到深夜一两点钟，他们有一个接一个的考试、一个比一个狠的老师，更需要穿梭在犯罪如麻、五方杂处的纽约市，如果说台湾的年轻人必须削尖了头钻，史岱文森的学生只怕犹有过之。

所以，在这本书中，许多言辞是激烈的，许多观点是现实的，许多故事是残酷的。正如我在《你不能失败》这篇文章中所说：

马断了腿，当然还能活！但是身为一匹马，不能跑了，就算活着，又有什么意义？！

你必须成功，因为你不能失败！

面对这个充满竞争的纷乱时代，我强调的是积极的人生观，发挥最大的潜能，将自己带上尖峰，虽死无悔、虽败犹荣。

在整个奋斗的过程中，我认为最大的敌人不是外面的，而是自己，尤其那些受尽呵护的年轻人，为了独立面对未来，他们必须战胜自己的惰性和依赖心。这种毛病若不革除，无论在父母的逼迫下，功课有多好，将来都难以成功。

也就因此，我在《现代青年》一文中，从一个"小游学生"的身上谈到了新的教育理念：

未来社会的成功者，必是那种以消费刺激生产，以速度争取时间，以时间争取知识，以知识争取财富，又以财富改善生活，以高级生活设备增加速度的人，而不再是农业时代，抱书慢慢啃，再以考试晋身的寒窗学子。

虽然这些信是写给我孩子的，实际上每个年轻人的发展，在其间生理的转变，和未来面对的世界，都差不多，对于那些父亲甚至母亲难得回家吃晚饭的青少年，我希望这本书能够引导出一些东西。对于为人父母的，我则希望提出一些个人的想法，供做教育子女的参考。

如我在前面所说，随着孩子逐渐步入成年，我觉得他不再是自己的财产，而属于社会、国家。同样，我觉得别人的孩子步入社会之后，不也是属于大家的吗？

对于孩子的理念，做父母的应该超越自己！

让年轻人发挥最大的潜能，超越他们自己！

则我们的社会也必能超越自己，开创出崭新的局面！

一九八八年冬于纽约

二〇〇六年六月修订

# 上课第一天

一个娇生惯养，从未出过远门的孩子，从今早开始，每天要坐三个多小时的车，穿过肮脏黑暗强盗出没的地区，到曼哈顿的高中上学……

今天是你上高中的第一天，虽然早晨我没有起来送你，却很清楚地听见你匆忙的脚步声，也知道你似乎有些胃不舒服，想必是因为紧张所引起的。

我知道，你必须先走到巷口去搭 Q17A，再转 Q44A 公交车，而后坐 F 线的地铁，穿过半个皇后区、曼哈顿中城的河底隧道，经过五十三街向南行，到十四街转 L 号车到学校。由前两天我带你试坐的经验得知，这单程就需要一个小时又四十分钟，无怪你的祖母整天坐立不安。

我也知道纽约的地铁，是世界上最乱且最不安全的。每天报上总有抢劫甚至杀人的新闻，前两日一个中国人被精神病患者推下站台碾死，上星期又有一个女人被车子拖了几十米而死。至于你所经过的地方，虽然有世界上最繁华的第五街，却也有最肮脏下流的四十二街，如果说你每天穿过毒蛇猛兽出没的森林去上学，是绝不为过的。

问题是，对于你这个过去从未一人离开家门超过三英里的孩子，我为什么放着眼前的高中不上，却让你冒那么大的危险，每天奔波于曼哈顿呢？

这一方面因为你考上了世界名校，有小哈佛之称的史岱文森高中，一方面更由于我认为这已是教你出去历练的时候了。在人生的旅途上，我们都要走这样的路，穿过这样的危险，去追求自己的理想。甚至应该说，人生的道路更危险，因为它只有去，没有回，走的是过去都不曾经历，且只可能经历一次的路。如此说来，你未来四年的通学，又算得了什么呢？

大概还是因为不放心吧，怕你在回程找不到公交车站的位置，我特别算准时间，到地铁的出口等你。知道吗？当我看到你怯怯地走出站时，心中百感交集，兴奋得有如多年不见的父子重逢。而你那惊喜的眼神中，竟也含着泪光。

回程的公交车上，你向我抱怨地铁最后两站间的距离好长，还以为坐错了车；而上次我带你试走时没能记下的站名，你居然今晚全能如数家珍地背出来。

是的，年轻人！你渐渐会发现，当你一人独行的时候，会变得更聪明；当你离开父母的时候，才知道父母是你的依靠、你的盼望。

崎岖而黑暗的道路，将使你真正成熟！

位于纽约市的史岱文森高中（Stuyvesant High School）。

# 忘不了的一天

想到将近二十年前的那一天，画面还是很鲜明！

我从八岁移民美国，就一直住在郊区，只是偶尔随着家人"进城"。那天第一次自己坐地铁，眼睛睁得大大的，书包紧紧抓在手中，像是闯入了蛮荒丛林。不久前有人被精神病患者推到地铁轨道上的新闻，我记得很清楚。到现在，我还尽量不站在站台边缘等车。

我老爸形容曼哈顿为"毒蛇猛兽出没的地方"，虽然有些夸张，但二十世纪八十年代的纽约的确比现在危险，犯罪率是现在的一倍多。时代广场（也就是四十二街的核心），是个复杂的地方，晚上更是一片狼藉，飘着浓浓的大麻烟味。有不少毒贩、皮条客、酒鬼逗留在色情电影院门口拦路乞讨、做生意，哪像是而今"合家欢"的观光胜地！

就在我上高中的那年，纽约地铁开始试用一种新的材质，让涂鸦喷漆无法附着。没多久，画得乱七八糟的车厢全变干净了。这只是开始，后来的市长增加了警力，整顿了许多问题地区，鼓励大企业进驻投资，逐渐把纽约变成一个体面又摩登的都市。

以前的纽约，像一块臭豆腐，先得皱着鼻子咬一大口，才会知道它臭得很香。当年离开皇后区湾边的单纯环境，一头栽入曼哈顿看人生百态，是我个人发展的重要转折点。上天保佑，我活着过来了！

地铁车站常是危机暗藏的所在。

## 幽默感

◆

一九八一年三月三十日，当里根总统被刺时，白宫新闻秘书詹姆斯·布莱狄也受了重伤，他的前额被子弹射入，血流满面扑倒在地。

没有人能相信，大脑受此重创的人还能活命。

但是今天，詹姆斯已经能骑马、谈笑。因为……

　　今天看电视时，当我发现你居然说得出每个演员的名字，甚至连他们的家庭生活也知之甚详的时候，开玩笑地问你："喂！请问布鲁克·雪德丝的电话几号？"你居然反问："对不起，爸爸！我不知道，但打听很久了，你知道吗？快告诉我！"

　　我大笑了起来，惊讶地发现，你居然有了幽默感。

　　有幽默感（with a sense of humor），这句话在东方或许并不重要，却是西方社会对人极高的赞赏，因为它不仅表示受赞美者的随和、可亲，能为严肃凝滞的气氛带来活力，更显示了高度的智慧、自信，与适应环境的能力。

　　幽默像是击石产生的火花，是瞬间的灵思，所以必须有高度的回应机智，才能擦出幽默的语句；那语言可能化解尴尬的场面，也可能在谈笑间有警世的作用，更可能作为不露骨的自卫与反击。

　　譬如在议会里发生了老议员以拐杖打人的事，有人提议进场者应该把拐杖挂在门口，这时议长若是接受而诉诸表决，无论结果如何，总是不愉快的，幸而他急中生智，笑着说："如果为了防止不正当的动作，就必须把拐杖挂在会场门口，那嘴也该挂在门口，手脚也该摆在保管处。"引得全场大笑，提议者也在莞尔的情况下，解决了尴尬的处境。

　　又譬如伏尔泰总是赞赏某人的作品，某人却总是刻薄地批评伏尔泰，当有人向伏尔泰说出这件事时，他只是一笑："我们双方都弄错了！"不过短短几个字，既幽默地解决了尴尬的场面，又做了有力的反击。

我还听过一个故事：美国工人到俄国工厂参观，看到停车场上的轿车，便问那些轿车是谁的。俄国工人回答："工厂是我们工人的，轿车是上面的。"随之反问美国工人，美国工人幽默地说："我们没有你们走运。工厂是上面的，轿车是我们的。"两句话对比，却有了深刻讽刺的意义。

但我必须强调，幽默并不是讽刺，它或许带有温和的嘲讽，却不刺伤人；它还可以消遣自己，在这当中更显示了幽默与被幽默的胸襟与自信。

我曾经看过一个秃头者，在别人对他的秃头幽默时，当场变了脸，这一方面可能因为对方的幽默不得体，刺伤了他，更可能因为他原本对秃头有极大的自卑。

相反，我也见过一位秃头的报纸主编，当别人笑称他聪明透顶时，居然笑答："你小看我也，早就聪明'绝顶'了！"你想，若不是他有相当的自信，又怎可能借别人的话，幽自己一默呢？

所以，愈是开放而富裕的社会，人们愈有幽默感；愈是闭锁的环境，愈难让幽默存在。不存在的原因，不是人们没有这份智慧，而是没有这份胸襟；不是因为人们有过强的自尊，而是因为色厉内荏的自卑。一个幽默者最重要的条件是完满健全的人格。

一九八一年三月三十日，当里根总统被刺时，白宫新闻秘书詹姆斯·布莱狄（James S.Brady）也受了重伤，他的前额被子弹射入，血流满面扑倒在地，当时许多媒体都报道了他死亡的消息，因为没有人能相信，大脑受此重创的人还能活命。

但是，年轻人！就在六年后的今天，我看到电视报道，詹姆斯不但已经逐步克服了半边大脑受损的行动不便，骑马与妻子出游，而且一如往日地幽默。访问中，令我印象最深的，是他说："幽默感，使我能撑下来。厄运是会打击我，但它打不到幽默感的那种深度！"

年轻人！你说，这幽默感是什么？

它是面对不同环境的乐观态度！

詹姆斯·布莱狄不但克服了伤痛，而且曾任美国伤残协会副主席。这是他送给作者的签名照，额头上仍见清楚的手术刀疤。

## 不同的幽默感

二十世纪八十年代的布鲁克·雪德丝,就像现在台湾的林志玲,是个玉女名模。很多学校的男生"哈"她,包括我在内。她后来跟不少名人(包括摩纳哥皇室)传出绯闻,现在已婚,有两个小孩,偶尔客串一些美国电视剧。而我,始终没要到她的电话。

"幽默感"这篇,应该是写给台湾地区读者的,因为我在美国长大,一向非常清楚幽默感在西方社会的重要性。后来我发觉,所有的文化都重视幽默感,只是表达方式不同。

我刚回台湾的时候,很是不能适应这里的社交方式,主要是因为幽默感不同。大家刚认识时很礼貌,好像没有许多幽默的空间,但熟了之后会很习惯互相调侃,不属于这个环境的人很难拿捏分寸。而且台湾人讲究的"热闹",其中"闹"占了很大的比例。西方人的幽默比较收敛,讲究的是字句之中的玩弄或逻辑的矛盾,不一定每句好笑的话都一定有个"爆点",所以初到"洋邦"的中国人,常觉得他们很"冷"。

总而言之,要在那里混,就得搞懂当地的幽默。

文章里提到的布莱狄先生虽然痊愈,但因半边大脑受损,终生还是有行动障碍。他成为美国反枪协会的领导者,极力推动限制民众购买枪支的法令。他的名言之中,有一句我特别喜欢。他说:"当命运给你柠檬（也就是不好的事情）时，你可以做柠檬汁。我这里有好几个柠檬汁的摊位呢！"

这种生活态度，应该全世界都适用吧！

# 防人之心

他被海关人员以携带毒品走私的罪名逮捕了，他大声对着还在另一个关口接受检查的朋友喊，那人却说不认识他。

一个学生去逛百货公司，临出门，突然有个女人，匆匆忙忙地跑来对她说："我的肚子痛，必须上厕所，可是我跟我先生约好，他就在门口的一辆白色的车子上等我，能不能麻烦您，告诉我先生一声？"说完塞了两包东西给她，"这也麻烦您交给他！"

学生才走出门，就被百货公司的人抓住了。她抱着两包没有付钱的贵重商品，吓得呆呆地站在那儿，因为人赃俱获而百口莫辩。至于那先前说肚子痛的妇人和所谓的白车，则消失了踪影。

某人单独旅行，在飞机上遇到一位投缘的乘客，两个人一起下机，提取行李，在过海关之前，那新认识的朋友说："我的行李真是太多了，能不能麻烦您帮我带一小件？"单独旅行的人，心想自己的东西反正不多，就一手接了过来。

跟着，他被海关人员以携带毒品走私的罪名逮捕了。

他大声对着还在另一个关口接受检查的朋友喊，那人却说不认识他。他被架出了海关大厅，悲愤的呼喊声仍然从长廊尽头传入，大厅里的人都摇头，说："罪有应得的贩毒者，过去不知道已经带进多少毒品了！"

那飞机上认识的朋友也叹气："好险哪，我差点被栽了赃！"

你今天对我说，一个许久未见的初中同学，知道你在曼哈顿读书，于是托你顺路带一包东西给下城的朋友，使我想到应该说以上的故事给你听。我并非教你不要帮助人，而是希望你慎重。尤其是许久未见的朋友，虽然以前有很好的交情，但由于并不了解他近来的生活，那早期建立的信任，也就应该重新评估。

再过二十年，你会发现，许多学校里的挚友，在久别重逢时，你或许仍然维持着以前的热情，对方却冷淡了。不是他没有了情，而是由于在社会上的种种遭遇，会麻木一个人的感觉，也可能改变他的价值观。相反，如果你自己遭遇重大的打击或步入歧途，也可能改变看这个世界的方法。

害人之心不可有，防人之心不可无。在这个人性光辉泯灭与人生价值观混乱的社会，你尤其应该慎重。记得有一次我采访"中华航空公司"在纽约的一个酒会，由于当晚正好有客机直飞台北，便赶到机场，将一包录影带交给华航的朋友，托他们转回"中视"。

那位朋友对我说："咱们是老朋友了，这又是'华航'的新闻，但是为了慎重，我必须打开检查一下。"

日后我经常想起这件事，我不是对那位航空公司朋友的做法感到不高兴，而是觉得自己理当主动打开包装，让对方检查，而不应该等对方提出。如果他碍于情面未讲，岂不是要在心中嘀咕很久吗？

往后的日子，你必有许多旅游的机会，别人可能托你带东西，你也可能请朋友传递，希望你以上面的几个真实故事做参考，保护自己，也减少朋友的困扰。

## 这是个可悲的事实

我老爸写这篇文章，其实有个更早的源头。在初中时，我和好友肯尼有次在回家的路上，碰到一位被锁在自己家门外的老头。肯尼站在我肩膀上，从二楼窗户爬进去帮他开门。这件事害我被父母狠狠骂了一顿："万一他是小偷怎么办？你们岂不是成了他的帮手？"

当时我有点不高兴。学校教我们要"日行一善"，怎么反而受到如此责备？但现在，我不得不认同父母的看法，因为时代大不同了。以前在万圣节，美国儿童都会打扮成小鬼，一家一家要糖果，但后来新闻上报道出有人因此而中毒之后，这种习俗就几乎消失了。

光是过去这几天，我就接到起码两通诈骗集团的电话。这个社会好像愈来愈复杂了。多可悲啊！纽约人本来就很小心了，"9·11"之后更是如此。当恐怖分子都可以在已怀孕的女友行李里面偷藏炸弹时（这是真事），还有谁能够相信？"防人之心不可无"已成为我们在二十一世纪生存的基本原则。

上礼拜我去台中，在一家餐厅前有人说他车子发动不起来，请我帮忙。我回答："对不起，我无法帮你。但我有手机，可以帮你叫拖车。"也许我太谨慎了，但就如美国人现在常说的："You can never be too careful these days."

至今想起初中的那件事，我还是相信那位老头，也觉得我和肯尼做了件好事，虽然我们当时的确太过天真。要是有一天我自己的小孩也碰到类似的状况，我八成不会骂他，但一定会叫他看看他爷爷当年给我写的这篇文章，并摸着他的头叹息："孩子，现在的社会比你想象的复杂！"

# 时间与金钱

在这个讲求速度的时代，同一时间永远只能做一件事的人，将可能被淘汰！但在何种情况下该一时两用、一心两用，必须由你自己去决定。

你问我"用时间的方法"。我的答案是："用时间好比用金钱，如果你知道怎样用钱，也就应该知道怎样用时间。"

金钱与时间，在"会用"与"不会用"者的手中，可能产生天壤之别。善于理财的人，能够用有限的钱，买到他需要的东西，甚至以钱滚钱，创造更多的财富。至于不懂理财的人，则可能毫无计划地使用，东买一点，西添一样，到头来买的东西不少，却该有的没有，既买了又无用处。

同样，会用时间的人，懂得安排时间，按照事情的缓急来支取，到头来，不但完成了他要做的，而且能够留下多余的时间。至于不会用的人，则东摸摸、西磨磨，时间一分一秒地过去，浪费的比利用的多，犹豫的比决断的多，时间永远不够用，事情永远做不成。

这样说，或许你还不懂。那么，让我举个例子吧！

如果我今天给你几千块钱美金，要你自己出去生活，你要怎样使用这些钱？你不会先去买电脑游戏，也不至于先去看百老汇舞台秀，而是在解决了衣食住行的问题，并缴完学杂费之后，才开始考虑娱乐支出，对不对？

于是，当你把自己的开销做成统计图时，会看到有大笔的开支，也有小笔的花费，必要的支出在先，非必要的支出在后。

同样的道理，今天老天给了你时间，你不能先拿去打电脑游戏和看电影，也不可以先去整理相册、看小说和胡思乱想，而应该先安排睡眠、上课、读书和通学的时间。因为没有充足的睡眠，你的身体状况不可能好；不花时间乘车，你到不了学校；至于上课、读书，则是你现阶段最重要的事。当然，除此之外，你必须吃饭、交际、消遣，并处理生活上的琐事。只是在整个时间的分配上，前面几项占的分量大，后面几项占得小。

我为什么会特别提出所占比例的问题呢？很简单，当你有一笔巨款，你可以考虑买贵的东西。相反，你钱少时，自然是买小的东西。一个永远只买小东西，钱多的时候也不买房子、汽车的人，不能算是懂得用钱的人。同样，如果你支配每一段时间，都用来做小事，也不能算是会用时间。必须既会利用长时间，完成较大的工作，又知道掌握零碎的时间，做小事情。譬如当有两个月的暑假时，你可以计划做一个参加"西屋科学奖"的大研究报告；当你有一个星期的假日时，你可以为校刊写篇专访；当你只有周末两天的时间时，你就只能做做功课、出去看场电影或邀几个朋友聚一下。如果你在暑假的"大时间"，天天用来聊天、看电影，在周末却想写研究报告，就是大小时间不分了！

有一个人总是急急忙忙地做事，朋友问他为什么这么赶，何不轻轻松松慢慢来。他回答："我做事快，正是为了争取多余的时间。你们看到的固然是我忙碌的一面，其实当我回到家，却有比你们更多的休闲时间，也利用它实现了许多梦想。"

这个人是以速度来争取时间的，他把零零碎碎的"小时间"集中，成为大时间，也就能做较大的用处。比起那些做事总是拖拖拉拉，永远没有较大"空闲"的人，当然要算是知道利用时间的。

我们也时常看见主妇们一边聊天、看电视，一边织毛衣，由于这两种事都属于较轻松的，不必百分之百集中精神于其中一项，所以她们在同一时间，做两件事。

不过我也知道，有位著名的女作家，在她年轻时为了争取时间写作，甚至一边煮菜，一边写稿。国画大师黄君璧更是一面跟来访的朋友聊天，一面作画。这就非要高人一等的功力不可了。

由于上帝给每个人的时间都一样，那些有过人成就的，往往都懂得这种一时两用的方法。

所以，当你假日起床之后，坐在桌前发呆，说是要想想那一天的时间该怎么安排，就已经是在浪费时间。你何不一边洗脸、刷牙、吃早餐，一边想这些事呢？

我过去作画到深夜，总是先把调色盘和砚台洗净，才安心去睡觉，但是后来改成了每天起床之后做这些事，因为前一夜已经疲惫，洗砚台时，脑海里一团迷糊，无法再想事情，不如省下时间，早早上床。第二天脑子清醒的时候，再一面洗一面想，许多写作和绘画的灵感，也就在这时产生了。

或许你要说，做事应该专心，同一时间只能做一件事。我想对于写文章、做数学题这些需要高度集中精神的事，确实如此，但如果说等公交车时不能一边看报，就没有道理了！在何种情况下该一时两用、一心两用，必须由你自己去决定。但我要强调，在这个讲求速度的时代，同一时间永远只能做一件事的人，将可能被淘汰！

综合我以上所说的，掌握时间的原则应该是：

一、决定事情缓急、轻重，以优先顺序来安排时间，免得该做的到头来没有做。

二、以大的时间做大事情，以小的时间做小事，绝不将大时间打碎，用来处理琐事。

三、以速度争取时间，将争取到的小时间，集中为较大的时间。

四、如果可能，在同一时间，做更多的事情，使时间多元化。

你说，这用时间与用钱的道理岂非相去不远吗？

## 放松和把握时间同等重要

这篇文章对我影响极大，但也是我最难实践的。

我几乎每天都发现自己的时间不够用。可能因为工作太多太杂，同时要兼顾创意和行销的角色，时常觉得自己总是在跟自己赛跑，一下子跟客户开会，一下子在工作室里敲 MIDI 键盘，同时还得赶稿。

现在看这篇文章，还是觉得自己有许多改进空间，不过我觉得"时间管理"这门学问，也得按每个人的工作性质及生理时钟作调整。例如我的脑袋都是晚上比较活跃，早上反而一团迷糊，所以我都尽量在中午之前处理比较不重要的事。可惜这跟一般人的生活习惯恰恰相反，所以有时候早上要开重要的会议，我也不得不妥协，只好出门前多喝杯咖啡。

我发现，很多事情是无法一心两用的。例如创作时，我需要一段完整并毫无干扰的时间。看起来像发呆，其实是在思考。我很羡慕老爸提到的那位女作家，可以一边炒菜，一边写稿。我写稿时连听音乐都不行！我老爸也一样，他可以一边跟我母亲聊天，一边浇花，但当他开始写作，书房门关上，谁也不敢吵他。

根据我的观察，现代人已经非常习惯同时做很多件事情。办公室里随便谁的电脑都不只有一个视窗开着，IE、Word、Excel 统统一起来，还可以跟 MSN 上的朋友聊天。分心已成为常态，专心才是比较困难的。

现代人流行静坐、练瑜伽，这都是为了让自己的生活能够慢下来。我以前看到有人在跑步机上打电话，觉得他们很厉害，但现在觉得那样很可怜。既然要跑步，就好好地跑；如果想放松，就完全让自己放松。所以，补充我老爸的时间观念，我要说："争取时间的时候极力争取，是为了让自己该停下来的时候，能够好好喘口气！"

# 面对抢匪

◆

在纽约，有个高中生连续被抢了五次，没抓到匪徒，学生却得到老师的赞扬，叫同学向他学习——如何面对抢匪，而不受伤害！

当你今天对我说，班上有个同学，已经在街上被人抢了五次时，我并没有对他遭抢这件事感到吃惊，倒讶异于他不曾受到一点伤害。

因为抢匪在动手时，往往先给对方一个下马威，使他失去反抗力。所以匪徒能够毫不动粗，抢了就走，必然由于你同学的瘦小，以及他回应模式的恰当。

或许你要说，面对暴徒，居然还要讲究"回应的模式"，是多么没出息的消极做法。但你也要知道，这消极的回应，却是使你免于伤害，进而能将暴徒绳之以法的积极态度。

正因此，以打击犯罪为职责的纽约市警察局，竟然公布过一项资料，教市民在四下无援的情况下，如何面对被抢，甚至如何面对非礼的暴徒。譬如：男人应立即拉开外套衣襟，露出上衣口袋，请抢匪过来拿或自己取出钱钞，交给抢匪。但千万不能在不先打开外套衣襟的情况下，伸手进去拿钱，以免对方误认为你在掏枪，而先将你撂倒。至于女人，最好自己将钱取出，而不可让对方动手，以免进一步引起暴徒劫色的非分之想。

他们更建议，当妇女遇到强暴时，可以将手指放进喉头，造成呕吐，甚至脱尿、脱粪，使对方看到恶心的东西，而失去"性趣"。

警方更叮嘱，受害者应该做出受害者的样子，不要表现得十分潇洒，更不可说"要拿吗？全都给你"这种蔑视的话，否则反而会挨揍。因为即使是强盗，也有自尊，他是要抢，不是要被施舍。

最重要的是，你必须记住他的特征，清点自己损失的财物，并立即报警！

请不要认为我在教你当懦夫、顺民。因为我要让你知道，如何在这个鱼龙杂处的社会中生存。我要你在无可避免、毫无反抗力的情况下，放弃年轻人的血气之勇，而留得青山，开拓未来。

　　孔子曾说："暴虎冯河，死而无悔者，吾不与也！"意思是他并不赞同那空手搏老虎和毫无凭借而渡河的人，这种人的死，是毫无意义的。

　　人生就是如此，我们既要有迎向光明、成功的胸怀，也要有面对厄运挫折的能耐；像韩信少年时由市井流氓的胯下爬过、勾践在被俘时尝夫差的粪便，反而是大勇的表现。

　　你要记住，只知刚的人，难免被折断；只有柔的人，到头来终是懦夫。只有那刚柔并济，认清方向，且在布满荆棘的人生道路上，以最恰当模式应对的，才可能是最后的成功者！

身在纽约，不时会心生"小心被抢"的危机感。

# Do something

我那两个可怜的高中同学雅费跟杰西！他们可能到现在还不知道，就因为我拍了他们耍帅的照片被我老爸用在书里，而使他们在地球的另一边成为成千上万青少年心中的"抢匪"！

我自己小时候曾经被抢过一次，不过是在家附近，不在曼哈顿。在纽约上高中时，我曾经数次发现自己处在危险的情况下，幸好都安全脱身，主要是因为感觉被人盯上后，赶紧跑到人多的地方。人多一定比较安全，纽约人虽然表面上很冷，但如果看到别人受害，一定会报警或前来制止，不会袖手旁观。

台北地区就不一样了。最近我有两个加拿大朋友骑车经过通化街附近，听到一个小姐大喊救命，他们马上跳下车跑过去，看到一个抢匪正消失在人群中。满街的人听到她叫，也目击那个抢匪，但大家只像看戏似的；抢匪逃跑，没人制止，反而闪开让他过，使我这两个外国朋友非常不解。可能周围的人都怕麻烦，或怕自己的力气不足以制伏抢匪，但起码他们可以打电话报警，或用手机拍下抢匪的照片，总比呆呆站着来得好！

我父亲的文章里呼吁年轻人如果碰到抢匪，不要为了"血气之勇"而惹上更大的麻烦，但我要补充：社会的安全靠大家互相帮助，如果你看到别人受害，可以不用冲上去当英雄，但起码要"Do something"，不要当个缩头乌龟！

# 如何事半功倍

一群记者抢新闻，为什么其中一位能提前发表，而且早了许多？一群导演抢拍动物片，为什么有人能提前推出，而且又快又好？

一架飞机撞山失事了！

成群的记者冲向深山，大家都希望能抢先报道失事现场的新闻，其中一位广播电台的记者拔得头筹，在电视、报纸都没有任何资料发布的情况下，他却做了连续十几分钟的独家现场报道。

电影圈突然一窝蜂地拍摄有动物参加演出的影片。虽然大家几乎是同时开拍，但是其中有一家，不但提早推出，而且动物的表演也远较别人精彩。

你知道为什么那位记者能抢个头条吗？

因为他未到现场之前，先请司机占据了附近唯一的电话，打到公司，假装有事通话的样子。所以当他做好现场报道的录音，跑到电话旁边，虽然已经有好几位记者等着，他却只是将录音机交给司机，就立刻通过电话对全国听众做了报道。

你知道那位导演为什么成功吗？

因为在同一时间，他找了许多只外形一样的动物演员，并各训练一两种表演。于是当别人唯一的动物演员费尽力气，也只能演几个动作时，他的动物演员却仿佛通灵的天才一般，变出许多高难度的把戏。而且因为好几组同时拍摄，剪辑好立刻就能推出。观众只见其中的小动物，爬高下梯、开门关窗、取花送报、装死搞怪，却没想到全是不同的小动物演的。

我讲这两个故事，是为了告诉你，这世间许多"非常的成功"，是以"非常的手段"达成的，那未动手之前的战略和构想，在一开始，就注定了他们的胜利。

　　同样的道理，我建议你在做每件事之前，甚至每一天的早晨，对将要做的事情制订个计划，而不是慌慌张张动手之后才去思想。

　　上帝给每个人同样的时间，只有那些事半功倍的人能有过人的成就，也只有知道计划的人能够事半功倍。

## 节省时间的目的

对于节省时间，我老爸是专家，不只是工作，连玩乐都一样。

小时候我们全家常去游迪士尼乐园。老爸总会先拿份地图，规划出最快的玩法。有别于一般人的习惯，我们总是采取相反的路线：入园后，先冲到最里头，再一路玩"出来"，或是以顺时针的方向游园（一般美国人习惯以逆时针方向行走，就是入园之后先玩靠右边的）。老实说，我当时并不喜欢老爸这么急着赶来赶去，但长大后愈来愈痛恨排队，想想老爸的方法确实省了不少时间。所以，将来有一天我带自己的小孩去迪士尼乐园，也一定会这么做。

现在的生活里，我尽量试着在一些小地方节省时间。像我从事DJ 工作，平时必须消化很多新兴的歌曲。我便会把大量的音乐先灌进 iPod，一边跑步一边听，这样不但做了功课，而且就运动的效率来说，总比听健身房的"芭乐歌"来得好。

# 你不能失败

马断了腿，当然还能活！但马不是人，人能残而不废，马不行。身为一匹马，不能跑了，就算活着，又有什么意义？

今天我在学校体育组见到一件怪事，当时球队正为晚上的比赛做练习，突然接到一个队员从地铁车站打来的电话，说是因为天气突然转凉，他穿的衣服太少，如果站在冷风里等公共汽车会感冒，所以希望队友开车去接他。

从学校到地铁只有十五分钟的路，真是再简单不过的事，可是你知道球队的教练怎么说吗？

他居然说："电话不要挂，先问他感冒没有，如果还没感冒，就立刻去接；假使已经感冒，再重一些也不要紧，就自己吹风，坐公共汽车来吧！"

我听了大吃一惊，颇不以为然。岂知教练有他的道理："如果已经感冒，今天晚上当然是泡汤了，又何必浪费别人的时间去接，而且影响了大家的练习。本来嘛！迟到就不应该，天气多变，不注意身体，更不应该。自己不小心，而且不以团契为重，谁又能管得了他！"

这件事，使我想起台湾的一位企业家朋友讲的话。他说："在我的公司里，如果一个人四十岁还没有升到主任，就永远不必再想这个位子。因为爬上来已经嫌迟了。既然不可能再由主任的位子往更高阶层爬，就乖乖待在下面，免得影响其他有冲力的人！"

他的理论虽不尽然对，但是跟下面西方哲学家赫伯特的这几句话，不是很相似吗？

一个人如果二十岁而不美丽、三十岁而不健壮、四十岁而不富有、五十岁而不聪明，就永远失去这些了！

这个世界是不等人的，它残酷得甚至不能给予失败者一点同情。

譬如在一组人执行秘密的战斗任务时，如果其中一个不幸受伤而无法继续前进，为了怕他被俘之后泄露军机，造成整个行动的失败，领导者可能不得不将那人灭口。

譬如几个人同去爬山，以绳索相连攀缘峭壁时，如果一人失足，悬在半空中，想尽办法不能解救，而其他人却可能因此都被拖下深谷时，只好割断绳索，将那人牺牲。

谁希望受伤？谁希望失足？

谁又能责怪他受伤与失足？

只能责怪命运！而命运常是残酷的！

相信你一定在电影里看过，当马腿关节受到重创时，主人常不得不将它一枪打死。我曾经问一位马术教练：难道那马断了腿，就活不成了吗？为什么非要置它于死地？

他说：当然能活！但马不是人，人能残而不废，马不行。身为一匹马，不能跑了！就算活着，又有什么意义？

以上，我讲了许多残酷的故事给你听，因为你已经到了可以接受这种事实的年龄，未来也将面对这些残酷的现实。

"你必须成功，因为你不能失败！"

这是一句非常莫名其妙的话，却有耐人寻味的道理！

## 输的感觉

读了这篇，许多人可能会觉得我老爸是个严厉的父亲。当年我听到这番话，也觉得太激烈、太残酷。但如果今天换成军队长官或球队教练，我绝不会对这话感到意外，因为打仗或比赛，非胜即败。

"你不能失败"这句话也反映了人生最戏剧性的一面。我们爱看体育比赛，心情随着选手们的拼斗而七上八下，因为运动场也像古罗马的竞技场，是输与赢、生与死的战斗。以后我教导自己的小孩，一定会让他们参加球队。要他们尝到输的感觉，这是除了打仗与当兵之外，体验真实人生的绝佳机会。

老爸对我说："你不能失败。"但对我妹妹却说："也给人家尝尝第一名的滋味嘛！"这么不同的教导，我认为不是重男轻女，而是因为当年在写《超越自己》时，我老爸也正处于年轻冲刺的时期，所以他对自己的态度是绝不能输，也急迫地想把这强烈的观念传递给儿子。如果这造成比较大的压力，我也只好认命。

当然还有另一个原因，就是我妹妹的个性很像老爸，她已经把自己逼得够呛了！

# 建立独特风格

名歌星唱得不如和音天使？

名书法家的作品可能被学校老师评为乙下？

大师的绘画可能被一般的美展退件？

"对门的马瑞诺，不过十七岁，但是他组成的合唱团，已经出了唱片，而且由全美国最著名的公司发行呢！"你在晚餐桌上艳羡又似乎不平地说，"其实马瑞诺的那一套，我比他强得多，他弹琴的技巧差远了！只是按按电子琴键而已。至于作曲，我也早就会……"

好！现在让我说个故事给你听，我今年夏天在台湾，有一天看歌唱综艺节目，主持人突发奇想，叫一位以声音高亢著称的名歌星，跟后面的和音者较量一下谁唱的声音高，结果起初几个音还难分高下，后来在不断提升起音的情况下，和音的女孩都毫无困难地通过了，名歌星却应付得愈来愈艰苦，结果声嘶力竭地败下阵来。

当时好几位一同看电视的朋友都说："真逊！名歌星还不如和音天使，只怕改天要让贤了！"

问题是，那位名歌星还是继续走红，且唱出许多叫好叫座的歌；而那位和音者，还总是站在台侧，偶尔被带到几个镜头而已。

我相信，和音的那个女孩子，不仅长得不差，声音又唱得高，她读谱的能力和对乐理的了解，大概也都在名歌星之上，但是为什么出头的却是看来较弱的那一位呢？

答案是：因为那位名歌星，有她独特的风格。而独特的风格，往往并不是由许多十全十美的东西所集合的。甚至可以说，有些独特的风格，从某个角度来看，反而是一种缺陷。譬如伊秉绶和金农的字，如果拿到中学交书法作业，只怕要得乙下；马蒂斯和塞尚如果参加早期学院派的美展，恐怕也会被踢出来；连那李恕权，我都怀疑他若参加合唱团，会不会因为嗓子太哑，而挤不进去。

可是，这些人都成名了！

　　这又使我想起美国一位著名的模特，她是被一个毫不特殊的男人，从乡下提携出来的，真可以说是飞上枝头，成为数百万年薪的凤凰。当有人问那个提携她的男人，如何"慧眼识英雄"时，他回答道："虽然她并不极漂亮，但是当我带她走进拥挤喧闹的场合时，发现人们都看她，于是知道她有一种特殊的吸引人的地方。"

　　这特殊的吸引力，就是每一位成功艺人的要件。所以当你比较自己与马瑞诺时，不能只拿单项的条件来比，而应该注意他整体的特质，进而建立属于你自己的风格。

　　此外，我们真该为马瑞诺高兴，过去我总觉得这个孩子有顽劣的倾向，所以限制你与他交往。但是最近发现他变得很有礼貌，这是因为人们越获得别人尊重，越懂得尊重自己。所以我们应该祝福这位曾令我们头痛的邻居，且分享他的光荣。

## 风格无法替代的事

这故事的背后，其实有一个说出来仍觉得丢脸的内幕。

当时我其实是被朋友骗了。那天正好是愚人节，马瑞诺找到一卷卡带，发现他自己与封面上的团员长得非常像，三四个朋友便联合起来糊弄我说他发唱片了，而我也因此被他们骗得团团转！

不知道现在的马瑞诺在做什么，反倒是我自己走上了音乐这条路。

这个故事让我想起周杰伦刚出道时，有制作人挑剔他咬字不清楚，王力宏刚发片时，也有唱片公司的老板跟他妈妈说，想在华语歌坛发展，唱腔不能带有这么浓的 R&B 味儿，但结果他们建立起自己的风格，成功了！

现今的世界丰富多元，你有太多机会表现自己，但风格终究不能替代真功夫。毕加索创造了很现代的画风，可是看他早期的作品，便知道他也是按部就班一步步走出来的。

成功的艺术家往往都是打了多年的硬底子，把传统技巧琢磨得炉火纯青后，才开创出个人风格。相反，很多人自以为拥有独特风格，但如果没有"底子"，往往会像没有结实地基的建筑，就算盖得高，也维持不了多久就会垮。

## 保护根本

他们希望你写最深入的作品，却可能整天整夜地打扰你！

他们希望球员精神饱满、场场报捷，却可能请球员饮酒通宵！

我有一位学术界的朋友，以写政论闻名，成为各大报社约稿的对象，他却对我发牢骚说："我真不了解那些约稿的人，他们白天不停地打电话，晚上又不断地请我吃饭喝酒，偏偏在喝得已经东倒西歪的时候向我约稿，不但要时事评论性的文章，而且急如星火，隔日就得交稿。他们也不想想，前一晚喝得酩酊大醉，如何有清醒的头脑写稿？整天应酬、接电话，又如何有时间查资料？所以我装了电话录音，有空再回电话。晚上应酬多半谢绝，因为今天我不赴约，只要稿子写得好，改天还有的约。相反，今天我去了，写作的水准降低，连着几次，就再也没人请了！"

听来像是个笑话，但是那最后两句话，却有极深的道理。你会发现人们常常很矛盾。他们希望你写最深入的作品，却可能整天整夜地干扰你；他们希望球员精神饱满、场场报捷，却可能请球员饮酒通宵，三更半夜才让他们休息；他们希望老人长寿，却可能在寿宴上灌酒，并强迫老人吃过量的食物。他们一方面要表现自己尽了奉承之力，使受者盛情难却，背负着情感的包袱；另一方面，却又因为对你有了狂热的招待，而跟着有了狂热的要求。

如果你失败了，他们则可能弃你而去。

所以他们心中的哲理可能是：

你成功，所以我们奉承你。由于我们如此奉承，所以你应该成功。如果你失败，则有负于我们的招待。

不知你听完这段话，会有什么感想？你觉得人们太现实，还是维系成功不易？

其实这世界本来如此，譬如看戏时，掌声会引来更多的掌声，嘘声也可能勾起更多的嘘声。不论我们怎么说"锦上添花，不如雪中送炭"，那添花的毕竟要比送炭的多。

所以，当你被奉承的时候，千万注意你为什么被奉承，而且应该知道，如果失去了那被奉承的东西，你也可能失去已获得的一切。

由于你在学校担任指导数学的工作，那些被指导的同学，为了表达谢意，纷纷请你看电影，你觉得盛情难却，而一一赴约，使我不得不讲以上的这段故事给你听。

请不要觉得我太现实，否定了人们超现实的一面与友情的价值，但我也必须强调，在任何情况下，你都要保护自己的根本，如同那位写时事评论的人所说："今天我不赴约，只要稿子写得好，改天还有的约。相反，今天我去了，写作的水准降低，连着几次，就再也没人请了！"

这种道理，不仅今天值得你深思，而且可能受用一辈子！

## 应酬与人情

这篇文章写得很真实，但我直到现在才能体会，尤其对于"应酬"与"人情"这部分。

人们会拥护成功者，大都是对他们有相应的期望。我也不断警惕自己：如果有人把我奉为VIP，我就必须更努力去赢得自己的地位。

人际社会，难免应酬，工作上必须花时间与客户维持良好关系，使日后有更多的合作机会，于是在工作与应酬间造成矛盾。我老爸习惯"隐居"的生活，就算他不去找人，自然有人找他。但我刚入社会，碰到该社交的场合，就算没空也得去。所以我觉得这篇所讲的，真是说来容易，做来难。

# 恒星的陨落

有一天你会发现总是拉你一把的那强有力的大手，居然孱弱而颤抖地伸出来，请求你扶持；有一天你心中永不衰颓的老人，可能写出最后两个已经难以辨认的字：『救我！』

上个星期天下午，看见你祖母坐教会的交通车回来，我叫你出去接，并从窗帘间察看，发现你站在车门前，盯着八十岁的老祖母，颤悠悠地从高大的车上溜下来，竟然不知道过去扶一把。天哪！我当时真是火冒三丈，如果只是这样，我又何必叫你出去接车呢？

多日来，我试着平复火气，思索这个问题，并从自己的成长经验中寻找答案，终于在报纸的一条新闻里找到了原因，我发现即使是今天的我自己，也可能犯跟你同样的错误。

"巨人离席——敬悼一代文学大师梁实秋先生"。

当我早晨在报纸的副刊上看到那巨大的黑字标题时，真是惊愕极了，不仅由于梁实秋先生曾是我们的旧识和家中常客，且是收藏我作品的知音，更因为他是我最敬重的一位学者。我常对朋友说，梁实秋教授才称得上是真正的才子，因为他不仅从年轻时，就成为文艺界的先锋，更毕生致力，直到八十多岁，仍然创作不懈。有些人是一闪即逝的流星，有些人是偶然出现的彗星，梁实秋先生却有如长久不衰的恒星。

但是恒星似乎也有陨落的时刻，虽然他是那么豁达，认为"人死即如烛灭"，更说"死欲速朽，何用铺张"，但在临终时，还是做出了最后的挣扎。

当我读到丘彦明小姐记录的梁教授在临终时写下"救我"的字条，又狂喊"我要死了""给我大量的氧"时，我有一种无比的悚动，我不敢相信，这是那位潇洒风流视生死如浮云的一代大师所说的话。我甚至有些发怒，责怪他为什么如此不够豁达。而真正应该说，我懊恼他居然毁坏了我心中的文学偶像——永不衰老、永不停笔的梁实秋。

但，人毕竟是要老的，即使在千万人心中不朽的英雄，也会像射出的箭，无论多么强劲，在飞越呼啸之后，总有坠地的一刻。对于崇拜他的人，或许会有短暂无法接受的时间，但终究要承认这个千古不易的定律。

同样，我发现把你从小照顾到大的祖母，在你的心中，即使已经八十高龄，仍然是那一如往昔伟大的奶奶。虽然过去，你曾是她一手抱在怀中，一手炒菜的娃娃，而今则已高出她两个头。但在她心中，你仍是娃娃；在你心中，她也仍然是能将你一手举起的超级祖母（Super Grandma）。

问题是，大家都错了！如同我一直到梁教授死去，仍难以接受现实般，我们都应该逐步调整自己的位置，即使这调整是痛苦的，带有英雄偶像破灭的感觉，但若不这样，世界如何继往开来、新旧交替呢？

年轻人！有一天你会发觉，总是跑在你前面，被你同学称为"不累的机器人"的父亲，居然会跟在你身后狂喘；有一天你会发现别人买你的面子，却不再买你父母的交情；有一天你会发现总是拉你一把的那强有力的大手，居然孱弱而颤抖地伸出来，请求你扶持；有一天你心中永不衰颓的老人，可能写出最后两个已经难以辨认的字：

"救我！"

年轻人！扶你的祖母一把！在外出时，为她探看前面的路，预警每一块不平的地面，并为她推开厚重的门，说："小心！别夹了手！该带的东西带了吗？"如同老人家以前对你说的一般。

这样，你就真正成熟了，而且老一辈也便可以安然离去。因为留在你心中的，是他们不朽的精神形象，而非暂时的肉体衰逝！

刘轩和小帆永远是奶奶心中的小孙子、小孙女。

# 那个信封

我奶奶一生个性好强又倔犟，人家想搀她一把，她总是硬说不要，我这个孙子更管不住她。老爸担心奶奶，奶奶还担心我呢！

许多年后奶奶中风了，完全无法自己行动。到医院去看她，看到好几个护士合力把奶奶从轮椅抬到床上，我的眼眶湿了，难过的不仅是她的样子，而且因为她已经完全不会反抗，还不如个小婴儿。

从我小时候开始，每次爸妈出远门，都会告诉我家里哪个抽屉里有个信封，里头装了遗嘱、房契、保险之类的文件。听到这话，我会浑身不自在，平时根本不敢靠近那个抽屉。

前阵子有一天忽然接到老爸的电话："我要去台安医院急诊室，快点过来！"当时我正在办一个活动，连忙赶过去，看到他脸色苍白地躺在病床上，摸他的手，是冰冷的。我找到医生问清楚病情，得知他是气喘发作，加上喝太多咖啡所致。第一次见到父亲如此衰弱，内心难以言喻的感触被彻底勾起，但难过的同时，却发现自己出奇冷静。那时我发现，这么多年来，我一直在做心理准备。如果有天必须打开"那个信封"，我相信我的心会是平静的。

谢天谢地，那天医生打了一针之后，老爸就好了。他现在还是每天要喝六杯咖啡，要管他跟管奶奶一样不容易。

# 读书的秘诀

◆

书印好了，就是死的，人脑则是活的，你必须将这些死的资料，用最有效的语言、方法，输入你的大脑中。

今天你问我该怎么读书。如果你指的是读课本、考高分，我想我是没资格回答的，因为我高中的学业成绩并不好，全靠联考之前的猛力冲刺，才进入师大。但是，我又想：说不定这种冲刺的经验，倒可以供你参考。

我觉得脑子里一定有个死角，因为念书时，常有些东西硬是读不进去。碰到这种情况，我绝不硬背，而将那正面的冲突改为消耗战。方法是将背不进去的要点，写在课本靠近页边的位置，每次读书之前，先快速翻阅一遍，使那些字闪过脑海，仿佛分期付款，一个月下来，自然就记住了，反比那硬背的东西结实。

我也利用谐音的模式来记东西，这是从初中时期就有许多学生使用的方法。譬如"危险"是"单脚拉屎"（dangerous），"大学"是"由你玩四年"（university）。又譬如我背长江沿岸的十个二等港，只用了一句话"政无安九月常常杀一万"，意思是"政治不安定，九月秋决时处死的人往往高达一万"，虽然句子没有道理，却让我到今天还能记得"镇江、芜湖、安庆、九江、岳阳、长沙、常德、沙市、宜昌、万县"，有人大为惊讶，封我为"电脑"，岂知我是用了特殊的读书方法。

如果你到我书架上找，还会发现一大包"方块字"。以小纸片做札记，和以方块字帮助记忆，是我至今仍用的方法。譬如近来临习明朝韩道亨的《草诀百韵歌》，由于草字与楷书的笔画顺序有很大差异，许多字不易记住，我就将它们制成方块字，正面写楷书，背面写草字，口袋里揣上一把，随时摸出来，看到楷书就想草书，见到草字则加以辨别，倒也能事半功倍。

此外，古人有所谓"锦囊集句"，方法是将平日的灵感写在小纸条上，先投入锦囊，有空时再取出来整理，将片断的灵感集合为大的篇章。我也采取这个方法，不论乘车、走路，甚至上厕所时，只要有灵感，就写在随身携带的小本子或名片背后，统统集中在一个地方。虽然很可能一两年之后，才有闲暇拿出来整理，但是就用这个方法，我在百忙中居然能写成七本《萤窗小语》和《点一盏心灯》。如果我不知道把握每一个小灵感而任它飞逝，怎么可能有这些成绩呢？

还有一点，在这个知识爆炸的时代，你会发现书念不完，在做学问时却又需要广泛涉猎，所以你必须懂得上网查询和整理繁杂的资料。书买回来，即使没时间细看，也要将前言、目录翻过。

同样的道理，百科全书的检索目录、各种字典、词典、植物典、句典、名典、世界历史年表、地图，也是必备的。甚至像《国家地理杂志》这类书，由于资料丰富，很具有参考价值，为了检索方便，你也可以去买一本数十年来的目录。《纽约时报》集合各种重大新闻的《首版集成》（Page One），百科全书的年鉴也很有用。

总之，书印好了，就是死的，人脑则是活的，你必须将这些死的资料，用最有效的语言、方法，输入你的大脑中。并将这些资料，放在身边，如同随身碟一般，随时等你插入，将你要的东西整理出来！

每个人都有自己读书的方法，我只是将我的方法提出来供你参考。如果你的程序语言（language）更适用，当然还是用你自己的比较好。

作者用来练习草书的方块字卡片。

## 所谓知识

现在资讯爆炸，透过网络，知识可以说是完全开放的。今天，最重要的已经不是如何得到资料，而是如何整理。尤其网络上充斥着真假难辨的事物，每个人各持立场、各有观点，我们要如何筛选，建立起自己的视野与眼光；如何在浩瀚的知识里，整理出整体的思想，才是真正的挑战。

# 活的历史

◆

最好的老师，不会只教你如何考高分，也不会严格规定你死背。

最好的老师，教你活的学问，并且领你进入更宽广的天地！

听完你讲述历史老师留的假期作业，实在令我佩服他。

相信你们现在正念到欧洲的百年战争，所以老师才会叫你们假设自己是生在那个时代，而又身为报纸的主编，以现代的模式，来编写一份当时的报纸。

于是你们要写社论，根据事实绘声绘色地写专访，配插图、漫画、气象预报，甚至杜撰几个广告。为此，你们必得熟读历史，找到当时的绘画作品，追索那时的风俗习惯，并了解地理位置，否则就画不出插图、弄不出气象、类比不出专访的内容。

在这过程中，你们兼习了报纸的编辑方法、加强了写作的能力、摸索了时事漫画的制作，甚至版面和广告设计，也成为必须注意的。尤其重要的是：他使你们发挥想象力，把课本上读到的史实，活生生地展现出来。

那看来冷冰冰的人名、地名和原先与你们毫无关系的事物，都将被重新赋予生命。你们甚至经过层层的推想，和当时的文献资料，感受到时局与个人的息息相关。于是人性流露出来，在大时代的变迁与小儿女的私情之间，你们也可能写出有血有肉的故事！

最好的老师，不会只教你如何考高分，也不会严格规定你死背。他要能引发你的兴趣，像磁铁般带出更多有意义的东西，且在这过程中发掘你的潜能。

最好的老师，教你活的学问，并且引领你进入更宽广的天地！

## 史岱文森老师万岁!

那位历史老师真是很有创意,当时我做这份作业也非常开心。

另一个令我印象深刻的功课是:一位英文老师在教导"如何写信"时,要求班上每个人写一封抗议信,对象自己找,而且必须真正寄出去。当时我想了好几天,最后去信给一本男性杂志,抗议里头某则不实广告有性别歧视之嫌。那杂志没理我,但有不少同学的确由不同地方收到回信,其中还有同学写信到"国防部"后,收到某位将军的亲笔回函! 一个简单的"complaint letter"作业,成了活生生的教育,而且跟社会连接,与政府互动,当然棒!

以我的观察,现今台湾地区的教育体制存在不少问题,例如很多作业最后落在家长头上,结果造成小朋友过度依赖。而且由于大家的作业都已经达到成人水准,老师在交代功课时,标准也愈来愈高,早已超出小朋友的能力范围,变成恶性循环。

在美国上小学时,我曾经因为一项制作房子模型的作业,让老爸插手,结果被同学狠K。从此之后,我打死都不再让他介入。另外值得一提的是,高中时期很爱造反的我,在一项科目上选择以拍电影短片取代交报告,居然非但没挨骂,还被老师送去校外比赛得了奖。日后回想,这也许是我能顺利申请进哈佛的原因之一。写到这儿,我要喊一句:"史岱文森老师万岁!"

# 贵人哪里来

每个人都可能遇到贵人，这些贵人不一定真的尊贵，他可能是陌生人，也可能是一面之缘的过客，甚至是你的敌人！

"贵人"这个名词，相信你早就知道了，因为三年前，有一次家里请客，我事先对你说，受邀的客人是我以前的贵人，因为他的帮助，使我有后来的成功。你当时虽然并不十分了解，却在餐桌上对客人说："我爸爸讲，你是他的贵人！"

我当时看得出来，那人听了有多么高兴，因为他知道我没忘记他以前的好处。但我后来也听说，他的太太回家跟他大吵一架，说他自己连个固定的工作都没有，怎么会是别人的"贵人"？

他的妻子错了！因为能做贵人的，自己不一定多么尊贵。当我们要找自己生命中的贵人时，也不见得要到世俗所谓荣华富贵的阶层去寻觅。许多贵人，都出奇的平凡。而平凡的我们，也随时可能成为别人生命中具有重大意义的"贵人"，甚至当我们成为别人的贵人时，自己还不知道。

从前有个人写信给燕国的丞相，因为光线太暗，就叫仆人举烛，一不留意，把"举烛"两个字，也写入了信中，等到燕国的丞相收到信，读到举烛两个字，竟然大为感动，说举烛的意思是追求光明，也就是要拔擢贤才，并以此呈请君王采用，使得燕国强盛起来。

传说李白起初做学问很没有耐性，直到某日，看见一位老妇，居然想将一根粗铁条磨成绣花针，才顿时醒悟，回头苦学，成为诗仙。

米开朗琪罗在画西斯廷教堂时，有些不满意自己的成绩，却又因为完成大半而舍不得重画，直到有一天去喝酒，看见老板毫不犹豫地把新开的一大桶酸酒倒掉，终于下定决心"重新画过"，成就了不朽的作品。

以上写"举烛"的郢人、磨针的老太太和酒店的老板，可知道自己无意中的行为，竟能造就别人？而他们何尝不是燕国、李白和米开朗琪罗的贵人？

又譬如我有位朋友外出旅行，临上飞机发现旅行社的小姐竟把他最重要的身份证明资料遗失了，他起初大发雷霆，要求赔偿损失，但是后来又跑去向旅行社道谢，说犯了错的小姐是他命中的贵人。原来他没赶上的那班飞机发生了空难。

你想想，由犯错，到成为别人的救命恩人，这当中有多大的转变，岂是当事人预先能知道的。

再拿我最近的遭遇来说吧！当我的《点一盏心灯》写到中途的时候，有位朋友来访，看了我写好的稿子说："这些东西太软，缺乏吸引人的力量！"

虽然你母亲说，那位朋友可能是嫉妒我的成绩，讲出酸葡萄的话，我当时也有些不悦，但细细检讨之后，发现确实有许多篇可以改变写作角度，以形成更大的戏剧性和说服力，所以将三十多篇全部抛弃重写，使《点一盏心灯》成为畅销而且长销的作品。

由此可知，到处都可能有自己的贵人，他们不一定是直接提拔你的尊长，反而可能是毫无关系的陌生者、一面之缘的过客，乃至你的敌人。只要你能从他们的身上有所领悟，并引导自己走向更美好的未来，或由于因缘，使你免于原本可能发生的厄运，他们就都是你的贵人。

所以，不要轻视任何人，也不要轻视自己，因为那平凡人可能是你的贵人，你也可能成为别人的贵人！

## 微妙的人际关系

这是一篇写给有人生历练的读者看的，现在的我，在阅读时也比以前更有体会。因为在现实生活中，常会发现有许多原先不喜欢，或相处不睦的人，最后却可能成为自己的贵人。例如我刚回到台湾工作时，有一次接办活动，被某夜店老板坑了一笔钱。当初几乎跟对方翻脸，但后来有一天，那个老板在他店里介绍了一位唱片制作人给我，那制作人又介绍了好几个业界朋友，让我很快打入台湾的音乐圈。没有那位老板牵线，我可能很不容易认识这些人，如此看来那老板岂不成了我的贵人？

# 无心的错误

一位留美学生，在飞机上跟空姐开了个小玩笑，却引来近百名警察，最后被铐上警车，并面临十五年的徒刑……

有一个年轻的留美学生，在从佛罗里达到纽约的飞机上，笑嘻嘻地递给空中小姐一张纸条，写着："我身上有炸弹，我要劫机。"

空中小姐笑了笑，把纸条还给那个留学生，便离开了。几分钟之后又转回来说："把你刚才那纸条再给我看看！"并取走了纸条。

当飞机降落时，地面已经有近百位荷枪实弹的警察，把飞机层层包围。虽然那留学生大喊："我只是开个小玩笑，当我递纸条时，四周的人都朝着我笑，知道只是闹着玩，他们可以作证！"但是他怎么说都没用。他被押上警车送审，并面临十五年的徒刑。

我刚从台北回到纽约，你的母亲就告诉我这个报上才登过的新闻，并在说完之后，十分感慨地说："这个年轻人多可怜哪！我相信如果坐在飞机上的是我们的儿子，他的朋友又怂恿他开这个玩笑，他也可能会做的！"

对！这是最令人心惊的一句话，也是她讲述那个新闻给我听的原因。我们都知道年轻人常犯无心之错，只是那错误又可能造成难以弥补的伤害。

问题是，什么是无心呢？醉酒驾车肇事的人是有心杀人吗？偶尔试一次毒品，作为体验生活方法的人是有心犯罪吗？考试时受不住朋友请求而传个纸条的人是恶意犯规吗？

但是这些都没有坏动机的行为，却可能犯下杀人、吸毒、考试作弊的罪，它们有重有轻，但同样在生命中留下污点。

至于今天我为什么要跟你说这一大篇，相信你早就心里有数。

因为我在后院整理园子时，发现地上插了许多冲天炮的细竹条，才知道你居然趁父母不在的时候，请你的朋友肯尼来放炮。

你明知在纽约放炮是违法的，也知道这种处处朽叶、天干物燥的冬天容易失火，却答应朋友用我们邻接树林的院子作掩护。可曾想想如果引起火灾，不论是烧了自己、别人或是后面的森林，我们所要承受的损失与法律责任会有多大！

你必然记得几年前，你经过一户人家，两个人正试着开门锁，你过去看，他们对你说不知是不是锁坏了，打不开，而你居然热心地帮着他们开。

你也必然记得有一回肯尼带着具有杀伤力的弓箭，拉你去小公园练习，结果邻人报警，一下子赶来三辆警车的事。

前两天，我居然看到你的朋友把几乎乱真的玩具枪留在我们的树丛里，又发现家里的花盆被他们当靶子，打得像蜂巢一般。

而对所有的事情，你给我的解释都是："他们没有恶意，我也无心！"

现在你应当知道，那无心却可能有恶果。如果开锁的人是贼，你就是共犯；若是肯尼的弓箭和朋友的气枪伤了人，你也脱不开关系。今天你还小，如果当你长大之后，还不能慎交朋友，又不懂得审度自己的行为，只怕那无心，就会惹下天大的麻烦。

最后，让我告诉你一个十年前的往事。

就在我来美之前，突然接到以前一个学生的电话，我清楚地记得他惊慌的声音，说一个朋友欠他钱不还，他明知对方是有钱想赖，所以找朋友帮忙，把欠钱的人抓住，逼那人家里还钱。他认为自己没有错，动机也只是想要回属于他的钱。可是对方家人报警，他成了绑架勒索的通缉犯。

之后我再没能跟他联系上，又很快去了美国，但是十年来每当我看到没有前科、家世良好的年轻人，因为一时糊涂而犯下大错时，都会想起他，想到他刚念一半的大学与暂时被断送的前途。

记住！年轻人，"无心"往往就是一种错误！

## Use your head

经历"9·11",再读这篇文章,又是不同的感觉了。现在如果还有人敢在飞机上拿炸弹开玩笑,那不只是"笨",而是"蠢到爆"!

我小时候住在纽约郊区,环境十分宁静,邻居也彼此认识,入夜后,青少年大多无事可做,仅有的娱乐就是看电影与逛街,学会开车后,则跟朋友出去兜风。无聊一点的青少年,可能会玩些恶作剧,在邻居大门上喷些刮须胡泡沫之类的,或是像我朋友肯尼那样,把冲天炮拿到公园里乱射。

纽约市不同,市区有比较严重的治安问题,一般的青少年反而不敢随便拿别人开玩笑——谁知道哪个人被搞毛了会掏出枪来?但这不表示无心的错误不会发生。套句我老朋友雅费(就是《面对抢匪》中照片上握拳头的那位)常说的话:"Use your head!"(用大脑想嘛!)

# 据理力争

有道德的人不少，有道德勇气的人不多。如果由于你在课堂上据理力争，得罪了老师，而被『死当』，我仍然要对你竖起大拇指！

这两天看你的神色不对，猜想一定在学校有了什么麻烦，而当你在我的逼问之下，说是因为跟新的英文老师辩论评分方法，老师词穷之后，似乎对你不满意，而不太理会你，甚至当你有疑问举手时，都装作没看到时，我不得不说："好极了！年轻人，我支持你！"

你一定十分惊讶我这个看似老古板的人，会有如此表示。但是你也要知道，向一切不合理的事务抗争到底，为维护真理绝不屈服，是我一贯的处事态度。我相信这种精神，是民主社会人人应该有的，而对于自己信仰和真理的坚持，更是每个成功者必备的条件。乡愿可以成功，但那成功必不够伟大；狂进的人可能失败，但那失败往往壮烈。所以只要你的态度和缓，做有风度的君子之争，即使是向威权不可侵犯的老师争，我也支持。

记得我在高中时，虽然考试成绩不错，作业也极佳，一个数学老师却因我经常去办校刊，或代表学校外出参加比赛，以上课缺席为由，给我很低的分数，当时我甚至气得想把实验解剖的青蛙放到她的抽屉里。

当我进入师大美术系的第一天，看见教室后面挂着一幅相当好的作品，问教授那张画在系展中得了第几名时，教授说画是可以得第一，但因为这个学生总逃课，所以给他第二。我立刻表示，如果比赛是就作品来论，画得好就应该给他第一，当场使教授不太高兴。

当我初来美国，有一次在南方坐长途客运车，位子被划在最后面，上车却发现前面有许多空位时，曾立刻去售票处询问，是不是因为种族歧视，把我这个黄种人放到厕所旁边，结果获得了前面的位子。

当我暑假回台湾发现我们住的大楼在管理上有许多不合理之处时，曾立刻邀集了两位住户，分别拜访一百多家，成立了管理委员会。其间遭遇许多阻力，连同楼住的亲戚都反对，认为我多管闲事。

正如你所说，老师评分方法不公平，虽然同学们都不服，却不敢说，只有你提出来，并逐项与老师辩论。随着年龄的增长，你会发现有道德的人不少，有道德勇气的人却不多。问题是如果没有人敢挺身抗争，不公的永远不公，委屈的永远委屈。所以我支持你做一个有风度的抗争者。

在此你要注意，我说"有风度的抗争者"，那"风度"是极重要的。当我们看美国总统大选辩论时，评论员往往把辩论者是否从头到尾面带笑容这件事列为优先。也就是说，即使在你激动而义正词严的时候，也要维持思路的清晰冷静，而且对事不对人，尊重那些与你抗争的人。因为你争的是理，不是去毁损对方的人格。

当然我也必须告诉你，作为一个带头的抗争者，往往也是最早牺牲的。我曾经在学校里因为跟两位教授辩论而失去做全 A 毕业生的机会，也曾经被"死当"而几乎无法毕业，我还是小学六年级班上两个被美术老师打手心的学生之一。但我并不恨他们，因为如果我自己理直，他们没有风度接受，是他们的错；如果我理屈，则我自己应该反省。在强烈的抗争之后，冷静地思考一下，作为改进或激励自己的一种方法，总是会有收获的。而我自己今天做教授，常被学生气得里面冒火，却不得不压下来，并回家自己思索，何尝不是由学生时代的经验中，得到了"同理心"。

我自己绝不会因为学生据理力争而扣那个学生的分数。我可能一时不高兴，但不会一直不高兴，尤其当我知道学生对的时候，更得感谢他的指正，甚至佩服他的勇气。我确实可能不喜欢他，但不能否定他，因为在未来的茫茫人海中，放出异彩的，往往不是书呆子，而是这种具有风骨与胆识的人。

所以只要你能心存恭敬，以学生应有的礼貌，举出自己坚信的道理，就算这一科"死当"，我也为你竖起大拇指，并希望你由愤懑不平中激发力量，未来在这一科有出色的成就。相反，如果因为老师不讲理，就使你意兴阑珊，放弃努力，你只好成为一个真正的失败者。

露出开朗的笑容！或许那老师明天也会对你这个不平凡的学生笑的。

作者大学一年级，在教室后面见到的巨幅国画，为画家林崇汉的作品。

# 原则之争

我老爸这篇文章应该是为台湾地区的读者写的。我记得刚回来时，发现台湾地区与美国存有很大的文化差异。美国人会主动争取权益，可是台湾人常不会，也许是怕浪费时间、怕麻烦，或怕因为争论而惹祸上身。

我最近在纽约收到法院寄来的通知，因为我使用的美国信用卡公司有一项隐藏的费用，造成消费者不满而告上法院。上诉人愿意花很多时间与精力为所有的信用卡会员争取权益，即使最后只是几块美金。但是争的人说："It's a matter of principle."（这是原则之争。）我相当认同这样的态度。

在美国社会，你要据理力争。我老爸在我小时候常教导我要争取自己的权益，甚至会在他跟对方理论时，叫我站在一边看。这种以前让我脸红的事，现在显得很有意义。更重要的是，其实我们要争取的是大原则，而非个人权益。

英国政治哲学家埃德蒙·伯克（Edmund Burke, 1729—1797）有句名言："邪恶胜利的唯一关键，就是当好人袖手旁观的时候。"道德很重要，但是有道德而没勇气，道德常是没用的。

# 当头棒喝

每年寒假，美国大学的入学组，常为一种转学生烦恼，因为那些孩子可能有特优的高中成绩，和最差的大一上学期分数。

你的母亲对我说，最近你常在车上以很坏的态度抱怨自己要到远处上学。她说若不是因为在开车，一定要赏你两记耳光。

你的祖母，最近也常对我表示，早上叫你起床，是件很难的事，因为总要喊四五次，你才能起得来。

我当时心想：如果你母亲在你抱怨时，立刻把车停在路边，赶你下去，由你决定回家还是上学，然后自己想办法的话，只要一次，你就再也不会在车上抱怨。因为你由处罚中知道，能有母亲开车送你到地铁，已经是很幸运的事。

至于你祖母，如果有一天，她只叫你一回，便不再催，妈妈的车子更不多等，使你迟到几次，你也会立刻改正那种屡催不起的毛病。

我几乎可以想象，当你站在高速公路旁，或自己突然从梦中惊醒，发现四顾无援时，会有多么慌乱。但我也相信，这种经验必使你终生难忘。

问题是，她们都不忍心这样做。也因此，造成你得不到教训，而不知改正；得不到棒喝，而不能顿悟。

每年在开学之后两个礼拜，理当已经没有人注册入学，却可能是美国大学入学组很忙的时刻。因为他们年年发现，这时会有许多原来怀着梦想，离开家门，到远方念书的学生，一把鼻涕一把眼泪地跑回家，再于父母的陪同下，到附近的学校申请紧急入学。原因很简单——他们发现离开家的日子不好过。

每年寒假，美国大学的入学组，常为一种转学生烦恼，因为那些孩子可能有特优的高中成绩和最差的大一上学期分数。原因也很简单——因为他们在家里被逼惯了，每天一进家门，父母先问有多少功课，然后便一样一样盯着做。他们的时间，理当由自己安排，却成为父母的事。有一天到外埠念书，没人逼，就事事失了方寸，成绩一落千丈。

我常想：今天这些孩子在父母的呵护下，进入附近的学校就读，固然又会被导上轨道，可是当他毕业之后，怎么办？也正因此，我们可以讲：学校里成绩好的学生，除非他是完全自动自发的，否则没有人能保证，他到社会上，还能站在前面。

因此，我今天作了个决定，尽量不问你学校的进度，不叮嘱你去做功课，不催你去弹琴，也不叫你起床。我也越发坚定了一个信念：让你到曼哈顿去上学，离家远一点，是正确的选择。

父母不能帮你走未来的路！

## 身为家长的抉择

虽然我妈妈不曾把我从车上踢下去，但如果她真这么做，我也不会怪她。

以后我教导自己的小孩，应该也会用这种态度，也就是说："你自己不负责任，我不会帮你擦屁股。"但这种教育方式的难处在于，家长虽然很想放手让小孩从错误中学习，却又怕小孩会吃亏。这是很大的矛盾。

在督促小朋友做功课这件事上，我倒觉得家长不能完全放手。因为小孩不懂得远程目标的重要性，"未来的成功"也只是个抽象的概念，这时候家长得引导。

这当中也蕴藏了一些教育上的文化差异。一般而言，美国家长较不会过问功课，看重的反而是小孩有无参加球队、人格发展是否健全、社交礼仪周不周到。又像我有个爱尔兰裔的朋友，提到他小时候跟其他小朋友发生争执，几乎要打架了，他爸爸知道后说："如果你不出去打，就不是我儿子。"

这位父亲的观念是："如果你有理，就要力争；若对方不讲理，你就去打。"这或许不是多半中国父母的观念，但其实也并不算错，文化差异造成不同的教养方式与观念，很值得思考。

# 两极的印象

研究所的一个教授，曾经在课堂上说：『秦始皇是坏人！』引起许多研究生的反感。因为那是研究所，不是幼稚园……

两个同在纽约做过短暂停留的朋友，提到他们的观感，一个人说纽约是世界上最浪漫的地方，他希望能有机会长住些时日，另一个却说纽约是人间地狱，要他多待一天也不愿意。

为什么他们对纽约有这么不同的感觉呢?

喜欢纽约的说，他下飞机之后，朋友先带他到皇后区的自宅歇脚，并叫计程车去大都会美术馆 (Metropolian Museum of Art)。在美术馆对面用过餐，然后沿着中央公园走到繁华的第五街，看了川普大厦 (Trump Tower)、IBM 的竹林庭园，转过洛克菲勒中心 (Rockefeller Center) 的溜冰场，再登上帝国大厦 (Empire State Building) 的顶楼，欣赏曼哈顿的夜景，而后叫车回家。

痛恨纽约的则说，他下飞机之后，朋友叫计程车送他去四十二街附近的一家旅馆，再带他由中央车站乘地铁到自然历史博物馆 (American Museum of Natural History)，而后坐地铁到下城吃饭，再去当时还存在的世界贸易大楼 (World Trade Center) 顶层欣赏曼哈顿夜景，又去时代广场逛了成人商店，而后送他回旅馆。

现在你应该知道，他们对纽约的观感为什么有那么大的差异了! 虽然接待的朋友都花了不少钱，也都带他们逛了世界最著名的博物馆和最高的建筑。但是前者住在安宁的住宅区，看到的是幽静的中央公园、豪华的商店、富丽的建筑和干净的市容。后者却见到肮脏的地铁、杂乱的下城、藏污纳垢的时代广场，且领教了旅馆附近的嘈杂。

问题是，若非再有机会到纽约，这种观感就可能留在他们心中一辈子。由于是他们亲眼所见、亲身所感，所以每当他们提到纽约，那好极了与坏极了的评语，必是斩钉截铁的。

我们不是常听人斩钉截铁地说"某人是好人"或"某人坏透了"一类的话吗？他们也是亲眼所见、亲身所感，但是如果以纽约的例子来想，你认为他们说得对不对呢？

请不要觉得我是小题大做。因为犯这种以偏概全毛病的人真是太多了，我们甚至可以讲每个人都会这样，甚至不经过亲自观察，就以推想或得来的小道消息作评断。

这样做，受损的是谁呢？

是那印象偏差的，也是那被偏差了印象的。因为前者很可能一辈子不会再想去接触、去了解，他失去了访问一个美丽的地方和结交一位好朋友的机会。后者则可能被永久误解，连申辩的机会都没有，且以讹传讹地遭到更大的伤害。

这世上有什么是十全十美的呢？愈干净的城市，它排污水的系统可能愈庞大；愈见不到垃圾的地方，愈可能有一个堆积成山的垃圾场。连人体都有动脉与静脉，谁能因为觉得那"青筋"看来讨厌而将静脉切除呢？

所以，我们不论看人、看事，甚至听别人论断事情，都要有客观审度的态度。古人说"尽信书，不如无书"，我们也可以讲"尽信人，则无己"，如果别人说的一切，我们都相信，自己的观察力不是白费了吗？

　　记得我在研究所的一个教授，曾经在课堂上说："秦始皇是坏人！"引起许多研究生的反感。因为那是研究所，不是幼稚园，研究的是客观的史实，而非主观的评断。当教授未举史实，而妄下评语，说"秦始皇是坏人"这句话的时候，除了显示他的强烈主观，也漠视了学生独立思考的能力。

　　由于听你十分主观地批评同学，我才说了这么一大番道理。因为它关系你的一生，也关系你一生接触到的人与事！

## 以一个客观的角度看世界

这篇文章隐隐透露了某种时代性。世界贸易大楼已经不存在了，四十二街也变得非常干净，如果从中央车站乘地铁到自然历史博物馆，会是一次非常美好的体验。

然而我对这篇文章也是深有感触的。"以客观的角度看世界。"这是我爸爸从小灌输给我的观念，影响我很深，并觉得这已变成自己的长处之一。

在哈佛念社会心理学时，学到的第一个概念就是我们都生活在一种错觉里，对彼此动机的解读经常是错误的。我们往往对每个人、每件事都抱着主观立场，这在我们与别人相处时，会导致复杂的因果关系。若我们将自身、他人、环境等种种因素综合考虑，会发现其实所有事物都具备多种方面，也都有不同的诠释角度。

# 空手道

每个男孩都会梦想成为除暴安良的侠客，我也不例外。

我曾经一次劈裂成堆的灰瓦，一巴掌打断学校的桌角，也曾一次劈断两块新烧的红砖。

但是……

今天下午我们在收拾完院子之后，你捡了两块瓦片来，要求我以空手道的模式劈断，而当我轻易做到之后，你眼睛里闪着异样的光彩，一再追问我该怎么学，以及我从什么时候开始练。

我想每个男孩子到了十三四岁，都会开始有尚武精神，我也不例外，常看武侠小说，梦想上山拜师习艺，成为除暴安良的侠客。羡慕那书中描述的剑眉星目、齿白唇红、鼻若悬胆，宛如玉树临风的青年高手，也便拿些棍棒挥舞，更试着劈砖，甚至买《少林秘笈》《易筋经》，依样比画。

劈砖应该是我练最久的了，主要的原因是可以炫耀。实际两年下来，也真有了一点成绩。我曾经一次劈裂成堆的灰瓦，一巴掌打断学校的桌角，也曾一次劈断两块新烧的红砖。但是有一回同学拿了拆老房子剩下的红砖，我却把手劈得通红，也伤不了砖块分毫。

你要知道，当我们空手劈东西的时候，如果东西应声而断，手上的力量完全出去了，自己便毫无损伤。相反，如果东西不断，那使出的力量，便完全弹了回来。用的力量愈大，伤害愈强。

记得高一的时候，同学常拿些木条、砖块来请我露一手。为了面子，我不得不硬着头皮，对付那自己没有把握的东西，而在回家之后，彻夜忍受手掌的疼痛，且在次日装作若无其事的样子。

渐渐我发觉，作画时有手抖的现象，甚至连画山水当中的小东西，都有了问题。我更渐渐想通，只有一只右手练成铁砂掌，真碰到状况，一心想对手把身子乖乖送过来让我对准了劈，不但不可能如愿，只怕自己会先吃亏。这种偏在一处的武功，实际是不值得仗恃的，也便停止了练习。

所以，当你今天问我该怎么练时，我再三强调，除非你能找到真有功夫的好老师，做整体的锻炼，如果只是像我当年拿肉掌劈砖头，练得几分硬功夫，反落得手抖，倒不如不练。

当然，在劈砖中，我也领悟了一些事情，那就是：

当我心里没把握时，生怕使出的力气又弹回来，便愈是劈不断。

当我一心表现，却再三无功而退时，便容易心浮气躁，斗血气之勇，到头来，使自己受到更大的伤害。

我不希望你学劈砖，却盼望你记住这两段话！

## 自我的纪律

许多小孩崇拜武功，其实都是希望建立自信，而不是为了四方除害或拯救世界。我想象自己以后有了儿子，也会鼓励他去练习空手道之类的武术，因为除了能够学到防身术，还可以学到更重要的"自律"。

在美国校园里，常会有些受欺侮的孩子，想通过练武以获得自信。但如果直接拿把枪，以极端的暴力去耀武扬威，例如日前弗吉尼亚理工学院发生的憾事，就太糟了！

此外，文末的几句话也让我受益良多，并且不时在日常生活中真切体验。我们在做一件事时，常是一股"气"在运行。平时如果把自己调整到恒常稳定的状况，遇事时全神贯注，把气势集中，便会力道十足，且不会因为犹豫而受伤。

## 做砚与做人

从溪流里捡回雕砚台的石头之后，先要放在烈日下曝晒！用砚石磨刀，再以刀雕砚台！而且不管雕什么砚台，都得从底开始修起！

今年寒假回台湾时，我去二水拜访了雕砚台的师傅，虽没买下多少砚台，却有了不少感悟。

雕砚师傅家的门口，堆了许多砚石，都是他从溪流里涉水挑选回来的。那些石块，表面看是灰色的，很难让人相信，居然能够刻出紫红、暗绿和深黑色的砚台。

师傅说，石头运回来，一定先要曝晒，因为许多石头在溪流里漂亮，却有难以觉察的裂缝，只有经过不断的日晒雨淋，才能显现，甚至自己就会崩裂。

师傅又说，未经琢磨的石头，因为表面粗糙，不容易看出色彩和纹理，淋上水之后，比较会显现，但是水一干，又不见了。必须切磨打光之后，才能完全且持久地呈现。他还说，其实这世上的每一块石头都很美，即使不适合做砚台，也各有特色，耐人赏玩。

我特别要求他，让我自己试着刻一方砚。师傅掏出一把平头的凿刀，又递给我一只锤子。我问如果这刀锋钝了怎么办，他说就用砚石来磨，因为好的砚石，质细而坚，也是最好的磨刀石。

我小心地由磨墨的砚面雕起。师傅赶紧纠正：不管雕什么砚台，都得先修底。底不平，上面不稳，很难雕得好。

回程的路上我一直想，砚石何尝不像人，无论表面怎么拙陋，经过琢磨，都会显现美丽的纹理。当然一方好砚，必须用石质细腻、触感润泽，又坚实耐磨的石头制作。那石块必须经过严格的考验，如同文质彬彬，外表敦和而心中耿介的君子，经过心志与肌肤的劳苦之后，才能承担大任。

　　我也想，在工作中锻炼，正如同在雕砚时磨砺。好的工作，就像好的砚石，不但成就了工作，也磨炼了工作者。

　　当然，最重要的，是雕砚先修底。多么细致的花纹与藻饰，都得由那基础的地方开始。

　　虽然修底的工作是最枯燥的！

## 自我充实的过程

十一二岁时，我常像个小书童一样，帮老爸磨墨、煮咖啡，他还说我煮的咖啡最好喝。老爸爱玩石头，旅行时常常沿途注意石头，所以他从砚台看到做人的道理，我一点也不意外。

我认为自己现在正是文中所提到的"打底阶段"。我的成长过程向来顺遂，又很早就受到瞩目，获得很多肯定。但这些肯定让我有些心虚，因为许多事情对我而言都是日常生活的一部分，不曾作过更大的努力，直到我走上音乐这条路。虽然小时候家人会逼我弹琴，但我现在从事的工作，都是靠自修。

专业要靠磨炼跟经验的累积。人生是不断自我充实与实践。今天，我因为创作与实践，而更能肯定自己。

# 聆听的学问

有位舞台剧演员，独白到舞台边，突然听见下面传来嗑瓜子的声音，虽然只有一声，他却气得差点儿从台上跳下去，掐住那人的喉咙。

在人们聊天的时候，经常会出现这么一个现象——

其中一人正兴高采烈地述说，却发现大家突然交头接耳，岔到别的话题，原来的听众似乎一下子全转向了。

正当他尴尬得不知如何是好的时候，如果你能做他唯一的忠实听众，甚至大声地追问："继续说啊！下面的事情怎么发展？"他一定仿佛溺水时突然抓到援手般，眉头一扬，又恢复了精神，续完他的故事。

每个人都可能碰到过这样的场面，都可能是那个故事说到一半，不知如何是好的人，也或许是那及时为人脱困的朋友，更可能是另起炉灶，岔开他人话题，换成自己发挥的人。

但是我相信，最令你感念的，应该是那追问你"继续说啊！下面事情怎么发展？"的朋友，最让你咬牙切齿的，则是泼你半盆冷水，大家突然转变话题的场面。

说话时，使听众注意力集中，是一门学问。

听话时，集中注意力于说话者，更是一门学问。

因为前者是才能，后者是德行。

这种德行，可能包含尊重、体谅与忍耐，并不是人人都能做到的。

当我们听演讲或音乐会时，知道要准时入场，中途不能讲话，也不该离座，因为这是对台上人的尊重。

如果这台上人的演出很差，你却能维持风度听下去，不是一种忍耐吗？

问题是，忍耐对你来讲只是一时的，如果你半途离场，对台上人的伤害，却可能是永远的。

有位舞台剧的演员对我说，他一辈子也不会忘记有一回在戏中独白到舞台边，突然听见下面传来嗑瓜子的声音，虽然只有一声，他却气得差点儿从台上跳下去，掐住那个人的喉咙。

他为什么那样气？

因为他觉得自己没有被尊重，那嗑瓜子的一声响，伤了他的自尊心，而这种伤害常是永远的。

至于我说聆听人讲话，也是一种体谅，就更值得你深思了。因为"事不关己，不关心"，你会发现许多在述说者心中最了不得的事，在外人耳中，却是极无聊的。

譬如遭遇情感问题的人，谈她少收到几封信，白打了几通电话；得意的父母，说他的孩子又考了多少第一，得了几个甲上；沉迷于宠物的人谈他的猫狗如何通灵懂事。如果你没有体谅，知道情人心、父母心，乃至宠物心，再加上忍耐与尊重，是极可能无法长久听下去的。

我有一位朋友，曾在长途车上，以几个钟头说他研究制作纸花的心得，仿佛他已经是世界上最伟大的纸花艺术家，并计划如何打开全球市场。

隔了几个月，他又改变话题，说他得到一种祖传秘方，将可以大量生产，且会得到诺贝尔奖。事后同行的人怪我，为什么一直听下去，而且有唱有和的，明明知道他在做梦，为什么不拆穿，又何苦做他的唯一听众。

我说，因为这是他再三遭遇挫折后，唯一做梦的机会。有些人的梦可以早早打断，有些人做梦的权利，却不是我们应该去剥夺的。

这种听话的忍耐力，是因为我了解他的苦，也可以说是一种体谅。

从以上这些例子，你应该知道，聆听人讲话，是一门多大的学问！你要学着去尊重、去容忍、去谅解，必能因此获得对方衷心的感念。

## 社交的秘诀

当有人在说话中途被打断，那个说出"请继续啊！"的人，常令人感激。

我自己也有很多类似的经验，像我在哈佛研究所念书时担任助教，与学生讨论时就很注意这点，让大家都有同等的发言机会。哈佛学生大多很有主见，因此常有学生在说话中途被他人打断，这时我会坚持让前面那人说完，或者想办法把话题接回去。教授和学生都因此很喜欢我。

平时我也会尽量当一名好听众，而且老实说，好的聆听者一定也是好的约会对象。常会听到一些女性朋友抱怨，很难遇到知心的约会对象，因为大部分男生都忙于卖弄自己。如果有个人愿意聆听，往往最能拉近关系。

# 远行的朋友

◆

失意人前，勿谈得意事；
得意人前，勿谈失意事。
失意时交的朋友，得意时常容易失去；
得意时得罪的朋友，失意时也难挽回。

今天当你跟亨利出去玩的时候，我特意把你叫进来，叮嘱你不要对他说，我们准备买新房子的事。

你似乎不太苟同地看看我，心不甘、情不愿地点头出去了。

不错！你可能认为我有一点假，既然是真实的事情，为什么不能说，何况亨利又是你那么要好的朋友。

但是你也知道，亨利跟他的父母就要被调往别的国家，对于这一块已经生活了十年的土地，他内心有着多少依恋、无奈与失落，他可能在家对着心情不定的父母说想留下，却换来斥责。他的父母何尝愿意走，心中又有多少矛盾？

况且当我们搬新家的时候，他们已经离开了，那么你对他说又有什么意义呢？表示你的父母有办法？表示你会生活得更体面？抑或表示你比他更得意？

他是你最要好的朋友，你能搬到更好的房子，他应该为你高兴，但是相反，他要到远方去，你是不是也该分担他的怅惘？

此刻你对一个将离去的朋友，说你不但能在美国安居，而且能够更上层楼，对你和他，都没什么好处，只有更增加彼此的距离。

所以，向他说一些你对他前去国家的向往，说我们将去那里看他们，说希望他每年回来玩玩，届时可以住在我们家。并告诉他，你们可以经常通信，并交换资讯，使他能够面对新环境，有更多的憧憬与勇气。

这些，才是你应该对朋友说的。

失意人前，勿谈得意事。因为那只可能加重对方的落寞。所以即使万事顺心，也要故意说些辛苦处给朋友听。

得意人前，勿谈失意事。因为得意人常不能体谅失意者的痛苦。所以即使有许多不如意，也要振作精神。

失意时交的朋友，得意时常会失去，因为他觉得你高升了，不再是他的一伙，他不愿意高攀，也高攀不上。你无心的一言一行，都可能引起他自卑的敏感。

得意时得罪的朋友，失意时也难挽回。因为他觉得你昔日气焰的消失，不是因为你变得谦和，而是因为走投无路，才回头攀老交情。昔日你不认他，他今天也不认你！

在未来的岁月，随着你的成长，将会逐渐了解我这番话的道理。

## 失意人前勿谈得意事

"失意人前勿谈得意事"的概念，蕴藏了老祖宗的深层智慧。

我有个很得意的朋友最近也遭遇了类似的情形。他在参加活动时碰到一位失意的朋友，说有信用卡的麻烦，我这朋友认识负责的经理，便自告奋勇地帮忙处理。岂料事后，那失意朋友竟传了一条简讯给他，说："你的强势让我愈来愈无法靠近你。"

失意人往往有自卑式的敏感。我老爸说得意人常无法体谅失意人的痛苦。但如果反向思考，得意人如虹的气势，遇上了失意人，也会像乌云，有碍气势。

这篇文章让我愈来愈了解东方社会。西方人常认为东方人说话时拐弯抹角，不表现真实情感，甚至觉得这是一种缺陷。他们如果读读这篇文章，应该有所领悟。

# 冤枉

在地铁车厢里，只为了换位子的时间不对，

就被打青了脸，甚至有失明之虞。

在地铁车站里，只为了撞人一下未说抱歉，

就被打裂嘴角，急诊缝了四针。

我有一个朋友，昨天在地铁的车厢里，被人打青了脸，甚至有视网膜剥离的危险，你知道是为什么吗？

当时他看到车厢另一端，有个靠窗的座位，于是移过去，才坐下，就被尾随的一个黑人壮汉狠狠地揍了两拳。

原因是在他换位子的前一刻，正好那个黑人上车，并坐在他的身边。他完全没注意到这件事，却引起黑人的误会，以为他有种族歧视，不愿跟黑人同坐而换位子。

那黑人是因为自卑而敏感，又因为敏感而愤怒。我的那个朋友，则毫不知情地遭到了殴打。

你的小姨夫，不也如此吗？他来纽约第一次乘地铁，居然还没上车，在票亭的前面，就被人一拳打裂嘴角，送急诊缝了四针。

只为了他的手提箱撞到对方，忘了说对不起，且以斜斜的目光，看了对方一眼。其实他偷看对方，是想查看对方被撞到的回应，生怕对方不高兴，岂知对方反而认为他有歧视和瞧不起的意味，好像说："怎么样？撞你一下又如何？"于是一拳挥了过来。

你说我的朋友和你的姨夫是不是很冤枉呢？

答案当然是肯定的。但在这个人际关系复杂、环境压力沉重的社会，因为看一眼而挨刀子，不小心说错一句话而结深仇的事真是太多了！

所以身为现代人，就好比开车，你除了自己守规矩，还得注意别人是否不守规；除了照自己认为正确的方向去做，还得留意是否会让别人多心。你必须保持高度的敏感，且常常设想别人的感觉，才可能过得愉快。

是的！这样已经不够愉快，但比起那更不愉快的遭遇，显然要愉快多了！

人愈多，愈挤，手脚愈不灵活，谁能说不是呢？

## 尊重与冷漠

在台湾，不时会看到这类社会新闻：两群年轻人在 KTV 错身而过，只为了互看一眼，就大打出手。相较之下，在纽约那样包容多元族群与文化的地方，每个人都既能自我防备，又能尊重他人。纽约客给人的印象常是冷漠的，但他们对人有基本的尊重。在尖峰时刻的地铁里，纽约客不会像许多台湾人一样不断推挤，而会不断地说"Excuse me"。如果真有人无理地推挤，马上会有人大声喝止。

## 非礼勿听，非礼勿言

某人暂住朋友家，朋友的妻子趁丈夫不在时，对某人示好。某人峻拒了，但朋友回家后非但未责怪妻子，反而将某人踢了出去……

今天你问我："讲话直，有没有错？"

我当时告诉你没错，但是几经思考之后，我要纠正自己的说法为："如果直言对事情有帮助，可以直言，否则不如不说。"

话虽然讲得简单，但即使我自己，在几年前也是办不到的，因为把事情压在心里不说，真会把人憋死！

记得有一回我用电话叫计程车，并站在门口等，眼看那计程车从我面前驶过，他居然把地址弄错，糊涂到找不到我所讲的地方，而往前直冲，完全没有注意到我挥舞的手势。

等了足足有十几分钟，才见他从另一头驶回。

上车之后，我抱怨地说："为什么这么久才来，不是在电话里说好五分钟就到吗？"

那司机居然回答："是啊，只怪路上交通太挤了！"

我当时正在气头上，毫不考虑地说："算了吧！我看到你从我面前驶过，你是'没找到'，不是'交通挤'！"

那司机没有再说话，我却一直记得他通红的耳根和下车时带有恨意的目光。为什么？因为我当面拆穿了他的谎言。问题是，这直言对事情有什么帮助？只怕反而伤了情、结了怨。

讲话的技巧何止于此！甚至当别人要直言时，我们也应该看情况而有所处置。记得十几年前的一个场合，有位朋友对我批评某人，偏偏某人是我的好朋友，而批评的人事先不知道，在他将我的好朋友说得一无是处之后，才有旁边的人提醒他，骂的正是我的挚友。

当场那骂人的，和我自己都尴尬极了！尤其糟糕的是，他猜想我必会告诉自己的老友，竟先去找我的好朋友，说我与他不和，只怕会搬弄是非。

现在让我们来检讨一下当时的状况，是谁不对。

大家都没有错！但是如果在他刚有意批评时，我就能察觉，而及时把话岔开，或是说："唉！各有长短，咱们不谈别人吧！"他自然会及时把话收住。

退一步想，他旁边的人就算不及时提醒、阻止，也犯不着当面拆穿，这样不是最少也可以免得当场尴尬吗？

我曾经听过这么一件事：

某人暂住朋友家，朋友的妻子趁丈夫不在时，对某人示好，起初只是微露神色，在言语上作些试探，看某人没有什么拒绝的样子，就渐渐放浪形骸，这时某人才起而峻拒，甚至说要告诉她的丈夫。

岂知那女人的丈夫回到家，不但没有责怪自己的老婆，反而狠狠把某人踢了出去，而且拒听任何解释。

原来那女人怕某人告状，竟先去告诉丈夫，说某人有非礼的举动。

你说，某人错在哪里？错在他应该在事情没有显明之前，先暗示自己的正派，甚至借故避出去，而不应该任那女人表白，失去挽回的机会。

我还听过一个故事：

某人夜宿旅店，在床上听见隔壁的人商谈谋反的事，商谈者讲到一半，突然警觉隔墙有耳，提刀冲过去，所幸床上的人装作酣睡而口沫横流的样子，才逃得杀身之祸。

更有一个老兵对我说，时局乱的时候，最要小心的是你曾经得罪和知晓他秘密的人，因为当那人拿到武器，多杀一个和少杀一个没什么不同，很可能因为你知道他的秘密，而对你下手。

由此可知，我们非但不该毫无城府地讲无济于事的话，而且应该避免去听可能引起纠纷的言语。孔子说："成事不说，遂事不谏，既往不咎。"又讲，"非礼勿听，非礼勿视，非礼勿言。"这三个"不"和三个"勿"的学问，真是太大了！

# 台阶

这篇是我老爸在成长过程中习得的道理，听说我老爸年轻时人缘不怎么样，因为他的行事作风锐利，经常不给人台阶。但年纪愈大，他处世态度愈柔和。

先前我们去大陆，碰到兜售假古董的商人，他一定当场揭穿。但现在他比较收敛含蓄了，碰到小贩向他推销假货，他还会说："嗯，好东西、好东西！"（接着便转头小声对我说："仿得真好。"）

给已经很尴尬的对方台阶下，知道什么时候不说，或什么时候不问，很需要一点智慧。

这也让我想起曾在美国看过的一个节目，记者访问在豪门工作，穿着燕尾服的男管家，若女主人问到男主人是否偷情，该如何回答。管家说："如果遇到这状况，我会说：'这真是个难答的问题。'"因为他既不能诚实又无法说谎。而当他这样回答时，希望女主人也就此了解他的尴尬，别再问下去。

# 进路与退路

◆

对已知的环境，作进一步想。

对未知的环境，作退一步想。

前进固然可喜，后退也未尝可悲。

　　你说想去征服高山，但当我问你登山者该带些什么东西时，你却答不上来。

　　现在让我告诉你吧！如果是攀登路径不熟的高山，即使原定一日往返，除了必备的指南针，你的行囊中也应该包括一把小刀、一条绳索、一盒用塑胶袋包好的火柴、一点盐巴、一块折起来不大的透明塑胶布或雨衣，和一只哨子。

　　这些东西多半不是为你的进路准备，而是为你的退路着想。不论登山的旅途，还是人生的旅途，"有退路"都是"寻进路"的必要条件。

　　于是那把小刀，在前进时可以帮助你切割猎物、削竹为箭、砍木为叉；在你被毒蛇咬伤时，更可以用来将伤口切开，以吸出毒血。

　　那条绳索，可以在前进时帮助攀爬；在山友遇险时，用来营救；在编织担架时，用来捆绑。

　　那盒火柴，在你前进时，可以用来烹食；在你遇难时，可以让你点起营火——熬过高山上寒冷的夜晚，并作为求救的信号。

　　那块透明的塑胶布或雨衣，在你前进时，可以用来防雨；当你困阻在深山时，可以使你减少地面或环境中潮冷的侵袭，甚至在缺水时，用来收集地面蒸发的水汽，使你免于干渴。

　　那块盐巴，可以在你前进时用来烹调鲜美的食物；在你受困时，用来消毒和补充体力，甚至帮助你吞下平时绝对难以接受的野生食物。

　　至于那只哨子，在你前进时，固然可以用来招呼队友，作为集合的信号；在你落难而饥寒交迫，喊不出声音时，更可能因为有这只哨子，隔几分钟吹一下，使搜救的人员找到你。

如此说来，哪一样东西可以少呢？它们占的空间不大，却是你行前不能疏忽，落难时可能保命的。

我过去曾多次对你说：旅游时，如果是旧地重游，不妨在既有的大道之外，再去寻访一些小路，发掘新的风景。相反，如果是到陌生的地方，则应该记住来时的道路，以便遇到困阻时能够脱身。

对已知的环境，作进一步想；对未知的环境，作退一步想。在人生的旅途上，前进固然可喜，后退也未尝可悲，最重要的是——

在前进时要知道自制，免得只能进而不能退；后退时则要知道自保，使得退却重整之后，能够再向前行！

## 深谋远虑

会想到退路，常是因为吃过苦头而得到教训。我老爸这些问题如果拿去问童子军，必定能得到不错的答案，但是拿来问我这个从未登过山的小孩，就完了。

我老爸是那种会预先做好各种准备的人。多年来，他可以持续创作，同时经营出版公司，都是由于他思虑缜密、谋划完备。又如旅行，如能在行前做功课，例如对旅馆环境、交通状况、餐馆推荐等细节都有大致的概念，玩起来会更尽兴而充实。也往往唯有在做好准备时，才有条件进一步探险。

# 真假世界

◆

盆景、小说、戏剧、电脑游戏，乃至迷幻药带给我们的，都不是真实的世界，它们很可能反映了真实世界的东西，却毕竟不等于真实。

今天在我批评你玩太多电脑游戏的时候，你不服气地说："知道吗？这是很复杂的游戏，里面有一整个宇宙呢！"

当时我没多说，只是现在要问你：你游戏中的那个宇宙有多大？它只是在一个电脑磁碟中的宇宙，一个别人创造的宇宙。

我还可以告诉你，据吃过迷幻药的人说："服药之后，世界变得五光十色，可以出现许多异象，感觉自己仿佛飘浮了起来。"那么，是不是他们也就拥有了另一个多彩多姿的宇宙了呢？

在这个世界上，确实还有许多不同的小世界。譬如盆景，当你面对它，让自己的想象在其中徜徉，那小小的石块、苔藓和迷你的亭台楼阁，就像是另一片真实的山水。

又譬如小说、戏剧，当你沉迷其中，自己就成了剧中人，随着他们生活、哭笑，那也便是另外一个想象的世界。

问题是，这盆景、小说、戏剧、电脑游戏，乃至迷幻药带给我们的，都不是真实的世界，它们很可能反映了真实世界的东西，却毕竟不等于真实。所以当你以它们为适当的消遣（不包括毒品），偶尔沉醉其间，使精神获得放松或驰骋自己的幻想时固然可以，如果错把那个由别人构筑的"假世界"，当作自己的"真世界"，就大错特错了！

好比曾经有不少吸食迷幻药的人，想象自己能飞，而真从楼顶向下跳一样，那结果是必然的——非死即伤。因为他飞的想象是在假世界中，而跳的行为却发生在真实的世界里。

　　更普遍的例子，是许多人举杯浇愁，希望在酒醉时能够浑然忘忧，飘飘然仿佛腾云驾雾一般。问题是，宿醉之后可能头痛，而头痛后，他还得面对真实的人生。他的困苦可曾因为一醉而消失呢？如果心想可以再醉几次，不断进入那酒后麻醉的世界，他便可能在真实的世界中永远站不起来。

　　所以我必须警告你，不可将假世界与真世界混为一谈，更不可将虚幻的价值观，移到现实生活中来！

## 在虚拟世界里暂歇

在网络如此发达的时代，真实世界与虚拟世界的界限愈来愈模糊。近年来有一个叫《Second Life》的网络游戏，在 3D 界面城市里，玩家可以拥有一个化身，过起另外一个人的生活。说它是游戏不完全正确，因为它没有特定的目标，没有怪兽要杀也没有宝藏要寻。每个玩家只是在虚拟世界里过着一般生活，认识别人，买卖东西，存钱买虚拟房屋、虚拟汽车，根本与实际的世界没两样，但《Second Life》却有百万会员加入。

我觉得《Second Life》会那么受欢迎，正因为我们都偶尔需要逃离现实。

就像进电影院，把自己关在黑盒子里，是为了短暂忘记自己、忘记世界。有些较严格的家长，会在考试期间完全禁止小孩看电视、打电子游戏等娱乐活动，但我觉得这应该因人而异。一直关在房间里啃书本，效率常会愈来愈差。短暂的放松与逃脱，反而常有助于提升效率。

# 真实的艺术

◆

他住在大统舱式的老屋里，搜藏各种古旧的机器，写豪放不羁的打油诗，还用街上捡到的废物，拼造了照相机、洗衣机和『电椅』。他似乎生活在想象的世界，却有着最真实的生活！

在纽约苏荷区有位兼修古董的中国艺术家，某日把一个由好几块碎片复原的瓷瓶送回古董店，出门时不小心绊了一跤，将那瓶子又摔成了十几片，他不慌不忙地将碎片连渣都不漏地捡起来，照样修理得毫无破绽地送回古董店。

这位艺术家就是夏阳。

今天下午，我带你到苏荷区拜访夏阳，相信你一定被他那大统舱式的老屋、五花八门的收藏、千奇百怪的发明和豪放不羁的打油诗所吸引。

我们看到夏阳如何用运货的推车，改装成上下电动的画椅；把电话、收音机、录音机、幻灯机，乃至控制画架升降的开关全部装在上面，使他能够坐在椅子上呼风唤雨。

我们也看到夏阳如何用木板和纸盒涂上黑墨，制成观景式的照相机，拍出效果绝佳的照片，更看到他以杠杆和帮浦原理制成的简易洗衣机。而那些东西的材料，居然多半是街上捡来的废弃物。无怪走出夏阳的家，你笑说好像进了迪士尼乐园"明日世界"（Epcot Center）里的想象世界，简直太奇妙了！问题是，那是一个想象的世界吗？

实在说，它比什么世界都真实。

那是一位坚持理想的艺术家，与现实环境奋斗的世界。那里的一桌一椅，都是攀爬艺术顶峰者，留下的血汗足迹。

不知你有没有注意到，他的鱼缸里，养的是一块钱一打，原本用来钓大鱼的小鱼。虽然那些鱼一点也不华丽，但在艺术家的眼中，却能从平凡中见到真趣。

你有没有注意到他的炉子，是可以进博物馆的老古董，可是他为我们烧水沏出来的茶，却是上好的乌龙。

在那看似简陋之中，他有着最精致的一面。对比他，这世上许多豪富人家，不是在数十万一条的红龙和数千元一两的茗茶间，却有着最粗俗的精神生活吗？

所以我说，夏阳在他破旧的小屋中，呈现给我们一个最真实而感性的世界。我们何尝不能说，他与凡·高、高更的世界一样伟大。

是的，在人类的历史上，真正享有不朽名声的艺术家是极少数的，却有着无数有理想、有抱负，甚至宁死不屈的艺术家，像是战场上捐躯的无名英雄一般，执著前进。

记得吗？当我临走时，问夏阳在纽约二十年的岁月，觉得如何，有没有什么遗憾。

他说："很好！"

当我问他的人生哲学时，他笑答："题目太大了！只觉得我们要为中国做的，实在太多！"

让我们咀嚼他的语言，并用他那真实的生活，来检讨一下自己，扪心自问：我们有没有生活得比他更真？

## 生活的艺术

以前纽约的苏荷区，都是老旧仓库改建的房子，因为租金便宜，空间又大，真是艺术家的世界。但现在苏荷区在纽约的房价已是数一数二，艺术家大都被逼到布鲁克林或新泽西。

夏阳先生跟我老爸可说是两个极端。我爸爸总是万事做足计划，生活有条不紊，家里永远收拾得干净妥当。但夏阳先生仿佛身在一个无秩序的世界，在纷乱中找寻灵感。

那时我在曼哈顿上学，初步接触杂乱中的美，那与郊区生活的悠然是截然不同的。我甚至觉得唯有这样的情调，才称得上是真正的艺术家生活。我还因此纳闷老爸跟这样的人怎么会是好朋友。但我后来发现，老爸很欣赏夏阳先生的生活态度，他甚至有点羡慕。大概因为他那时非常忙碌，内心渴望无羁的生活吧！

坐在"电椅"上的艺术家夏阳（李小镜摄影）。

# 当下的成功

◆

没有豆子在上面，就不认它是豆子！

不要以为自己成功一次就可以了。『现在的

成功』是重要的，而『现在』马上便成为『过

去』……

今天下午我请你母亲到后园小坐，难得出去晒一下太阳的她，居然指着零落将残的四季豆，问我是什么植物。我大吃一惊地说，那是她已经享用了一整个夏天的四季豆，并且责怪她居然五谷不辨。

你知道她怎么回答吗？

她说："我不管！只因为我看不到结着豆子，所以不认它是豆子。"

这两句话使我大有感触，因为它们代表了世上大多数人的价值观，也显示了现实的冷酷无情。

是的，没有豆子，就不认它！不管它过去有多大的贡献，只因为没有亲眼见到，或现在看不出，就无法认同。对人来说，不论你过去多么成功，如果此时没有表现，也便往往被否定。

洛克菲勒每天晚上都要对自己说同样几句话："你虽然有了一点成就，但只要不继续努力、虚心学习，就会被人击倒……"

西方有句谚语："没有失败的成功者，只有成功的失败者；没有失败，只有失败者。"更说，"没有成功的叛国者！"因为叛国者若成功了，便是革命家。这不正是中国的"成则为王，败则为寇"的道理吗？

所以，不要以为自己成功一次就可以了，也不要认为过去的光荣可以被永久肯定。在这个世上，"现在的成功"是重要的，而"现在"马上便成为"过去"，下一刻又得有下一刻的成功。

记住！没有豆子在上面，就不认它是豆子。这是你母亲说的，也是大多数人会说的一句话。

## 头衔的重要

"没有结豆子，就不认它是豆子。"我自高中时代，就总听老爸说。

以前我认为，如果你从事的工作内容已到某种程度，人们就会认定你是符合那个标准的人，为什么还要受到头衔的约束。但现在，我开始相信一些让你获得头衔的工作经验是重要的，因为那像奖杯一样，说明你曾经做过的事、达到的成就。也因此在工作上，现在的我会尽量留下完整的记录与作品集，也会不吝争取该有的头衔，因为那表示别人对你的认知。

所以我要在这儿加一句："即使你知道自己结了豆子，也一定要让大家看见，否则人家会以为你只是豆苗！"

# 尊敬大地

攀在篱墙上的黄瓜须蔓，虽然已经干枯，仍然紧紧地缠绕着，为了下一代的绵延，即使在死后，也不放弃自己的责任！

你知道我为什么最爱到屋后的园圃去吗？那并非由于它是我挖土施肥活动筋骨的地方，更不是因为它能提供我们半年所需的蔬菜，而是由于它充满教训！

从小，我就爱种菜，也自自然然地学会了尊敬土地、尊敬自然。我觉得没有土地，就长不出植物；没有植物，鸟兽就难以生存；没有鸟兽，食肉类的动物便无法存在。所以这世上的每一种生物，都是由土地养育的。

一直到今天，我仍然相信，如果能常常光着脚，站在土地上，让我们的脚心，像植物般吸取泥土的精华，感受那大地的脉动，会有益健康。因为在人类史上，穿鞋只是晚近的事，我们绝大多数的祖先，都是日夜与土地赤裸裸接触的。

所以你常看见我赤脚在园中穿梭。我仔细观察每一棵植物的消长，由其中仿佛听到自然的律动与大地的呼吸，更由其中得到许多启示。

今早，黄瓜藤就给我极大的触动，我先是发现上个星期才开花结蒂的小黄瓜不见了，经过寻找，才知道原来它已经改变了位置，落到瓜藤的下方，且成为一根大黄瓜。

最令我惊讶的是，那一整棵瓜藤，和它原来攀爬的小树，居然都改变了原先的样子——

小树的枝子因为黄瓜的重量而下垂，瓜藤随着倾斜，新的叶子为了追求阳光而向上发展，在黄瓜的四周则长出许多须蔓，紧紧地攀住树枝。

直到此刻我才知道，原来那看来纤细的须蔓，竟然非常坚韧。尽管小树枝倾斜得近乎垂直而不易攀附，它们还能一枝又一枝地伸出，紧紧缠住不放，使那比初生时大上许多倍的黄瓜，能够安然成长。

那许多须蔓，有些已经因为苍老而完全干枯，但是当我试着拉动它们的时候，竟仍然坚持而强有力地"不松脱"。

生命多伟大啊！它的尊贵与光辉，是不仅为今生而存在，且为下一代的绵延而支撑，甚至在死后，都不放下自己的责任。

同样，每一个生命的成长，都不是它自己的事情，就像那个黄瓜，从土地萌芽，孕育出它的母体，攀上篱墙，再转到旁边的小树上。而后在开花时，用它艳黄的花瓣吸引蜂蝶虫媒，再于受孕后，在母株极力维护下，一日日成长……

孩子！当我们晚餐的盘中，有着鲜嫩的凉拌黄瓜时，请别忘了谢谢种黄瓜的人、谢谢土地、谢谢篱墙、谢谢蜂蝶，谢谢牺牲自己，至死不谢的须蔓，也谢谢那棵曾被压弯的小树吧！

## 大山大水大感触

我有位朋友是个"虔诚"的无神论者。我问他，这样的观念会不会让生命显得很没意义。他说每次感觉茫然时，就去爬山，因为当他登上山顶时，放眼壮阔的景象，心里会不禁赞叹：上帝啊！他说："虽然我不相信上帝的存在，但是大自然总能给我近乎宗教的感觉。"

见识过大山大水，感觉自我的渺小，尊敬大地之心就会自然产生。像我去西藏时，在海拔四五千米的地方，看到大自然的壮阔，那种感动与敬畏是难以言喻的。

但下山之后怎么办？生活在城市里，只有小花小草的感触。我很佩服我老爸。他可以养两只螳螂，种一些菜，就有足够的灵感写出一大本《杀手正传》。而我，还是得爬到山巅上，才能体会"尊敬大地"的感觉。

# 寻找灵感

当灵感突然出现，会使你惊艳。问题是，如果你一天到晚往男生堆里钻，怎么能有惊艳的机会呢？

今天当我问你为什么许久没写作时，你回答："因为没有灵感。"话说得很轻松，却使我相当吃惊，因为我发现你患了一种没有严重症状，却最糟糕的病，一种使许多原本具有潜力的作家，到头来一无所成的毛病。

什么叫作"没有灵感"？这只是人们没创作时的一种托词。

有句名言——

> 若你呼唤那山，
> 而山不来，
> 你便向它走去！

同样的道理，当你没有灵感时，为什么不去寻找呢？

"日有所思，夜有所梦"，你会发现灵感也如此，你愈是寻找它，它愈会出现。虽然好像在意外中突然涌现，实际却是因为你在不断地寻找，所以它的出现才会使你惊艳！

惊艳，对的！我们可以说灵感来临时，会像你突然看到一个出奇美丽的女孩子一般惊喜。但是你也要知道，如果你希望看到漂亮的女孩子，最好常参加交际，或往女生比较容易出现的场所跑。如果天天待在家里，或往男生堆里钻，是很难有惊艳的机会的。

所以惊艳看来是一种机遇，但是这机遇却可以创造。灵感好像是一种"天外飞来"，可遇不可求的东西，却可以因为我们的努力寻找而变得容易。

有个人带了一台傻瓜相机在公园里闲坐，看到一群可爱的孩子从面前跑过，突发灵感，举起相机拍下来，参加摄影展居然得了大奖。

　　另外有个人，早上起来突然想要出去摄影，又接着灵光一闪地想到何不拍小孩子，再飞来一个灵感是：何不到贫民窟去拍穿着破衣，却满面天真，惹人怜爱的孩子？于是准备好各种器材，转两三班车到了贫民窟，又守了一整天，从上百张照片中选出一张参加摄影展，也获得了大奖。

　　他们的结果相同——都拍到好的作品，得了奖。过程却有多大的不同？

　　你当然会向往前者，因为那灵感来得巧，几乎不费力气，举起傻瓜照相机，咔嚓一声就成功了。问题是，那种机会是不是常会出现呢？比较起来，反而后者容易把握，也更能保证成功。因为守株待兔的人，可能不费力气地得到一只自己撞死的兔子，却绝不会像猎兔人一样，虽然辛苦，但总能有所斩获。

　　"天若有情天亦老"，这流传千古的名句，想必你早知道。但是你晓得它的作者李贺，是用什么方法寻找灵感吗？他每天一大早便骑着瘦马出去，到处发掘灵感，并把得到的感触记下来投入锦囊之中，直到晚上回家之后，再把那许多灵感加以整理，成为完美的作品。当你没有灵感时，何不学学李贺，出去寻找呢？

　　当然也不是说灵感非要到外面去找，丰富的生活体验固然可以带给我们灵感，前人的作品也可以引发我们的情思。所以古人说：

终日之思，不如须臾之所学也。当我们整天苦苦寻找灵感，发现灵感的泉源依然枯竭的时候，另一个泉源往往就在你的身边。你可以由再充实、再学习，加深自己内涵的过程中，获得新的灵感。

> 疏影横斜水清浅，
> 暗香浮动月黄昏。

当我们吟咏宋代诗人林逋的这两句诗时，有谁会想到它实际是出自五代南唐江为的"竹影横斜水清浅，桂香浮动月黄昏"呢？

当我们看莎翁名剧《奥赛罗》时，有谁会想到那是出于意大利钦蒂欧（Cinthio）的作品《故事百则》（Heca tommithi）中的《夫与妻之不忠实》？

如同吃东西，当我们把外来的食物消化之后，它就能成为自己的血肉；当我们阅读前人作品的时候，也能勾起灵感，创作出属于自己的作品。

年轻人！灵感就像我卧室窗外不断来访的小鸟，它们成群地来，是因为我放了喂食器和谷子。我能够清楚地观察它们，是因为我挂上了可以隐蔽自己的百叶窗。至于能够把它们搬上画纸，成为我作品的一部分，则是由于我总准备好纸笔，随时速写它们的生态。

你说，我是因为总有灵感来找我，才能不断创作，还是因为我不断寻找灵感，以至于有所收获呢？

所以从今天开始，我希望你再也不要说"没有灵感"！

## 听听自己脑袋里的声音

对一个创意人来说，这是经常会碰到的话题。我觉得最大的问题不是没有灵感，而是生活里没有空间让灵感进来。我们最缺乏灵感的时候，常常正是我们稿债最多、琐事最杂的时候。坚持保留自己的心灵空间是很不容易的，也难怪很多艺术家会选择隐居。

寻找灵感的另一挑战是要打破生活的惯性，唯有这样才能找到新的灵感泉源。

我现在教授音乐制作时，学生有时会反映，学了许多新的软件跟混音技巧之后，反而不会作曲了。这时我会告诉他们："关掉电脑，也关掉音响。给自己一点宁静，才有机会听到自己脑袋里的声音！"

# 把握时间

上帝给每个人的时间都一样，但是每个人使用的效果却不相同。如果你没有崇高的理想，就不能战胜自己的惰性；无法战胜惰性，就很难把握时间。

今天我在杂志上看到一则有关美国华裔体操名将马思明的报道，感到非常惊讶。我并非对她以十七岁的小小年纪，获得泛美运动会体操全能金牌感到吃惊，而是佩服她运用时间的能力。

马思明每天早上五点半起床，六点出门，六点四十至七点做热身运动，然后练习到九点半。十点开始上学校的正规课程，下课之后再去体育馆练习，从四点一直到七八点，才开车回家做功课，并在十一点钟就寝。

我暗自想——

当我的孩子还在被催着起床，或坐在床边发呆的时候，马思明已经做完热身运动。

当我的孩子正在浴室挤青春痘和吹头发的时候，马思明已经在平衡木上跳跃。

当我的孩子在电视机前吃着零食，嘿嘿傻笑时，马思明正离开体育馆，驾车穿过黑暗的夜色。

当我的孩子坐在餐桌前细细品味他的夜宵，一刀一刀往小饼干上涂起司时，马思明已经做完功课，上床睡觉了！

我相信马思明的筋肉是比你疲惫的，但是她疲惫得健康，第二天的早上，又以一副清爽的身躯，投向新的战斗。

我也相信马思明的时间是不够用的，但是她安排得有条不紊，由于都在计划之中，所以反而从容。

我更相信马思明会希望像一般十七岁少女一样，细细装扮之后，赴一个又一个约会。但是追求更高境界的理想，使她不能也不敢有一刻松懈。

记住！上帝给每个人的时间都一样，但是每个人使用的效果却不相同。如果你没有崇高的理想，就不能战胜自己的惰性；无法战胜惰性，就很难把握时间。我尤其欣赏马思明的教练唐·彼得斯所说的两句话："我认为她是美国最好的体操选手，她有能力把握每一天的时间！"

　　他没用任何词语形容马思明辛苦的练习，却强调她有能力把握每一天的时间。是因为每一个堪称"最佳体操选手"的人，必然都经过辛苦的锻炼。其中唯独"有能力把握每一天时间"的，才能站到巅峰。

## 或许我还不够忙吧!

在大学,我很佩服那些参加校队的同学。他们每天练习至少三个小时,回家已经累得半死,怎么有时间做功课?他们说:"久了,就知道怎么利用琐碎的时间,即使只有五分钟,也可以读两页课本,哪怕一页也好。"

快速切换思考模式,让每分钟都有效率,而不是等到有一大段完整的时间再动,我觉得这一点最难。我甚至在想,这或许是在逼不得已的状况下才能熬出的功力,就像马思明,大部分时间被占据,除了善用每一秒,没有其他的选择。

所以回头看我自己为什么办不到,我只能苦笑说:"或许我还不够忙吧!"

# 早熟

前年种的两株牡丹，虽然当初一样大，但是去年开花的那株，今年却比未开花的另一株瘦小了一半，而后者今年开的花也比前者更多。为什么？

"我小时候就想学画，但是没能学，高中毕业后又想学画，还是没能做到，所以一直拖到今天！"

夜间部一位中年妇人对我说，她的眼睛里闪着智慧的光彩，虽然只是上第二堂课，已经看得出过人的才学，我敢说如果她早早学画，一定能有不错的成就。

"为什么两次都没能如愿学画呢？"我问她。

"因为我父母十几岁就结婚生了我，能养活我已经够辛苦了，怎么还可能花钱让我学画？"

"那么你高中毕业时，为什么又没能走上学艺术的道路呢？"

"因为我也早早结婚怀了小孩！"她有点不太好意思地说，"只怪我父母结婚太早，两个人情感都不成熟，总是吵架，家里没有温暖，所以我希望愈早离开家愈好。问题是既然结婚成家，也就没能实现学艺术的理想。"

我没有继续追问她的子女又如何，只是把这段故事告诉你，供你思考。

一对十七八岁就结婚生育的父母，不仅没能完成他们年轻时的理想，也没能实现他们子女的梦想，甚至一连串地影响了许多人。那么，这个早婚是不是值得斟酌呢？

记得我有一天叫你到后园看前年种的两株牡丹吗？虽然当初一样大，但是去年开花的那株，今年却比未开花的另一株瘦小了一半，而后者今年开的花也比前者更多。是什么原因，使它们有那样大的分别？

因为有一株太早绽放，虽然抢了先，却也伤了本。

　　每年夏天，蔷薇开过后，你总会看见我把它们结的籽一个个剪掉，你也会看到我把君子兰粗大的花茎齐根切去，因为当它们以大量的养分支持果实和种子的时候，下一季的花朵就可能减少许多。

　　你已经是个十足的青少年，甚至可以说是正走向血气方刚的青年；你的骨骼开始变得粗壮，胸肩变得宽阔而厚实，你卧室的墙上开始悬挂女星的照片，早上可以听见我去年送你的电动剃须刀愈来愈频繁的声响；你梳头洗头和挤痘子的时间成倍增长，头发的花样不断地翻新，当你坐在我对面时，那发胶的香味经常令我敏感得有些气喘。

　　这表示，你将成熟。成熟得准备绽开花朵，引来蜂蝶，甚至使一株雌花受孕。

　　所以在此刻，我说以上的故事给你听，希望你了解其中的意思！

画面上方是早一年绽放的牡丹，
枝叶显然比下方那株来得瘦弱。

## 牡丹花的比喻

听父母谈性，总是有点别扭。对这点，我老爸倒是能说得脸不红气不喘。记得我第一次回台湾时，我老爸直接带我到屈臣氏，对我说："这里可以买到安全套。"那时我心想：如果可以用到当然最好！那时我十九岁，仍是个处男。

这篇文章，我老爸倒是写得很含蓄，意思不难懂，但是对当时十四五岁的我，其实很想回头问："老爸，有没有比牡丹更好的比喻？"

# 师生之间

当我初到美国大学教课时，对学生说：『尽管我教得多，并不表示会考那么深，所以大家不必担心。重要的是知识，而非成绩，我不会在分数上为难你们。』

从此，学生上课就不专心了。

今天下午，你母亲到学校见了你的各科老师。我原先认为以你的成绩而言，是没有必要去的，但是现在不得不承认，你母亲的决定对，因为她带回了一些我们没想到的信息，也带去了许多老师不知道的资料，更解除了一些师生之间原有的疑惑。譬如你的音乐老师发现，你曾经要求他准许你使用钢琴是有道理的，而他原先误以为你只是想捣蛋，所以与你母亲谈过之后，他不但特别约你谈话，还要为你介绍钢琴名师。

我们原以为会由于你在堂上与他抗辩而宰你的英文老师，则一见面就赞美你善于写作，表示虽然他只读过你一两篇东西，却早已发现。而当你母亲提到你在堂上冲动抗辩的事，他更认为那没有错，同时解释了他的评分观点，而显然他是对的。如果你母亲不去，只怕我们会一直认为错在他，你也可能在心头有个挥不去的阴影，认为他会记恨呢！

最令我们惊讶的，是你法文老师的评语。当他说你上课表现不好时，你母亲不敢相信，居然连问了两次："您没搞错吧？"直到他举出上课时总跟你讲话的同学霍华的名字时，你母亲才不得不相信，因为她知道霍华是你法文班上最要好的同学。

你的法文老师还举出实例，说今天为了开家长会，法文课缩短到只有十五分钟，而你居然讲了十分钟话，还没打开课本！

天哪！你要知道，相信你也早知道，我在大学教课时，最痛恨的就是在下面讲话的学生，因为他们非但注意力不集中且成绩总是不好，还影响其他同学听讲。尤其糟糕的，是他们会弄坏我授课的情绪，使教的内容也打了折扣。

　　而今天，居然这种捣蛋鬼，令我心里恨得牙痒痒的学生，也包括了我自己的孩子。你叫我怎么说，又对你法文老师有多大的亏欠呢？

　　不错！你说你讲话都是在老师闲聊而非教正课的时候。你的老师也说，可能因为他上课用的方法太轻松，使你把他看成了自己的哥哥，而变得毫无顾忌。

　　但是你也要知道，正因为他用这种轻松的教法，你愈要与他合作，使他的每个幽默都获得回应，使他的亲切能获得回馈。他不把你们当学生，而看成自己的小弟弟妹妹，是他对你们的尊重，你们怎能因此而不自重呢？

　　记得我初到美国大学教课时，第一堂课就对学生说："为了使你们学得多，我可能会提到不少人名、地名和年代，但尽管我教得多，并不表示会考那么深，所以大家不必担心。重要的是知识，而非成绩，只要努力地学习，我不会在分数上为难学生。"

　　几乎每一班，只要我这么一讲，秩序就突然变坏了。学生们开始聊天，缺席的人数也愈来愈多，使我不得不板起面孔，宣布随时可能测验，才将学生控制下来。

　　每次我不得不改为采取严厉态度之前，都想：为什么当我尊重他们时，他们反而不知好歹？他们是不尊重老师、不尊重知识，更不尊重自己。

　　同样，今天你的法文老师会不会也这么想？当他希望在轻松的谈笑间教导你们，让师生融成一片时，会不会事与愿违呢？当他想利用三天假期，带你们去加拿大法语区魁北克旅游学习时，会不会自忖控制不住你们，而到头来放弃呢？

记住！老师永远是老师，不论他看来像你的哥哥，或跳坐在讲台上聊天，他都是老师。你们也都应当以他为中心，让他觉得自己说出的每个字、讲出的每个笑话，都获得"满堂"的回响。这是他的收获，也将是你们的收获！

最后，让我告诉你，尽管你在堂上有许多不对的表现，你的法语老师非但给你最好的成绩，而且高达一百零八分。你的英文老师不但没宰你，还给了你最高的分数，而且愿意在课后特别指导你写作。

我不想赞美你，但不得不佩服你的老师们，还有你那从百忙中抽空去学校的母亲。

老师、家长与学生的这种沟通，真是太重要了！

## 严师与名师

我是在当老师之后，才知道当老师的难处，以及作为学生的幸福。

我老爸这篇文章除了提到要尊师重道外，也触及另一个重点，就是老师、家长和学生，应该保持良性的互动。在台湾，有许多老师跟家长报告孩子的不是，家长回家后便一味责备孩子；也有一种家长听到孩子在学校不开心，就冲去向老师理论。在这三方的沟通中，家长应该尽量保持客观，先把事情弄清楚，不要一开始就选边站。

学生时代的我，喜欢开放的老师，觉得很酷，但现在，也能够了解严格教育的好处。其实当严师很辛苦，因为严师要掌握原则、有所坚持，才能得到尊敬。

# 最高指导原则

◆

如果有一天你在亚马孙丛林里迷了路……

如果有一天你在伸手不见五指的建筑中要逃生……

如果有一天你在半山腰遇到了山洪……

如果有一天，你在亚马孙丛林迷了路，举头只见树叶蔽天，使你认不出太阳的方向，森林里又是一片平坦，没有让你可以四处眺望的高山，加上亚马孙丛林是广达七百零五万平方公里的蛮荒之地，你要怎么找到逃出丛林的路呢？

如果有一天晚上，你在电影院、办公大楼或超级市场这类的宽广建筑物中碰到了火警，所有的电灯突然熄灭了，人们在黑暗中狂奔尖叫，你要怎样找到逃生的路？

如果有一天你在登山途中遇到大雨，而山洪暴发，只见洪流从山上滚滚而下，你正置身半山腰，该怎么办？

当我告诉你，今年暑假我在台北住的英伦大楼地下室发生火警，管理员从楼顶搭电梯赶下去救火，中途停电，使电梯停在半空，管理员在漆黑中跳出电梯折断大腿骨，而送去急救的事情之后，考了你以上的问题，却发现你没能给我最满意的答案。

你想到从树干上的苔藓和年轮分辨方向，想到在地上爬行以免被浓烟呛晕，想到抱紧大树以免被山洪冲走，答案都没错，却差在你没有说出最要紧的应变原则。也就是说，所有的小举动，都应该在那个大原则的指导下进行。你提出了战术，却没有提出战略。

现在让我告诉你，专家们建议的大原则。

在广大的丛林里迷路，如果没有指南针或辨别方向的可能，走出丛林最好的方法，是顺着小水流前进，从小流走向小溪，从小溪进入小河，转入大河，最后自然会流向江海，脱出丛林的围困。

在黑暗的建筑中，找出逃生之路的最好方法，不是东跑西撞地狂奔，而是朝固定的方向一直走，自然会碰到墙，再沿着墙一步步朝同一方向摸索，自然可以找到逃生的门窗。

在山洪暴发的半山腰，逃避的最高原则，是绝不能往山下的地方跑，因为愈向下，山洪汇集得愈多，夹带的沙石也愈多。唯有朝山顶的方向前进，才能减少山洪的威胁。所以登山家有句名言："没有一个山顶会有山洪。"

如同上面所说的情况，在我们遇险时，有许多"最高指导原则"，它们听来非常简单，却可能带给你最大的希望。

在你心中，有多少这样的指导原则，使你在最紧要的关头，可以立刻作出正确的抉择？

## 勿惊慌

我老爸一定是看准我不知道标准答案，才问我这些问题。

这些"最高指导原则"不难懂，但如何碰到状况时懂得运用它们，不但要靠应变能力与机智，而且要靠冷静的思考。所以我的最高指导原则是："不要惊慌！"因为人惊慌时，什么原则都乱了。

## 腻了就甩

美国高中女孩流行一句话，交朋友是为了认识更多的人，不断换，就不断认识！

于是男生也说：为了乐子嘛！腻了就甩！

"我高一交的女朋友，到毕业的时候，早就不可能跟我在一起了！"

今天下午，当我们一同给车库刷漆的时候，你不经意地对我说。

"那么你又何必交呢？"我问。

"为了乐子（for fun）！所以没乐子，就吹了！"你说。

我差点把油漆刷子掉在地上，张大嘴望着你："天哪！这就是你的交友观或恋爱观吗？"

"大家都这样！这是流行，我只是跟着走。"

"服装 fashion 可以跟着走，难道连交友的态度也要跟着流行走吗？"我问，"当你觉得没有乐子时，可以跟女朋友说再见，是不是当你的女朋友觉得你不够吸引时，也可以把你甩掉？"

"当然！"你居然好像想都没想，就答。

"那么，你被甩掉之后会不会伤心呢？"

"如果她是我的第一个女朋友，当然会伤心！"

"相同，如果你是她的第一个男朋友，她也会伤心。如果你是她不知道第几任的男朋友，她就会比较不在乎，对不对？"

"在理论上是对的！"

"所以你们在交往之初，就已经有了没乐子便分手的想法。这样，你们之间可能有真正的友谊吗？一段在一开始就不诚恳，就不敞开胸怀，就准备甩掉对方，或被对方甩的友情，是有价值的吗？"我又要问你，"你以不认真的态度交朋友，是不是也能确定，所有与你交往的女孩子，在态度上同样是不认真的呢？"

"女孩流行一句话，交朋友是为了认识更多的人，不断换，就不断认识！"

"是不是所有的女孩子都如此呢？百分之百？"

"当然不是！"

"那么当你以一种游戏的态度交朋友，对方却是全心投入时，从一开始，岂不是就不平等吗？你们一向讲求平等，为什么连交朋友的态度都不平等呢？如果你是认真的，对方不认真，是不平等！如果她认真，你不认真，也不平等！如果双方都不认真，你们这种友谊，又算什么？"我还要告诉你，"友情，不论同性或异性之间，最基本的条件，就是真，就是信。如果没有这两者，就不必说那是交朋友，不如讲只是找个暂时的玩伴！问题是，在这个世纪之病泛滥的时候，你说不定已经是对方的第 N 个男友，这种玩伴你能要吗？"

"所以我应该找那老实的、认真的！"

"可是如果那认真的女孩子，知道你过去交友的态度是找乐子，而且不信实，她无法确定她不是你的第 N 个女友，也难保证你有没有毛病，她又会肯跟你深交吗？所以当你交友的态度只是为了乐子，只怕你便只能找到那同一类型的人。若非你欺骗了对方，或对方欺骗了你，就是彼此欺骗。"

从种菜当中，我体会了一件事。有些人喜欢从撒种、育苗开始，种成一畦畦菜，有些人喜欢到苗圃买保证成活的幼株回去种，还有些人干脆去市场买收割来的成品。

我发现许多人或因为苗床的养分处理不当，苗株常长得太细；

或由于日光不正，而苗株倾斜；又或因为不耐烦搬进挪出，让幼苗适应外面的环境，而在移植后死亡。经过几次失败，便宁愿去买现成的幼株，从半途开始。

日久之后，他又可能觉得由幼株开始也太费力，不值得，而放弃种菜，干脆要吃的时候去菜场买。

没错！这三种人都吃到了菜。也没错！买现成菜的人，可能多花不了多少钱，却省了许多力气。问题是那由播种，看着冒出新绿、茁壮、成熟的种菜之乐，恐怕只有第一种人享受得到。

如果将吃菜比喻为性关系，我相信在今天的社会，有许多人宁愿买现成的，因为省时，而且可以换许多花样。可是在肉欲的满足之外，他享受了多少精神生活的美好呢？

人可以多情，但不能滥情；可以多交朋友，但不能滥交朋友。而且交朋友最起码的条件是：你要真诚与信实！

我把今天的对话记下来，供你再思考！

## 青涩的成长

当时的我，其实是因为刚被女友甩了，才说出那段很酸的话。现在回想，当时交男女朋友不是为"爱情"，而是一种对于"自我价值"的渴望：有一个人喜欢你，愿意跟你交往，这样子肯定比什么都实在！

初中的我是个书呆子，又很不时髦，我喜欢的女生都懒得看我一眼。直到上高中，远离了初中的世界跟之前被锁定的形象，开始耍酷，装个吊儿郎当的样子，说些自认为很成熟世故的话，居然吸引了一票女生。怪不得有句俗话说："男人不坏，女人不爱。"

# 忧患意识

同样听见一声枪响，在贝鲁特的人，会立刻扑倒；在纽约哈林区的人会弯下腰去；在夏威夷的人，只怕会东张西望，以为是什么车子爆了胎。

我十三岁那年的寒假，有一天跟朋友去爬阳明山，回家才吃过晚饭，家里就失了火，瞬时火舌冲出屋顶，当救火队赶到时，已经烧成平地，唯有几根焦黑的房柱，立在颓圮的断垣间。

逃出火场的我，眉毛都已经烧掉，呆立在人群中，却发现手上还攥着一样东西，原来是白天从阳明山摘回的小橘子。

二十多年来，那失火的一幕，总在我眼前浮现，仿佛昨天才发生的一般清晰，甚至连那天在阳明山的种种，也历历在目。

我常想，如果没有失火，那一天不过是我人生中的一日，平凡得不可能留下记忆。问题是，为什么晚上发生火灾，却能使我对白天的事情，也铭记不忘？痛苦的打击，难道能把许多已经淡化的东西，再染上一层深重的色彩吗？

从这一点出发，我渐渐有了更深的体会。

我发现参加联考之前几个月准备的东西，即使不再温习，考试时也可能想起来。偏偏在放榜录取之后，没几天就忘了一大半。可见在脑海储存资料，是分为第一、二、三等不同优先登记的。当我遭遇失火的灾变时，原本列为最不重要资料的日间记忆，立刻被移入第一优先。相对，当考试放榜之后，那原本最重要的资料，又可能被移了出来。

记得当我头一年回台湾时，你的母亲在信中告诉我，每天晚上你必定像我一样检查门窗，夜里楼下有一点异响，你也会立刻注意到，好像听觉突然变得敏锐了。

你的听力真是增强了吗？答案当然不是。而是你增加了关心的程度，你 care（在意）、你 alert（警醒），甚至可以讲：你有了忧患意识！

什么是忧患意识？

忧患意识所涵括的真是太广了！往大处想，可以是民众对国家、社会、时局变迁的担忧；往小处看，可以是学生对考试的担心、居民对盗窃的警戒。总之，凡是认为环境与个人的命运休戚相关而有所警惕，都可以称为有忧患意识。

忧患意识能使涣散的人心振作起来，使淡忘的记忆清晰起来，使迟钝的感觉敏锐起来。当我们细细观察时，可以明显地看出有忧患意识与缺乏忧患意识的差异。譬如同样听见一声枪响，在贝鲁特的人，会立刻扑倒；在纽约哈林区的人会弯下腰去；至于在夏威夷，人们只怕会东张西望，以为是什么车子爆了胎。这种表现的差异，就是因为前者更有忧患意识。

❧

你或许要问，我说这么一番大道理的目的是什么。

我的答案很简单。

我希望随着年龄的增长，你能对许多事情具有忧患意识。你应该开始关心环境污染的问题、国家施政的方针、世界局势的变化。更应该对自己未来的发展有忧患意识，考虑未来求学的方向，乃至人生的目标。也可以说，你要把自己放到这个世界的大环境中，而不再一切等父母师长的安排。

你会发觉，当你有忧患意识之后，许多潜力都能获得发挥，你也能看得更深、更广，且计划得更长远！

# Y2K 与温室效应

这篇文章让我想到在进入千禧年之前，媒体突然爆出的 Y2K 危机。根据统计，全球的公私机构花了超过三千亿美元处理这个问题。

值得吗？很难说。起码当我们正式进入二十一世纪的那一刻，没有因为电脑故障而天下大乱。后来，有不少专家指出，当时为了处理 Y2K 的问题，许多企业都做了彻底的备份及系统更新，因而预防了许多电脑问题发生，那些花费都是值得的。

现在，"温室效应"已经成为全球瞩目的新危机。其实它一点也不新，只是现在成了热门话题。有些科学家甚至认为媒体已经把这个现象炒得过火了，其实不用那么大惊小怪。不管事实如何，如果这个危机意识可以有连带效应，让大家不但更注意节约能源，而且对整个地球的自然生态更加关注，绝对是好事。

# 重新来过

◆

名书法家曹秋圃先生，十八岁就教人写字，但是三十二岁才自觉不足，而真正下功夫练字。

林玉山教授二十二岁担任书画社指导老师，二十七岁获得『免审查』殊荣，之后亦自觉不足，再赴日本深造。

我常觉得你不是不够聪明，而是不够傻，今天朱丽叶音乐学院艾司纳（Leonard Eisner）教授对你演奏的评语，就印证了我的话。

艾司纳教授说，他发现你有非常好的音感和记忆力，什么曲调只要听一遍，就能模仿得很像，但是你不在乐理上用功，所以如果没有老师的指点，拿到一本深的乐谱，常不知如何下手。他又批评，你似乎不爱弹巴赫和莫扎特这些作曲家的古典乐曲，而偏爱抒情和浪漫的东西，却又常不老老实实地照谱弹，而加入太多自己的见解。对于伟大的钢琴家或许可以，但对你而言，那却是不正确的学习态度。最后，他下的评语是：你弹得很好，但是不够用功！

这句话或许你一时不易了解，因为同样的评语，也曾发生在我身上，经过很长时间，我才真正知道它的含义。

记得我大二时修篆刻，王壮为教授看了我草草交差的功课时，一面为我修改，一面感慨地说："你刻得不错，就是不够用功！"

当时我很纳闷，心想：既然说我刻得不错，又为什么批评我不够用功呢？

第二年，当我在美术系画廊展出作品时，王老师看到我所画的《桃花源》图，笑着说："'桃花林'画的感觉很好，问题是，那枝子属不属于桃树呢？

我又心想：既然知道是桃花林，又说画得好，为什么还评论我的桃枝不对呢？

又过了几年，我在新公园开第一次个展，王老师莅临会场，在看我一幅有长题的作品时，频频点头说："字写得很好，但是练得不够！"

前后连续三次，他讲的几乎是同一类的话，我终于了解那话中的意思。也就是说我的聪明确实可以创作出看起来不差的东西，但是也由于过度倚仗聪明，缺乏平实的努力，使展现出来的作品，骨子里不够结实。就像是在那篆刻之中，刀落得潇洒，丰神也不差，但是因为技巧不够熟练，而"刀法"欠佳。在那《桃花源》作品之中，气氛构图都不错，却因为疏于观察，而把握不住桃树的特色和精神。至于书法，看起来不错的行草，实际却因为临帖不足，以致笔画顺序不合章法。

这也使我想起大学毕业不久，有一次参加在台北武昌街精工画廊举办的一个当代名家画展。要知道，那已经是名家展，包括了张大千、黄君璧、林玉山等大师，而我居然能在被邀请之列，岂不沾沾自喜。但是就在这时候，也参展的张德文教授，在看了我的作品之后，赞赏地说："画得真不错！"并指着画上的远山松树说，"还是过去画的样子。"

张教授的这句话也给了我很大的震撼，我回家之后不断想"还是你过去画的样子"，是说那已经成为我的风格特色，抑或表示我没有新的突破？

我开始了解，由于自己在大学时的作品就已经被历史博物馆送去亚细亚现代美展，而毕业的第二年就应邀参加美展，靠着聪明得来的虚名，使我在自满中不知反省，结果连基础都有问题，居然还不自知。

同年，我在一篇介绍书法名师曹秋圃先生的文章上，看到"曹秋圃十八岁就教人写字，但是三十二岁才自觉不足，而真正下功夫练字"；又在与林玉山教授的谈话中，知道他二十二岁从日本游学三年归来，开始担任两个书画社的指导老师，并因连续获奖，在二十七岁获得台展"免审查"的殊荣之后，自觉不足，而结束家里的业务，再去日本京都深造。

不久之后，我也辞去了"中视"的工作，来美国游学。因为我知道自己的不足，在台湾岛内的得意，与四周的掌声，更使我难以自省。

而今天，我的孩子居然犯了跟我同样的毛病。其实这是我早觉察到的。譬如我听你弹琴，初学一首曲子，往往觉得感性不差，但是当你熟练之后，在那十指齐飞、使人炫目的技巧之外，内容却变得贫乏。

我每每在你的演奏会中，大家高呼"Bravo！"时，看到你面有得意之色，也回想到自己的大学时代。所以常对你说，你是"山中无大木，小草也为尊"。实际跟大师比，可能连一个小节都听得出差异。

也就因此，我曾提出俄裔钢琴大师霍洛维兹（Vladimir Horowitz）的演奏和你讨论。发现高龄八十多岁的他，直挺挺地坐着，十指似乎轻松地搭在琴键上，面部和身体的表情不多，指下却流动出如此紧密、清晰而含蕴无穷的琴音。说实在话，他所弹的曲子，许多都是你早就练过的，问题是，他在同样的琴键和音符中，却弹出了那么多微妙的东西。他快速的音阶如果表现得像是一颗颗圆熟完美的葡萄，你所表现的却可能有葡萄果酱之嫌。

年轻人！我相信艾司纳教授对你的感觉，就像是我看到一个已经学画十年，又来拜师的学生，面有得意之色地展开他的巨幅作品，在看来云烟暧叇、气势磅礴的画面中，却发现他连树枝都画不好的惋惜。

站定脚步，从头开始！你会发现在那华丽的音符和看来娴熟的技巧之后，还有太多欠缺的东西。当你退回起点，沿着以前的路再走一遍的时候，会发现那路边有许多珍宝，是你过去只顾一味向前冲而忽略的。于是同样的路，你再走到今天同样的位置，可能已经是极富有的人。

所以我说，你现在需要的不是聪明，而是那甘愿重新来过的傻劲儿！

艾司纳教授与刘轩合影留念。

## 基本功之必要

在学习过程中，磨炼基本功是很重要的。

就像学音乐，即使你已能驾驭技巧，是大师级的演奏家，还是得练习基本技巧。

打个比方：我有"绝对音准"，听到一个音符便能马上辨识出来，所以小时候我从来没专心学过乐理，凭耳朵就可以过关。但现在，当我跟人做音乐上的沟通时，会发现若无乐理知识，比较难说明白，也比较难发展。因此，我现在反而回头复习乐理，补足先前的不足。

# 最后的堡垒

每个人心中都应该有这么一个堡垒。在人生的战场上，他可以一站一站地败退，但是到那最后的堡垒时，就算下面仍有退路，也要坚决与那堡垒共存亡。

昨天晚上菲司来上课的时候，又是"空手到"，连半张作业也交不出来，而且在我为别的学生改作业时，她还不断打哈欠，真是失礼极了！但是下课的时候，她对我讲了一番耐人寻味的话，使我一扫心中的不快。

她说："自从到房地产公司做事，每天一大早就开车带着客户看房子，往往要忙到天黑，回家还得整理房地产的资料，实在是筋疲力尽，没有能力继续学画。可是想想，如果把这已经从事四五年的唯一嗜好放弃，我的人生还有什么呢？所以告诉自己，无论多忙多累，绝不停止学画，就算拿不出作业，看看别人的也好！"

这使我想起宋代女词人李清照在《金石录后序》里的一段话。当时北方的金人入侵中原，宋室南渡，兵荒马乱之际，李清照的丈夫赵明诚突然奉命独自到湖州去上任。临行时李清照问她的丈夫，如果情势不好该怎么办。赵明诚回答："跟着大家逃难，非不得已的时候，先抛弃辎重，其次丢掉衣被，再次将画籍卷轴放弃，甚至古器物也可以扔。唯有所谓宗器，绝不能失去，宁可自己背着、抱着，与身共存亡。"

每当我看到这一段，都觉得赵明诚未免有大男人沙文主义，把收藏看得比妻子的命还重要。但是又想，如果换成赵明诚本人，恐怕也会有同样的抉择。这是因为在他心中，"宗器"是绝不可失去的。仿佛作战时，在许多军人的心里，都有自己最后的堡垒，他们可以一站一站地败退，但是到那最后的堡垒时，就算下面仍有退路，也坚决与那堡垒共存亡。

我们每个人的心中都应该有这么一件宝物，或这么一个堡垒，在平常或许并不显明，唯有紧要的关头，才突出它无可动摇的地位。

在你的心中，可有这么一处堡垒，永远维护着，固守着，绝不退让？

# 寻求宁静与自由

如果问我自己最后的堡垒是什么，我想应该是宁静与自由。

现实环境中充满杂讯，我常觉得如果要创作，先得聆听自己脑中与心里的声音。我在家很少听音乐，尽量留给自己宁静的空间。而所谓的自由，指的是心灵上的自在。例如上周，我行程很满，原本周日该彻底休息，却接下假日的工作，结果表现不好，身体也疲惫不堪。之后自我检讨，觉得该休息时就得休息。我们如果连保留给自己的领土都捐出去，就真丧失了最后的堡垒。

也有人声称最后的堡垒是家人，但我看到很多人言行不一，假日还在外地奔波，小孩跟着菲佣长大。

最后的堡垒需要用心守护与经营。不在外面"舍"的人，很难在家里"得"。

# 快乐是什么

◆

快乐的条件，非但不是无忧无虑，而且可能是有忧有虑。快乐是要付出代价的！要被爱，更要去爱；要获得，更得付出！

"快乐是什么？"

"快乐是无忧无虑，没有负担！"

这是你给我的答案。但是我要说："快乐很可能正是在有忧虑、有负担之间所能享有的欣悦，如果真无忧无虑，只怕反不知什么是快乐了！"

记得我在你的这个年龄，常看着大学生心想：要是我进入大学之后，没有了大专联考的压力，该多快乐！但是既成了大学生，又羡慕踏入社会的人，想他们不用应付功课、考试，该多快乐！而在自己真正进入社会，又想如果能每天不用固定上下班，该多快乐！可是来美之后，学校的课不多，大半的时间可以由我自己支配，要怎么睡都成，却发现因为闲而发慌。直至找到研究的目标，才觉得快乐。

所以我常想：快乐是什么？我认为快乐就像安宁的感觉，如果把我们放在完全隔音的房间里，一点声音都没有，我们不见得感觉宁静，甚至因为从体内会有一种嗡嗡的声音进入脑海，而心里发慌。反倒是置身林野之间，鸟语、虫鸣、竹韵、松涛不断传入耳际，能给予我们宁静的感觉。

同样的道理，如果一点让我们费心的东西都没有，固然会有短暂的快乐，接着却可能手足无措，发觉生活失去了重心。

这又使我想起，或许可以用"爱"的道理来解释。

当我们小的时候，觉得快乐就是被爱、被呵护、被照顾得无微不至，但是年长之后，却渐渐发觉，快乐是要"去爱"。所以会养小动物，明明知道它们不懂，却对着宠物讲话。我们更会爱子女，明明知道他们回报的与父母付出的不成比例，却一厢情愿地爱。甚至当子女成家之后，年老的父母还为他们操心。至于没有子女的人，则可能参加公益活动，照顾残障、孤老，乃至保护野生动物。

看那些抱着孩子跑医院的父母，和每天睡晚赶早，忙着公益事业的人，谁说他们无忧无虑？谁又能说他们不快乐呢？

有人研究什么是最快乐的工作，结论是"能够从头到尾都参与的工作"。譬如你自己盖房子，从设计、选料、施工到装潢，当房子终于落成的时候，便是最快乐的时刻。

又譬如你接到公司交下来的一个工作，由构思、人事安排、联系运作，到验收成果，看着从无到有，是最快乐的。

同样，由孩子的诞生、哺育、教养，到长大成人、成家立业，那付出无数心血的父母也是最快乐的。

可是你想想，盖房子时设计、选料、施工、装潢，工作的构思、人事、推展，乃至孩子的哺育、教导，哪一样是不令我们操心，而没有负担的呢？

从以上这些点归纳起来，你应该知道：

快乐是要付出代价的！要被爱，更要去爱；要获得，更得付出。快乐是在我们的生活中先建立目标，并完成它。而就在这完成的过程中，在那忧心与释怀、走入困境与突破万难之间，我们享有了真正的快乐。

快乐就是完成理想、完成使命，就是从无到有的创造，由这一站到下一站的旅程。

快乐也就是积极的生活！

幼时的刘轩与名叫刘猫的虎斑爱猫。

## 暗藏的悲伤

快乐是什么？我家的猫！

我的猫叫 Bijou，大小姐一只，每天咕噜咕噜的，吃饱了睡，睡醒了吃。看它懒洋洋的样子，我常想自己下辈子一定要投胎做猫。

我相信动物的快乐很单纯，有食物、有睡眠、能交配，应该就很满足吧！相比之下，人类的快乐复杂多了。

不知道猫在追老鼠、猴子在找香蕉、小鸟在筑巢的时候是否快乐，但起码可以确定，人在工作时可以快乐，也可以在享受时莫名其妙的不快乐。这，不就是我们做人的福气和悲哀吗？

# 体能与技巧

◆

运动的精神，是达到体能的极限，并发挥身体的最大潜能，而非不自量力地硬拼。

如果举重的人压伤了脊柱，赛跑的人拉伤了肌肉，投球的人扭伤了手肘……

你对我抱怨说，虽然练了一个暑假的篮球，却在比赛时打不了多久就体力不支，似乎体力不如人。

我想这固然显示你的体力较差，也表示你的技术有问题。

因为体育活动除了是体能的活动之外，更包含了技巧与智慧，如同用杠杆和滑轮举东西，当你使用恰当的工具时，能有"四两拨千斤"的效果。也就因此，练网球的人，第一件要学的是握拍的方法和手臂的曲直，如果起步的基本动作不对，非但球打不好，而且可能伤到身体。相反，当你用力的方法正确时，则能以较少的力气，击出较佳的球。

记得今年暑假，我有一次跟朋友去游泳，我游的是多年前自己练出来的蛙式，虽然在岸上的体力绝不比同行的朋友差，可是在水中，非但游得不如他快，而且游不久就累了。朋友笑问我，为什么每次拨水时手臂都不伸开，又不拨到底，看起来十分忙碌而滑稽。我想这应该是我容易累的原因。我以为手动得快，就能游得快，岂知用出去的力量，多半被自己匆忙而不完整的动作抵消了。

这也使我想起刚进"中视"报新闻的情况，许多人都批评我播得太快，给人气急的感觉。但是当我播久了之后，虽然速度丝毫未减，却从容而游刃有余了。这是因为我掌握了节奏，将不重要的句子瞬间带过，碰到重要的字眼儿，又放慢速度，使观众听得特别清楚。

同样，我像你这个年岁时，也不擅长打篮球。每次比赛，抢球时猛跳，却因为抓不准时间，而总是抢不到。截球时，又双手乱舞，想以密不透风的动作拦阻对方传球，碰到差的对手固然有效，遇见高手却毫无用处，最后往往累得上气不接下气而先退场。

其实这种运动技巧的问题，不仅发生在初学者的身上，许多资深甚至已经跻身顶峰的选手也可能遇到。譬如华裔溜冰好手，被称为"中国搪瓷娃娃"的陈婷婷，就因为使用肌肉位置不当，而再三遭遇挫折。

运动应该是刚柔并济的，如果举重的人压伤了脊柱，赛跑的人拉伤了肌肉，投球的人扭伤了手肘，不是由于他们过度练习，就是有了技术上的误差。因此，拳击赛时，有一方已显然不支，虽未倒地，裁判也会判定比赛结束；当医学界发现少年棒球选手投变化球，可能有碍手臂的发育时，更会建议禁止小选手练习变化球。

运动的精神，是达到体能的极限，并发挥身体的最大潜能，而非不自量力地硬拼。所以当你觉得体能不支的时候，应该以渐进的模式提升，而不要勉强。更应该检讨是否基本技巧有问题，而非逞一时之勇。

## 掌握诀窍

我认识一个乐团鼓手，自己学会打鼓，打得不错，只是方法不对。其他的团员都建议他找个老师学习，他说："只要打得准，谁管？"后来他得了关节炎。

有不少歌手，刚开始练的时候只懂得用蛮力飙高音，但其实唱歌有胸音、喉音、头音三种技巧。不懂得转换，很容易造成喉咙受伤。

我以前打字很快，因为练过钢琴，手指比较灵活。但我从来没有学过所谓的 touch typing，所以打字要一直看着键盘。后来在大学，去应征打字员的工作，老板说我虽然速度快，但因为方式不对，容易打错，所以没有聘我。

一旦养成了习惯，就很难再改，不如一开始先多花一点时间，学会正确的方法！

# 在风雨中成长

◆

生命不总是风和日丽，但是有些人在凄风苦雨里，却能咀嚼出另外一种美，也只有这种人最经得起打击，也才称得上懂得人生的情趣。

我知道你今天有些失望，因为经过长久计划的环河之游，却遇上难得一见的风雨，虽然我们由甲板移入船篷内，还是被斜斜飘入的雨水淋湿了。

或许你会想，如果不为等妈妈有空，而在上星期风和日丽，学校未开课时去该多好；或许你会想，何不下个月，等我有空时，再挑个日子前往。

但你要想想，什么是一家人，什么叫 Family Ties，上星期如果在没有你母亲同行的情况下，我们去游河，当你看到美丽的景色时，会不会想，如果妈妈也能看到该多好？

而如果我们延到下个月，纽约的天气转入寒冷的暮秋，在你观赏自由女神海湾的景色时，会不会担心，海上来的寒风，会使八十岁的祖母受凉？

如此说来，我宁愿一家人，在今天的风雨中同行。

况且，风雨中的景色也很美。当密雨像轻纱般在河面上牵过，远远的帝国大厦尖端隐入浓云，岂不是比晴朗的日子，更有味道吗？

当自由女神生着铜绿的身躯，被雨水淋透，在后面灰暗天空的衬托下，不是更来得明艳吗？

还有当我们穿过哥伦比亚大学的北方，看到哈得孙河时，近处岸边树木盎然的翠绿，与远方凄迷的河谷相比，不是更来得悠远，而令人有一种怆然的情怀吗？

而当我们坐的大游船经过小船时，特别放慢速度，使水波不至于过度激荡，每一艘帆船，都降下一半船帆，使自己不会因为强风而墙倾楹折的做法，不都给我们最好的教育吗？

你要知道，在我们的生命中，不总是风和日丽的。但是有些人在凄风苦雨里，却能咀嚼出另外一种美，也只有这种人最经得起打击，也才称得上懂得人生的情趣。

记得我在你这个年岁，曾经看过一部叫《日瓦戈医生》的电影。其中最令我难忘的，是当日瓦戈医生的家被充公，只身逃往西伯利亚的途中，车内拥挤嘈杂，日瓦戈却拉开小车窗，静静欣赏外面乌拉山的雪景。

我初到美国的时候，正逢冬天，有一次站在露天等车，突然下起大雪，我便学日瓦戈医生苦中作乐，静静欣赏附近枯树在雪中的变化，还有小鸟们如何不断抖动翅膀、扑落雪花的样子。而当车子在四十分钟之后，从密雪中缓缓驶近时，我才发现自己竟已陷入半尺深的雪中。

所以，我爱今天这样的风雨，也希望你爱它，因为我们都要经历雨雪风霜，才能长大。

纽约哈得孙河上的游船。

## 亲情最可贵

最近我们全家去迪士尼乐园度假。我妹妹很早便开始规划行程，结果出发当天，我们居然误掉了班机，打乱了既定的计划。妹妹一开始很不高兴，让我想起当年的我。

人生不如意的事，原本十之八九。现在的我，很诧异自己高中时还闹这种别扭。但我也真的愈来愈重视家庭生活。从独自搬到离家四小时车程的波士顿，到现在长住台湾，一年只回去一两次，这促使我更加珍惜与家人相聚的时间。在迪士尼，老爸感慨地说这样的家庭旅行实在难得，不如以后每年固定一次到不同的地方游玩。我举双手赞成！

因为不是常相守，愈来愈重视与家人欢聚的时光。
图为 2007 年作者全家共游迪士尼乐园的快乐情景。

# 只问收获

有一个老农，每日带孩子下田在农地工作，有一天突然把田地交给孩子说：『过去，我只逼你辛勤工作，要你只问耕耘，不问收获。但是从今天起，我不逼你工作，却要只问收获，不问耕耘。』

昨天晚上你抱怨地对我说："明明讲现在我长大了，可以自己支配时间，不再逼着我去弹琴和读书，可是却要不断地问我成绩，使我有压力。"

现在让我告诉你，那没错！当我不再叮嘱你去做每一件事的时候，并不表示我不再要求你，而是希望你能用自己的判断力，决定事情的缓急轻重。当我不催你去睡觉时，不是不再顾虑你的健康，而是希望你由前一天迟睡，第二天疲困的经验中得到教训。当我不逼问你过几天可能考哪些科目时，是希望你由拖延积压，以致临时抱佛脚的困窘中得到教训。

所以对于你，我好比一个总是带着孩子下田的老农，有一天将田地交到孩子手中，要他自己看日子播种，看情况浇灌施肥。我试着不再即刻纠正你的错误，以免除你长久养成的依赖，却要告诉你："过去，我只逼你辛勤工作，要你只问耕耘，不问收获。但是从今天起，我不逼你工作，却要只问收获，不问耕耘。"

这个世界就是如此，我们对于自己，固然可以讲"只问耕耘"，以求心安。但是别人对我们，却常常"只问收获"。即使是赌徒，都只问他下桌时，能带走多少筹码，又何必计较他上桌时有多么阔绰。

所以就短程而言，不论你用什么模式读书，或玩耍占去你多少时间，只要你诚诚实实地考试，成绩好，就是成功。就中程而言，不论你高中几年的表现如何，只要你能进入好的大学，就是成功。就长程而言，就算你根本没进过什么学校，只要有成就，对社会人群有贡献，就是成功。

现在我看的是短程。你尽可支配你的时间，做你要做的事，拖到一两点钟不睡，打几十分钟电话不放，只要你的成绩好，我就没话说。因为那是你的本事，你有条件玩，有资格拖！而非父母一步一步逼出来的。

尽管如此，我还是无法保证你以后成功，因为今天我可以逼你取得好成绩，明天可以逼你上好的大学，当有一天你进入社会，有谁能继续逼你？如果你不给自己压力，要求自己出人头地，到后来，还是可能失败。

所以，我承认，仍然在给你压力，只是由问耕耘，到问收获。而我相信，这种压力绝对是好的，只要我知道怎么将短程目标的要求转为中程，再逐渐交到你自己手中，使你能自我要求，必能帮助你在人生的旅程获得成功。

我常想，在美国的中国孩子多半比西方孩子表现好，不只是因为中国人聪明，主要还是因为父母的要求。换成你的话说，就是父母施加子女功课上的压力。问题是，那些子女进入了好的大学，后来得到研究所学位的比例远超过西方人，而今更在各界崭露头角，你能说这压力没有用吗？

当你昨晚向我抱怨时，你应该记得电视上正转播冬季奥林匹克运动会的花样滑冰，你可曾看见那些选手比赛后等着看成绩的大特写？他们的手腿都在轻微地颤抖。你又可曾看见，当溜冰者滑倒在冰上，立刻挺身而起，追上音乐节拍，扮出笑容溜完全程的样子？

在他们优美的舞蹈、可爱的笑脸后面，隐藏的是什么？

是压力！来自国家、来自对手、来自现场、来自他们自己，也来自每一个爱他们，以及他们所爱的人！

在这种强大的心理压力下，他们只要有一块肌肉稍稍僵硬，有一点速度微微减慢，可能就会在全世界数亿的观众面前摔倒。最重要的是，金牌只有一枚，最后绝大多数的人，都将黯然归去。

年轻人！生物就是在竞争中成长与进化的。有竞争，就有压力；只有具备最强的实力，又能忍耐最大压力的人，才能站到巅峰。

# 如果人们不爱吃豆子

我对这篇文章的概念没有意见，但是我还是不免要追问：我们的"收获"是由谁来评估？以什么标准来衡量？今天认为不长豆子便不是豆子，那是因为人们爱吃豆子。但是如果今天人们爱吃的是豆苗呢？

每个人拥有不同的抗压力与竞争力，有些人生下来就好强，有些人是被逼出来的，但我相信并不是不爱竞争的人就没有发展，只是或许适合做不同的事。虽然媒体上看到的多半都是好斗，喜爱受人注意的强势角色，但这个世界上也有许多平常人正默默耕耘，按部就班地过日子。他们的成就或许不是那么辉煌，但是一个大机器没有小螺丝钉也无法运作。一个真正民主的社会，不能忽视这一点。

# 在工作中学习

如果你只是在餐馆短期打工，当然无可厚非，但是假使长期打下去，十年之后的你，除了能多记几道菜名、多端几只碟子，对你原来所学的有什么帮助？

　　你在信中告诉我，暑假以来打工已经赚了五百块美金，真是让我高兴。不是因为你赚了钱，而是由于其中所具有的意义。

　　首先，我相信当你拿到第一笔报酬时，一定非常兴奋，因为那是你十五年来，靠自己劳力赚取的第一笔钱，表示在你向这个世界索取了十多年之后，开始能够回馈，开始有了贡献。

　　你要知道，一个生命真正被肯定，绝不是在他的消耗期，而是在他的贡献期。我们甚至可以说，如果一个人成年之后，离群索居地隐世，就算他有高深的学问，如果从来不能发挥，死后也不能留下什么，那么他的存在，对这个世界就毫无意义。所以，今天你拿到报酬，它是酬劳，也是回报，是社会对你付出的一切给予的回报。对我而言，那酬劳不重要，你付出的这个行为，才是要紧的。

　　其次，相信当你拿着自己辛苦赚来的钱时，会觉得那特别重，也特别轻。特别重是因为它是你早起晚睡、奔波劳累之后的成果，所以你会珍视它。特别轻的原因，是它完完全全属于你，所以你有最大的支配权，不必像从父母处拿到的钱，随时要考虑使用的方法合不合旨意。如果能这样，钱对于你才真算是钱，因为一个不劳而获的人，钱对他没有意义；一个拿着钱不敢用的守财奴，钱对他也没有意义。只有赚取它、珍视它、把握它、使用它的人，才算是懂得钱的意义。

　　至于你这暑假打工最让我高兴的，是你工作的性质，虽然那只是帮助希腊人协会设计电脑程序，并输入会员资料，但必然使你处理电脑程序和打字输入的能力增加。这让我想起初来美国时，看见一位学长批评他的弟弟："如果你只是在餐馆短期打工，当然无可厚非，但是假使长期打下去，十年之后的你，除了能多记几道菜名、多端几只碟子，对你原来所学的有什么帮助？只怕还退步了！所以打工的钱再多，如果与所学的无关，又不能成为一项事业，就不值得长期做下去！"

他的这几句话，虽是用来教训弟弟的，却让我听在耳里，成为自己打工时取舍的原则。在美十年来，我也确实发现，那些学法商而在律师楼、会计师事务所打工的大学生，和在医院、药局、实验室打工的中学生，往往在工作中学到许多东西，引导他们走上未来的成功之路。

在学习间工作，是一般人所谓的打工。在工作中学习，则是打工者应有的态度。

## 接轨的准备

我对自己的第一份工作还真的蛮得意的。

当时的邻居海伦是纽约希腊居民协会的秘书长。我帮她输入会员资料，一份一毛钱。印象深刻的是，希腊人的姓名都很长，甚至会到十五六个英文字母，所以赚这个钱还不是很容易。

在美国郊区，很多十几岁的孩子都会自己打工，帮人铲雪、剪草、刷油漆等，家长都非常鼓励，觉得这是对体力跟人格的锻炼。但是像我这样小时候就当了"白领"的，还真的不多！

我觉得每个阶段都有合适的打工工作。十几岁可以靠体力，长大了就应该靠脑力。高中时即使帮老板打杂、煮咖啡，都会学到东西，但如果大学毕业后，还在帮老板煮咖啡，就显得可惜了。

## 预留退路

◆

有一个艺术家，带着他画的心血之作，坐飞机出国展览。临行，他交给妻子一套作品的幻灯片，说：『如果飞机失事，我与作品俱焚，就把这些幻灯制版印刷出来，为我的绘画生命留个见证！』

今天当我知道你把设计一个多月才完成的电脑资料借给同学，自己却没留底，真是吃惊极了！因为我发现你犯了一个不为自己留后路的严重错误。

记得当我像你这个年岁，初参加登山队的时候，每次在树林里遇见岔路，领队总命令我在路边折一根小树枝，指向来时的方位。至于草木不生的荒山野岭，则叫我四处找小石块，排列出先前道路的指示标记。

每当我看见队伍已经开拔，而自己仍在四处找石块时，都抱怨这无谓的做法。直到有一天，大伙在深山里迷了路，无法到达终点站，而不得不退回原路时，才改变了我的想法。

当时天色已经转暗，我们不得不以最快的速度撤退。大家几乎是用跑的方式穿越密林，而每当遇到岔路口，我立刻由断枝的记号指出方向，使全队能及时退到安全地点。而我，这个总在后面做指示标记的小子，居然变成当时的领队，全队的安危竟系于我一身呢！

你说，那折树枝与排石块，能说是无谓的举动吗？何况对你而言，只是将电脑磁碟片插进机器，用不了几秒钟就可以拷贝完成的事了！

谈到拷贝，我又想起影印机，自从它普及之后，许多人都"不可一日无此君"。但是如果你做个统计就会发现，人们影印的东西，实际大部分都没有绝对的必要。他们付款之后，常把账单留个影本，送出各种申请表格之前，也总是影印留底，信件更是影印存档，甚至做成好几份影本分送有关人员。我们可以说，不影印，事情不会停摆，但更可以讲，由于件件存底，便于查考，使繁忙的事务，能被安排得有条理，也做得更顺。尤其重要的是，当送出的资料遗失，因为存有影本，而能获得补救。

所以，影印机普遍之后，挂号信的数量便减少了，这并非由于平信的邮误降低，而是因为寄信的预留了退路。

退路就是这么简单，它只是退一步想，做一个相反的假设。譬如办游园会时设遮雨棚，跳伞时带备用伞，飞机上准备逃生器，高楼设置防火梯。虽然没有人希望用这些东西，即使用，也不见得百分之百管用，设置时反而增加许多麻烦，但是，毕竟退路可以使你不至于一败涂地，而为你在绝望时带来希望。如此说来，"退路"何尝不是另一种"进路"。

我有一个朋友，带着他画的心血之作，坐飞机出国展览。临行，他交给妻子一套作品的幻灯片，说："如果飞机失事，我与作品俱焚，就把这些幻灯制版印刷出来，为我的绘画生命留个见证！"

希望你能由这几句话中思考，有一天了解，退路不仅是为活着的时候，也为死了之后；不仅为有限的生命，也为千古的事业！

# 与墨菲相处

我有一个相当惨痛的经验。大约七八年前，我回台湾过暑假，有一天晚上，跟朋友到台北六条通一带吃烧肉，车子停在高架桥下。当我们用完餐走回高架桥，没想到我放在后备厢的手提电脑不见了！电脑里有我博士论文的研究资料以及音乐。当时的我真是全身一阵冷。因为我半年的作曲成果全没了。现代人愈来愈依赖电脑，也更体会做备份、预留退路的重要。像我从事音乐工作，有时甚至需要用到第三个备份档案。

但在我的日常生活中，更常遇到所谓墨菲定律，例如在交报告的前一刻，打印机的墨水用罄之类。对我而言，不管怎么小心，墨菲还是会出现。

# 天才是什么

在第二次世界大战的纳粹集中营里，有些犹太艺术家，明明知道自己即将被推进瓦斯室，却伸出他们骨瘦如柴的臂膀，以自己仅有的一点食物，向人换取炭条和铅笔，创作出他们生命中最后的作品。

最近常有人赞美你是天才，我听了只是摇头苦笑。

因为若没有父母盯着你练琴，你就不会去弹；没有我把石膏像放在你面前，并递上纸笔，你就不会去画；没有我逼你作文，你就不会动手；没有我交给你一本世界名著，你就不会主动去念；没有父母逼你读书，你也可能马马虎虎去应付。

所以虽然你在各方面的表现都很杰出，我却私下对你母亲说，你只是有过人的聪明，仍然算不得天才，如今小时了了，长大之后未必能成。除非你有那种自行激发的能力、不断超越自己的冲动和锲而不舍的精神。

这就是天才的特质，它不见得是过目不忘、一目十行的高智商，而是一种说不出的，对任何事都有的怀疑态度、好奇的想法，与不达目的绝不终止，近于傻的冲劲。

中国有个形容词——苦心孤诣，非常适合用来形容天才做事的态度。因为天才追求的目标，常常难为外人了解，他们做事的方法，也常难为一般人接受，他们更常因为孤诣而孤独。

但是若不能忍耐孤独，又如何站到巅峰呢？巅峰只有一点点，容不下许多人站，所以不仅遭遇的风大，而且旁边难有扶持，受不了风寒与孤寂的人，就无法成为天才。

记得在一九八八年冬季奥运会闭幕式的时候，负责转播的美国ABC电视台评论员说了一句耐人寻味的话，他说奥运的真正精神，是把我们自己硬推到自己的极限之外（Push your own limits）。

这句话也适合形容天才，只有那种不向自己既有的能力屈服，不满足于既有的成就，总是试图超越自己，抱着一种不服、不平，甚至愤懑，以自己为敌，追求突破的人，才能称得上天才。

也就因此，天才才会有几分神经质，或被人看成疯子，当然他们加诸自己身上的压力过大，也确实常会使他们崩溃。譬如爱迪生小的时候，曾经被学校老师怀疑为低能儿；有诗鬼之称的唐代诗人李贺，由于早晚不停地写作，连他母亲都忧心他，只怕要呕出血来才能停止；印象派大师凡·高，不但割下自己的耳朵，更结束了自己的生命。

我说这许多话，不是要教你去效法李贺、凡·高般透支自己，而是告诉你，你虽然是一个学什么像什么，甚至能青出于蓝的人，但是不论你的文章、绘画、琴艺目前有多么好，只要那不是出于你内在的学习冲动而获得的成就，便不算一回事。

年轻人！如果有一天，我不准你写作、不准你弹琴、不准你绘画，甚至不准你读书，而你却千方百计地自己追求，如果有一天，你工作繁重，乃至生计无着，拖着疲惫饥饿的身子回来，却仍会提笔，一吐你胸中的块垒，虽然你不一定能成功，也不一定会被人肯定，却可以自己对自己说：我是个锲而不舍的天才。

在第二次世界大战的纳粹集中营里，有些犹太艺术家，明明知道自己即将被推进瓦斯室，却伸出他们骨瘦如柴的臂膀，以自己仅有的一点食物，向人换取炭条和铅笔，创作出他们生命中最后的作品。

当你被我硬是塞上纸笔，画出一幅好画时，我要问：在你心底可有他们那种"生死与之"的创作原动力？

如果没有，你就不可能成为天才！

## 天才头衔

我从来不认为自己有什么了不起，以前也只有钢琴老师会说我很有"天分"。我觉得天才是个很高的头衔，那像是上天的一个礼物，若有人说你是天才，几乎就把你跟莫扎特相提并论。此外，天才是使命、是负担。因为你天生比别人多了一些东西，别人当然对你有更高的期待，久而久之就成了负担。

使命感，加上莫名其妙的强迫症，天才会把自己推展到极限之外，甚至可能丧失健康与性命，换来传世不朽的作品。

我并不想当天才，那头衔太大、太重，只能赋予历史上极少数的奇人，而且仔细回想，天才们的生活似乎都有些坎坷。也因为我把天才的条件设得很苛刻，我宁可当一个扎扎实实、努力工作的人。

## 现代青年

一个『小游学生』，穿 GUCCI 名牌服饰，拿 NIKON 单反相机，开 TOYOTA 双门跑车，是高中辩论队代表、校刊编辑和曲棍球队员，得全 A 的学业成绩，被加州大学柏克莱分校录取，且兼了九个家教，月入千元美金，父母却不在美国……

昨天在大都会美术馆，我遇见了一位台湾"小游学生"。

他留着时髦但不流气的发型，看来成年，脸上却还带着几分稚气；穿着米白色印着 GUCCI 大字的休闲上装，配白色的长裤和皮面的运动鞋，不时举起 NIKON 相机，以非常娴熟的动作测光、对焦。虽然初次从加州到纽约玩，却对美术馆有很深的认识，因为他在没来之前，已经阅读了有关的书籍。

中午我邀他在馆里共进了午餐，看得出他有极佳的餐桌教养，说话的音量和对侍者的态度，都表现得恰到好处。谈话中，我知道他马上就要进入著名的加州大学柏克莱分校，并立志将来从医。我好奇地问他怎么申请到柏克莱，高中的成绩如何，他先谦虚地告诉我在加州的居民比较容易申请，又说他高中拿了四点二，接着解说——四代表 A 的成绩，多出来的零点二，则因为在高中已经选了大学的课程，所以获得加分。

我又问他高中参加了什么课外活动，因为像春藤联盟（Ivy League）这类名校，如果没有好的课外活动（Extracurricular Activities）记录，学业成绩再高，也不能保证录取。

他说他参加了辩论队，代表学校出席了许多学术竞赛，编了一年校刊，并且是曲棍球队的中锋。

我举杯向他致敬，说很高兴遇见这么一位杰出的青年，也无怪他申请每所名校都会被录取。我尤其佩服的是，他居然是一个父母都不在身边，来自台湾的"小游学生"。

虽然家里的经济情况并不太好，但是他开着一辆时髦的TOYOTA跑车，他说买日本车的目的是省油，因为高中最后一年，他平均每周要赶九个家教，指导邻镇中国孩子英数理化的功课。这虽然使他一个月有上千美元的收入，但是大半的时间都花在往返途中。

"您知道吗？我的车子才买半年，就超过了一万英里了！"他对我说。

而我真正好奇的，是他怎么还能有时间，在学业及课外活动上，获得如此卓越的成绩。

从大都会美术馆回来的路上，我细细思索这个问题，发觉对你的教育方法似乎应该调整，这并非我过去督导的模式有偏差，而是因为时代已经不同。

在台湾，我常看到同样收入的家庭，却过着完全不同水准的生活。

一种人节俭持家，连张擦过嘴的卫生纸都舍不得扔，要再拿去擦桌子；锅铲的把子都已脱落，还要包上废布将就使用。一种人则看来有些浪费——东西过时，立刻换新；报纸隔日，立即抛弃；厨房一尘不染，锅碗非常简单却永远光亮如新。

依照过去的理论，当然是前面那户俭朴的人家，能够有较佳的生活。但事实却是后者不仅生活品质好得多，经济状况也显然比前者强。而据我观察的结果，是因为后者不但在生活上有现代理念，在理财上也有较新的方法，使他们在孳息、投资上都获得不错的利润。渐渐这两种家庭走入了不同的社会层次，新者愈新，旧者愈旧，距离愈拉愈远。

同样，农业时代，靠招牌、信用的老店，如果依旧维持过去那种堆货的方法、昏暗的灯光、缓慢的速度和一成不变的样式，可能也将被新式的经营所取代。

因为过去百货杂陈，表示店里东西多，今天看来却显得乱而缺乏管理；过去一边跟顾客磕牙，一边慢慢包装算账，表示优雅而有人情味，如今却显示效率差；过去一成不变，表示老字号货真价实，现在看却是不求改进。当环境不断变迁，凡是不跟着适应的就将落伍而被淘汰。

现在回到正题，过去读书成绩好的学生，往往能成功，在今天这个时代，却可能因为无法适应周遭的环境，即使以第一名毕业，也难有杰出的成就。

如果现代经营的理论是以促进消费来刺激生产，过去是以节约消费来积蓄财富，那么过去设法少让子女参加活动及打工，以集中精神念书的态度，是不是也应该改为多让子女在外发展，从发展中获得更大的冲力，对知识更深切地求取，也对未来产生更大的憧憬呢？

过去常是父母为子女计划未来，现在是否应该让子女到相当的年龄之后，就自己计划未来，父母只担任参谋的角色呢？

从那个年轻人的身上，我看到了一个以环境激发潜力，将时间做最有效分配，以积极态度投入社会，而不是"被动"走向社会的新典范。

他穿最讲究的服饰、用名牌的相机、开流线型的跑车、做九个家教、在高中修大学的课程，且参加许多活动。他以服饰、车子满足了年轻人的虚荣，以做家教来付每月五百多块的分期付款及保险费，又以车子载着自己参加活动、担任家教，争取了许多时间，且能够掌握每一分钟，在学业上有最佳的成绩，并用他的成绩，征得信任而获得家教，不正是以促进消费来刺激生产吗？

过去我一直使用大部分中国家长的方法，推着你向前走，今天突然对自己的模式产生怀疑。站在上一个时代，与瞬息万变的未来之间，我有了许多彷徨。

如果我把这问题交给你，你认为应该选择哪一种生活模式呢？

# 走向独立

记得第一次听我老爸提起这个人时，我觉得他真的蛮厉害的，可说是"小游学生"的一个典范。很多家长把小孩送出去，都是希望他们之后可以成为这样的人：开朗、独立、时髦，而且人生目标明确。

"小游学生"有很多种，念研究所时，我认识一个台湾同学，节省到在极冷的冬天也不开暖气。但走到波士顿的精品街，总是可以看到不少其他的亚裔"游学生"，开着跑车、穿着名牌。这其实没什么不好，但是现在在台湾一天到晚听说有人出去"游学"，花了一大笔钱，回来却一无是处，而且因为在外面成天跟华人混，连英文也没学好。

所以我觉得"小游学生"在外面的造化，朋友扮演了很重要的因素。是可以彼此帮助，还是只会帮助彼此偷懒，经常是"游学"成败的关键因素。

# 美好的星图

◆

一个赴大陆探亲归来的老兵感慨地说：『我已经去看过八十岁的老母。四十年，母亲还是母亲！可是四十年，母亲又已经不是母亲了！』

明天一大早，我就要陪着你的祖母回大陆去了！住在香港的华商酒店，我一时无法成眠，于是提笔写这封信给你。

旅馆的窗外，正对着香江，白日繁忙穿梭的船只显然减少了，但是原本并不十分抢眼的九龙建筑，却织起了一片灿烂的灯海。那片灯海之后，则是我即将叩访的故乡。

今天上午，当飞机经过一个钟头又十五分钟，抵达香港的时候，你的祖母惊讶地问："怎么这么快就到了？"

"因为近哪！从这儿飞北京，只要不到三个小时，如果有一天从台北能直飞上海，恐怕一个多钟头就够了！"我回答。

确实，四十年的分隔，使绝大多数的中国人，都以为台湾与大陆是非常遥远的，远到父母、夫妻、兄弟，和那许许多多的亲人，一别就是四十年，甚至天人永隔。

这也是为什么你的祖母坚持要在今年回去，她怕再不去，那剩下的几个亲人也见不到了！

今早我们在台北起程时，楼下管理员一面帮着搬行李，一边说："我已经去看过了八十岁的老母。四十年，母亲还是母亲！可是四十年，母亲又已经不是母亲了！"

听来多么没道理，却又有着无限道理，动人的一句话啊！从那个十九岁离开故乡，而今已经白发的退伍老兵的嘴里说出来！

但是，你知道吗？也有一个老兵的妻子对我说："小心被剥光了！我的丈夫连鞋子、裤子都脱给了他的兄弟，穿一双破布鞋回来，差点让我不认得！"

我没注意她说话时鄙夷的眼神，却想象到，那老兵临别时，将鞋子脱下来与兄弟交换的画面，是多么感人！多么凄怆！而那情，又是何等深长！岂是他那年轻妻子所能理解的。

这也使我想起纽约的一个朋友，七年前第一次由祖国大陆返回美国，立刻大病一场之后，所说的话：

"我不是身体病了，而是心灵病了！从大陆回来之后，我夜夜做噩梦，常常从梦中哭醒。我不了解上帝为什么那样不公平，为什么有的人要接受如此的苦难？"

所以当那老兵的妻子对我抱怨她的丈夫之后，我不客气地说：

"怎能怪你先生呢？在他的兄弟遭遇四十年的苦难，在他的亲人可能因为他而被打为'黑五类'，自己不能有好的工作，子女不能进高等学府，甚至下放到农村，人生最珍贵的四十年，只换来一场噩梦之后，你的丈夫不过留下他穿去的衣裤、鞋子，对于他是随时可以买到的东西，对于他的兄弟却是奢侈品，难道这一点心意，也是罪过吗？"

凭什么我们的同胞要受到如此的苦难？凭什么我们要享受如此的富足？我们应该觉得惭愧，愧对自己未能及早帮助的亲人。我们非但不能瞧不起这些历经浩劫的同胞，反而应该觉得亏欠了他们才对啊！

福祉不能独占，正如同满天的星子，不是只有高楼上的人才得欣赏。此刻香江的灯火，像是地上的一片星海，明灭闪烁。我却衷心盼望，那地上繁华的星海，能像天空一样均匀，从这里，从香港、九龙、新界，一路铺下去，到杭州、上海、北京，到甘肃、新疆、内蒙古……

哪怕山间小小的村落，有一天，也能展现一片美好的星图！

庭院及屋檐上长满秋草的北京紫禁城。

# 真正的家书

我老爸把这篇文章放在此书的最后是很耐人寻味的，对我而言，这篇仿佛才真的是我老爸写给我的家书，字里行间都是他的真感情。

我们家是所谓的外省人，在战乱中来到台湾，现在的我们回到大陆，也都仍有不少亲戚在那里。从家族到民族，这段有如史诗般的动荡时代，蕴藏了多少情感与记忆。

当我爸爸提到"美好的星图"时，他强调的是"包容"，是我们该如何面对世界。我家过去六十年间，从祖国大陆到台湾再到美国，已经漂流过三地，我们对这三个地方都有情感。而我老爸的感触尤其深。

在这篇文章之后，我老爸写了《爱就注定了一生的漂泊》这本书，应是他情怀的延伸。

作者与刘轩父子感情深厚，同样喜爱艺术，热心公益。